Porcelain Moon and Pomegranates

Porcelain Moon and Pomegranates

A WOMAN'S TREK THROUGH TURKEY

Üstün Bilgen-Reinart

THE DUNDURN GROUP
TORONTO

Copyright © Üstün Bilgen-Reinart, 2007

Editor: Michael Carroll
Design: Alison Carr
Printer: Webcom

Library and Archives Canada Cataloguing in Publication

Bilgen-Reinart, Üstün, 1947-
        Porcelain moon and pomegranates : a woman's trek through turkey / Üstün Bilgen-Reinart.

ISBN 10: 1-55002-658-5
ISBN 13: 978-1-55002-658-0

        1. Bilgen-Reinart, Üstün--Travel--Turkey.   2. Turkey--Description and travel.   I. Title.

DR429.4.B54 2006   915.6104'4   C2006-904594-1

1   2   3   4   5   11   10   09   08   07

Conseil des Arts
du Canada
Canada Council
for the Arts

Canada

ONTARIO ARTS COUNCIL
CONSEIL DES ARTS DE L'ONTARIO

We acknowledge the support of the Canada Council for the Arts and the Ontario Arts Council for our publishing program. We also acknowledge the financial support of the Government of Canada through the Book Publishing Industry Development Program and The Association for the Export of Canadian Books, and the Government of Ontario through the Ontario Book Publishers Tax Credit program, and the Ontario Media Development Corporation.

Printed and bound in Canada.
Printed on recycled paper.

www.dundurn.com

Dundurn Press
3 Church Street, Suite 500
Toronto, Ontario, Canada
M5E 1M2

Gazelle Book Services Limited
White Cross Mills
High Town, Lancaster, England
LA1 4XS

Dundurn Press
2250 Military Road
Tonawanda, NY
U.S.A. 14150

To past, present, and future Anatolian women of all creeds

Contents

Acknowledgements

I gratefully acknowledge the Canada Council for the Arts grant that enabled me to write this book.

I thank my father, Samim Bilgen, and my mother, Hidayet Bilgen, for sharing their memories; my brother, Semih Bilgen (who took some of the photos in this book); my sister, Gülsün Bilgen-Konuray, for love I've always counted on; my son, Errol Reinart, for rapidly dispatching a laptop to me when my old computer broke down; and my son, Ronan Reinart, for reading an early draft of some sections.

I owe a debt of gratitude to my friends, Maureen Hunter, Susan Riley, Karen McElrea, Heather Frayne, and Michael Riordon, for encouraging me and for commenting on various sections.

I thank Dr. Reşit Ergener; writer Kürşat Başdemir; Dr. Fatmagül Berktay; archaeologist Shahina Farid; lawyer Feride Laçin; anthropologist Dr. Hanife Aliefendioğlu (who became my first friend in Turkey); my forgotten relatives, Eleni and Eftalya Kanaki; whirling dervish Didem Edman; Necla Hattapoğlu of the Women's Platform in Diyarbakır; the women at the brothel in Ankara, including Hacer, Nuray, Songül, Naciye, and Zeynep; the Kurdish refugees in the squatter houses of Diyarbakır, including Feride, Remziye, and Hamza; Naime and Mehmet Yılmaz in Antalya for their time and their willingness to talk to me; the dozens of villagers of Bergama, including Oktay Konyar, Günseli Zeybek, Rahime Özyaylalı, Tahsin Sezer, Ayşe Kurhan, Mustafa and Gülizar Umaç, Şahsine Dikmenoğlu, Ayşe Yüksel, Sebahat Gökçeoğlu, Ayşe

Girgin, and Münir Aldaş, who not only told me their stories, but also offered me a place to sleep, fed me, and gave me precious jars of olives.

I thank the administrators of the School of Foreign Languages and the Department of Modern Languages at the Middle East Technical University, for their flexibility and support.

I am grateful to Michael Carroll, editorial director of The Dundurn Group, for believing in this book.

I thank "Rosinante," the yellow motorcycle, for taking us to forgotten shrines on so many dusty roads. And Jeancığım, I thank you for your love.

An excerpt from Chapter 4 was previously published in *Prairie Fire*. "A Dirge for Zeugma," one of the sections in Chapter 6, and a shorter version of Chapter 1 were previously published in *Descant*.

And, finally, the photographs in this book were taken by me or are family pictures except where credited otherwise.

Chapter One
ANCYRA, ODD NAME FOR AN INLAND CITY

wake up disoriented in the small hours of the night. It is raining outside. The wind that comes in through the open window smells of damp elm leaves, just as it did in Winnipeg, but I hear the hum of traffic instead of the rustle of elm branches. Then a distant sound spills from the sky — the call of the *muezzin* to the predawn prayer. This is Ankara.

In the dark, dreams scurry away and leave me with a sense of loss: Canada is in another world that gets farther and farther away from me. I worry that Canadian sounds and smells will keep receding in my memory until they become irretrievable, that my Canadian self may also be slipping away, that this ancient land will draw me into itself, absorb me and crush the self that was formed in Manitoba.

For more than thirty years, as a Canadian, I secretly grieved for my Turkish self. Now I wear that Turkish self deliberately, like a new skin, but a new regret takes me by surprise.

Oh, the prairies of Saskatchewan, I moan before a photograph in the lobby of the Canadian embassy — *those long, snow-covered, desolate stretches*. I remember a church service at Ponteix, Saskatchewan, a town where families were losing their farms. Sunlight streamed in through the stained-glass windows while the congregation sang, "So sings my soul, my Saviour unto thee. How great Thou art, how great Thou art." And I had tears.

Was it in another life that I stood beside the grave of a murdered Cree teenager, Helen Betty Osborne, at the Norway House Reserve in northern

Manitoba? The grave had an ornate wrought-iron border, painted white, and the sky was aflame with the evening sun. Stiff, frozen laundry swung on lines behind prefabricated houses.

In Ankara I speak Turkish without a foreign accent, but my love for Canada — my habits and values formed in that northern country — make me a foreigner. In Quebec I spoke French with an accent and was considered anglophone. My dearest friends and most cherished memories are in Winnipeg. My sons live in Vancouver and Toronto.

For fifteen years, as a journalist, I told Canada's stories. My own days were woven into the texture of life in Canada. It was my country — it still is. But Turkey is also my country, and it also has stories: mysterious, compelling, dark ones. Until now I haven't attempted to tell any of them. Now I want words to connect my two worlds.

☾

For 2,000 years the fortress of Ankara has brooded over the city. (Semih Bilgen)

It's a late afternoon in October. The taxi taking me home after a rain shower turns a corner, and suddenly the shanty-covered hills of Ulus and the 2,000-year-old-fortress of Ankara loom before me in the distance. The sight is dramatic and magical, like a stage setting — the hills glow in the sunlight while charcoal clouds still hang over them. I gasp, struck by the beauty and the mystery of the land rising behind the concrete blocks that fill my neighbourhood.

The taxi driver doesn't even notice the sight. The crowds rushing through the congested sidewalks don't seem to pay attention to it, either. Had I not left this country as an adolescent and stayed away for many years, perhaps I, too, would be blind to the quality of light on Ankara's ancient fortress hill after the rain. But more than thirty years in Canada have made me see this land through the eyes of an outsider.

Ankara, whose name derives from the 3,000-year-old Phrygian word *ancyra*, meaning "anchor" (odd name for an inland city), is the place of my birth and my childhood. Two thousand years ago the settlement was inside the walls of the fortress that rises on a rugged hill. Now it sprawls for miles — block upon block of concrete on the central Anatolian hills.

Anatolia is the ancient name of the rectangular piece of land that extends from Asia towards Europe between the Black Sea and the Mediterranean. It has been home to different civilizations for more than 10,000 years. Arid and lunar in summer but splashed with blood-red poppies in spring, Anatolia gave me my first images of earth and sky and life and people. As a child, I loved its friendly seas, dusty roads, and sweet fruits with an unconscious and uncritical love, assuming they were mine. Then I left. I matured into adulthood in a spacious northern country — Canada — whose fierce winters, wide spaces, and black soil I also came to love.

For someone who is eighteen, travelling to the other end of the world is not a life decision; it's an adventure. I didn't know then that I had crossed a significant junction and chosen a path. I hadn't made a conscious decision to stay in Canada — I was absorbed with living, and fell in love with a Canadian man in Winnipeg.

I went to university in Winnipeg, got married, and became a journalist. I grew used to rituals of survival in ferocious winters. The rhythmic scraping of snow shovels on cold, still nights after a blizzard. The slow grind and hiccup of cars needing a jump-start. The fog and frost on my glasses when I covered my face with a scarf.

As a television reporter for the Canadian Broadcasting Corporation (CBC), I covered aboriginal issues, Canadian social affairs, and agro-economics. I never wrote about the country of my origin, never explored my own cultural identity. I felt at home in Winnipeg.

But after each trip to Turkey, as soon as I entered the plane that would carry me back to Canada, I felt an aching loss, only made worse when my mother tongue was replaced with English or French and the noisy, chaotic, hot streets of Ankara disappeared as if a curtain had descended on them.

On the ride home from the Winnipeg airport, I always noticed how different the quality of light was in Canada: sharp and crisp as if the trees, the earth, and the houses were all in clearer focus, while in Anatolia the light was whiter and a haze blurred the edges of trees, land, and sky. The crowds, energy, and even disorder of Anatolia drew me like magnets as if this were the *real* world, while affluent, spacious Canada seemed remote, insulated, and immune.

I was frantic to take things back from the country I was leaving to the country where I was going: olives, tablecloths from the marketplace (as if a cotton tablecloth could ever transport the smell of melons and the shouts of sellers at the sun-drenched market), laurel branches from my parents' garden in Seferihisar on the Aegean coast — ridiculous items that could easily be purchased in Canada. From Canada I carried boxes of pancake mix, maple syrup, and even long-grain rice to Turkey! Not because I couldn't live without pancakes or Canadian-style rice, but because I needed to bridge my two countries with familiar items of daily use.

In 1977 spring arrived early in Manitoba. Icicles were beginning to drip and daffodils were on sale at Safeway in early March when my husband died. My two sons were at primary school, and I was earning a pittance as a freelancer at the CBC. My parents rushed to my side for a visit, urging me to return to Turkey. But as a young widow I couldn't face the restrictions Turkish society would force on me. It was then that I chose Canada.

But deep inside me there was division and there was loss. There were chambers that had to remain closed. My Anatolian self was suppressed, my memories of that land — its rhythms, its smells, its temperament, its ancient joys and pains (for what is culture if it is not collective memory that is somehow transmitted through the generations?), the pleasure of my mother tongue — all these lay buried under the psychological layers that formed an efficient, adaptive Canadian self.

In 1995 I left CBC-TV to write *Night Spirits*, a book about a Dene community in northern Manitoba. I also remarried and moved to Quebec City. In Quebec it was impossible to avoid issues of ethnic identity. After thirty years of smooth adjustment to Canadian society, I was now a double "outsider" — an anglophone woman of Turkish origin. I found myself sharply aware of my own foreignness, wanting to reclaim my ethnic origins. During and after the October 1995 Quebec referendum, I had to think about ethnic nationalism and about what it meant to be Canadian. I had to think about the relationship between land and people. I began to acknowledge how deeply my birth and childhood in Turkey had marked me.

"What have we got to lose?" my husband Jean's daughter, Annie, asked one night while we were having dinner with a group of friends. "*Nous gagnerons un pays.* We'll gain a country." Each one of our friends at that table was going to vote yes to separation from Canada.

I remained silent, confusion and anxiety stirring in my guts. The concepts of community, culture, and identity danced in my head, but their values were blurred. I was frightened of ethnic nationalism and uneasy about issues related to ethnic identity, because in Anatolia, ethnic diversity is a taboo subject — a source of terrible pain.

Occasionally, there were news reports about Turkey. My friends knew very little about Anatolia. They asked me about Kurdish separatism or the rise of political Islam. I also wanted to understand the tensions in my country of origin. At middle age I was filled with a need to write about Anatolia, to bridge my two worlds, to try to reduce the "otherness" of the Turks — to make the country and its people accessible to my own Canadian friends and to other curious, intelligent Canadians.

As I sat beside the dormer windows of our apartment in Quebec City reading, thinking, and transcribing interviews with Anatolians, a longing for those dust-coloured hills and ruined cities took hold of me. My parents had grown old. I had lived all my adult life away from them. Now, while they were still alive, I wanted to be near them.

Jean took a leave from the College of Limoilou in Quebec City where he was teaching mathematics. His leave was for only one session, but I accepted a job teaching English at Middle East Technical University (METU). This meant that for a while, until Jean's retirement, we would keep a home in Quebec City and one in Ankara, that we would go back and forth between the two places and accept periods of separation from each other.

We left Quebec City in December during a blizzard. Snow had piled up in the parking lot of our apartment building, blocking the door. We lifted our scarves to our faces, and during the drive to Montreal's Dorval Airport, I watched a world made opaque by snow blowing across the highway.

The compartment of the sleeping car from Istanbul to Ankara — not as opulent as the Orient Express but quainter and much more spacious than the VIA Rail roomette in which I had once travelled from Winnipeg to Montreal — took me to a world I thought was lost. Nostalgic and as excited as a child, I stayed awake between the crisp sheets in the lower bunk.

My brother and his wife met us at the Ankara train station the next morning and took us to the modest, minimally furnished apartment they had rented for us in Bahçelievler, the neighbourhood of my childhood, on a street lined with acacias and parked cars. In Ankara there was no winter. The acacia branches were bare, but the ground was dry.

There were parked cars everywhere: on the street, on the sidewalks, beside apartment blocks, on driveways. Ankara's streets and uneven pavements offered very little space to pedestrians.

Jean had dreamt of a motorcycle all his life. He had owned one years ago in Quebec City, but the Canadian weather was so unsuitable to bike riding that his Honda had rusted in the garage. After our first winter in Ankara, he declared Anatolia *the* land to be explored on a bike. I protested in vain about wild drivers on congested roads. In May he bought a yellow BMW and two helmets. Willy-nilly, I took my place on the back seat.

The motorbike transported us on country roads to remote villages and forgotten shrines. I learned to relax and daydream while sitting still behind Jean in the wind. Sometimes I would take a bus to a town and meet Jean there to venture into uncharted territory with him. I came to love the freedom the bike offered us.

As a child, I took Anatolia's immense human past for granted. Layers of civilizations — the Stone Age, the Bronze Age, the Hattis, the Hittites, the Phrygians, the Lycians, the Ionians, the Romans, the Byzantines, et cetera, et cetera. Names in history books. Lizards darting between tumbled stones.

After thirty years in the "New World" (where Manitoba's 150-year-old Lower Fort Garry is a "historic" monument), though, the richness and the mystery of Anatolian history and prehistory began to thrill me. When I visited the ruins of historic sites, I was filled with awe, as if the layers of buried civilizations had an urgent meaning for today.

But now my excitement is tinged with sadness. While I rediscover Anatolia's distant past, several industrial projects are destroying ancient sites. I realize for the first time that the frenzied plunder of resources that provokes wars and damages ecological balance around the world also erases ancient memory. Concrete shopping centres rise over ancient Roman columns in Ankara, olive groves and nut-bearing pine forests have been razed by a gold mine that poisons the land and water in Pergamon, a dam lake has flooded the exquisite mosaics of the ancient Roman city of Zeugma on the banks of the Euphrates River. The medieval town of Hasankeyf on the shores of the Tigris

River will be flooded for the sake of another dam within a couple of years. Concrete blocks, quarries, and mines mushroom along the Aegean and Mediterranean coasts. On the Black Sea, a four-lane highway slashes the forests that might have sheltered the Amazons thousands of years ago.

Ecological balance represents survival — the human race can't live without air, land, and water. I knew that in Canada, too. But it is only here that I begin to discern the relationship between ecological damage and the loss of distant memory. So many layers of civilizations have lived and died here that I feel as if spirits hover over Anatolia. But if their traces are destroyed, if no one remembers those who once lived and died here, we are not even going to know what we have lost. Without insights into the past, can we fully live in the present? Can we imagine a fulfilling future?

As I reflect on these questions and research Anatolian secrets, something else comes to my attention. I notice that I often turn to women for stories about taboo themes and about the buried past. Is it true then that women are the bearers of collective memory?

That question leads me to the issue of the suppression of female voices, female memories, and female sexuality in Anatolia, and I see another connection that should have been obvious all along: the killing of nature and the suppression of ancient memory are related to the silencing of women's voices. Perhaps women could have defended the earth if they hadn't been robbed of power thousands of years ago.

Taboos surrounding female sexuality in Anatolia are forces that have formed me. As a lively and rebellious girl, I grew up with a sense of danger (and shame) associated with my body. Those feelings probably contributed to my decision to stay in Canada. Now that I am back here as a middle-aged woman, I want to explore and expose their roots.

On this land at the dawn of history, a different vision shaped human societies. An ancient great goddess reigned in Anatolia for thousands of years. The traces of her worship remain all over this mountainous land. The Phrygians, during the Iron Age, called her *Matar* (Mother) or *Matar Kubileya* (Mountain Mother).

People often feel an urge to understand their own past in order to gain insights into the present. I feel compelled to delve into Anatolia's past. A long and loaded human past must affect the people who now live on this land in the same way that a family history going back many generations will affect someone who knows nothing of the secrets buried with those generations.

17

☾

"*İyi günler.* Good day," an elderly woman calls to me from the terrace of the apartment building next to ours. "I've noticed your husband is a foreigner. He hangs laundry. Turkish men wouldn't do that."

Nadire *Hanım* (Lady) putters on that terrace, tending lemon trees and geraniums that grow in large tin cans. My desk faces her apartment. She drinks tea in the evenings and hangs laundry on her clothesline several times a week. Jean and I have gotten to know all her bed sheets, towels, and nightgowns, and she has come to know ours. We frequently exchange small talk.

Seventh Avenue, near our apartment, is like a fairgrounds every evening. The smell of grilled meat drifts from *kebapçı*s. Crowds pour in and out of pastry shops. Strolling people lick ice-cream cones as they jostle one another. Clusters of young men hang around smoking, eyeing slender teenage girls in bell-bottom jeans who sway on platform shoes. People mill in front of shop windows displaying Levi's and Tommy Hilfiger shirts. Street sellers spread their wares on the sidewalk. Cars honk. Commercial pop music spills out of stores.

"*Écoute!*" Jean says one day while we search for canned chickpeas in GIMA, the supermarket at the corner of our street and Seventh Avenue. "*Tu connais cette voix ...*"

"Please, no," I say. "Not Céline Dion!"

"*Si. Céline à Ankara!*" He giggles and cheers at the triumph of the girl from Quebec, while I cringe at "canned" culture, a marvel of globalization.

In January it frequently rains in Ankara. The acacias on our street, and the lindens, ashes, willows, and Judas trees on the METU campus, sparkle after each downpour. "They're laughing," a student once said about the dripping trees. In late February, the large weeping willow in front of the cafeteria begins to grow green shoots. Buds form on the horse chestnuts and on the oleasters beside the social sciences building. I stand outside in the sunlight, feeling the warmth of spring and thinking about ice storms in Quebec.

The mixture of foreignness and familiarity of Bahçelievler fascinates me. On a cloudy evening in February, as Jean and I return from GIMA, the clouds suddenly part above the apartment blocks and a full moon like a porcelain plate appears between the branches. The sight is so astonishing

These school boys earn their allowance by working as porters at the weekly market in Ankara's Emek neighbourhood.

that we stop in the middle of the street. I feel grateful to be there, on that street, before that moon, not as a tourist but as a resident, catching a glimpse of the life I haven't lived.

☾

I remember an ordinary young man coming out of a movie theatre in Winnipeg after seeing the film *Midnight Express* in the autumn of 1978.

"Why do you think the Turks are so ugly?" I asked him.

He didn't hesitate to speak into the microphone in my hand. "I guess it's because they eat raw meat."

"Would you ever want to meet a Turk or go to Turkey?" I continued.

"No," he said.

"What if I tell you that I'm Turkish and that you've just seen a racist film?"

"Well, I suppose all films exaggerate some things."

I was interviewing people for the CBC Radio program *Morningside*. The comments were all frightening.

"Those people are evil because they have a strange religion," one person said.

"The Turks are different from us," another said. "I wouldn't want to go to their country."

"This is a true story," a third said. "Everyone knows the Turks have terrible prisons."

Those words remain etched in my mind. So do the terrible images of pig-like children and corrupt lawyers and grotesque judges in that film, and the unrecognizable Turkish spoken by people who had no knowledge of or love for my native language.

Many of the accusations hurled against Turkey of human-rights violations, ethnic repression, and the suppression of women are well founded. But some Latin American countries have committed similar crimes, and no one vilifies the entire population, say, of Argentina. Why then do people so easily vilify the Turks? When did the "otherness" of the Turks begin? Was it in the Dark Ages when they were galloping on horseback in the steppes of Central Asia?

That was where they came from. Various Turkic tribes galloped westwards during the tenth and eleventh centuries searching for pastures for their livestock. Some of them entered Isphahan (Iran) and Baghdad and converted to Islam. The descendants of a tribal chief named Seljuk formed the first Islamic Turkish empire, which extended from Central Asia all the way to Anatolia.

I try to imagine the chaos that prevailed in medieval Anatolia. Vassal princes warred with one another all the time. In the west, the Byzantines (the Christian heirs of the Roman Empire) were in disarray and at war with the Armenians in the east. The Turks (men and women) were skilled equestrians and archers. Some Turkic tribes fought on the side of the Byzantines against the Armenians or against rebellious Byzantine princes. Some bickered with one another.

In 1069 the Byzantine king Romanos Diogenes set out on a campaign against the Seljuk Turks. It led him to disaster. In 1071 Seljuk leader Alpaslan defeated Diogenes at a crucial battle at Manzikert in eastern Anatolia. Our high-school history books gave such glorified accounts of that battle that to this day I have an image of the Seljuk sultan Alpaslan looking valiant and severe with his wrought-iron helmet and his drooping moustache, greeting the captured Diogenes in his tent and treating him with all the decorum due to a monarch.

"What should I do with you now?" Alpaslan asked the Byzantine king. "If it had been you who had won and captured me, what would you have done to me?"

"As I see it," Diogenes answered, "you have three options. The first is to kill me. That would be butchery. Your second option is to display me in the streets to boast of your victory, and that would be crass." Here Diogenes paused, then said, "It would be madness for me to tell you your third option."

"Go ahead," Alpaslan urged.

"Your third option would be to let me go back to my throne unharmed," Diogenes said. "I would pay you taxes and remain your friend for life."

"You are a free man," Alpaslan replied. "Go in peace."

That decisive Seljuk victory opened Anatolia to the Turks. They captured the Byzantine city of Iconium in central Anatolia, called it Konya, and made it the capital of their Anatolian sultanate. In the thirteenth century, the Mongolians invaded Anatolia and dominated the peninsula until the fourteenth century. Their arrival destroyed the Seljuk Empire.

In the early fourteenth century, one of the small Turkic states in western Anatolia succeeded in uniting all the others. Named after its ruler, Osman, the Ottoman (*Osmanlı*) state eventually became a formidable Islamic empire. In 1453 the Ottoman conquest of Constantinople, the capital and bastion of Orthodox Christianity, was a disaster for medieval Christendom. The story of the siege and fall of Constantinople is one of such heroism and doom that I often wonder if the West's fear and hatred of the Turks began with that event.

At its height, during the early eighteenth century, the western boundaries of the Ottoman Empire extended all the way to the gates of Vienna, and the Mediterranean was an Ottoman lake. The Ottomans seemed so invincible and were so different from the Europeans that the latter were terrified of, and at the same time, fascinated with them. Ottoman themes in the work of Wolfgang Amadeus Mozart and Antonio Rossini — *The Turkish March*, *The Abduction from the Seraglio*, and *Il Turco in Italia* — give us a glimpse of the European preoccupation with the frightening and exotic "other" — the Turk.

By the eighteenth century, however, the balance between the Ottoman Empire and Europe changed. The creative energy that suffused Europe during the Renaissance transformed that continent. Voyages of discovery produced colonies and led to an accumulation of capital that propelled Europe into the Age of Enlightenment. By that time the Ottoman Empire had become unwieldy. Its treasury could no longer finance its military campaigns, yet the sultans wallowed in luxury in Istanbul at the opulent Dolmabahçe Palace whose glamour matched that of Versailles. Decay had set in.

In 1911 Ottoman territories in North Africa were lost to the Italians. In 1913 the Balkan Wars ended with defeat for the Ottomans, and as the Bulgarians and Serbs won their independence (after the Greeks, who gained their independence in 1832), close to five million impoverished and bitter Muslim Turks fled from

Eastern Europe to seek refuge in Anatolia. Then World War I broke out, and European empires collapsed while uprisings shook the Ottoman Empire. The ailing Ottoman Empire allied itself with Germany and the Austro-Hungarian Empire. For the anglophone and francophone worlds, once again, the Turks were "the enemy."

In eastern Anatolia, some Armenian nationalists took up arms for independence and some joined the invading Russian army. The hard-line leaders of the Committee of Union and Progress in the Ottoman government, known as Young Turks, were all from Balkan stock. They felt betrayed by the non-Muslim peoples of the empire. As Professor Doğu Ergil recounts in *Ottoman Armenians During the Decline of the Empire*, a paper he presented at a conference at İstanbul's Bilgi University in 2005, the Young Turks "promised the remaining lands would not become a second 'Macedonia,' as they called the bulk of the Balkans." They decided to rid Anatolia of its Armenian population.

The majority of Anatolia's two million Armenians were deported in 1915 to Syria and Mesopotamia. Hundreds of thousands (the highest estimate is 1.5 million) died or were killed in the process. This terrible massacre of Armenians that happened during World War I, partly as a result of the Russian invasion of eastern Anatolia in which some Armenians welcomed the Russian army, is denied in Turkey, something that has reinforced the Western view of the Turks as "other."

((

On a sunny autumn morning as I linger on the curb, daydreaming while I wait for the university bus, a siren begins to ring and the people on the street suddenly stand still in an eerie freeze-frame. It was 9:05 a.m. on November 10, 1938, when the founder of the Republic of Turkey, Mustafa Kemal Atatürk, died in Dolmabahçe Palace in İstanbul. Decades later on this November morning, a country that owes its existence to the dead man still pauses every year at the exact moment of his death. While everyone around me honours Kemal's memory, I think about the blond, blue-eyed commander who during the ANZAC landing at Gallipoli in World War I called out to the outnumbered Ottoman troops: "I'm not ordering you to advance. I'm ordering you to die!"

They did — by the thousands. That was what it took to repel the Allies who were set on reconquering Constantinople.

By the turn of the twentieth century, the Ottoman Empire was bankrupt and in decay. Westerners called it the Sick Man of Europe. At the end of World War I the Ottomans were defeated along with their German and Austrian allies. In 1918 the victors of the war partitioned Anatolia between themselves, and British, Italian, and French troops invaded the country with the cooperation of the Ottoman sultan. The British invited the Greeks, who had long nurtured the dream of reconquering the Aegean coast of Anatolia, to occupy western Anatolia. On May 15, 1919, the Greek army arrived in İzmir, which the Greeks called Smyrna.

Four days later the brilliant young soldier who had commanded the Turkish troops at Gallipoli left Constantinople in a rickety boat and stepped onto Anatolian soil in Samsun on the Black Sea coast. Away from the occupied imperial capital, he renounced his rank, and in the impoverished and demoralized country, he set out to organize resistance against both the invaders and the Ottomans.

By April 23, 1920, Kemal set up a provisionary government in the sleepy central Anatolian town of Ankara. He ordered local committees in ancient Cilicia (southeastern Anatolia) to repulse the French. In May 1920, France signed a treaty with him and withdrew its troops. A year later Kemal sent his rebel troops to eastern Anatolia to rid that region of the Georgian and Armenian invaders. A strategic alliance with the Bolsheviks helped him to push the Georgians and Armenians back to their current borders. Next the nationalist rebels forced the Italians to evacuate the Mediterranean coast. But in western Anatolia the war against the Greek army took close to two years. Finally, in September 1922, the Greek soldiers retreated in disarray, setting fire to the towns and cities they vacated. The British fled from the Dardanelles. As news of the decisive victory spread, the last Ottoman sultan, Vahideddin, sneaked away from Constantinople one evening on a British boat.

In October 1923, Mustafa Kemal proclaimed the secular Republic of Turkey. He abolished the Islamic caliphate, adopted the Latin alphabet, and set Turkish women free of chadors. The grateful nation gave him the name Atatürk, Father Turk.

As the sirens start to fade, I think about the hopeful young republic born of the tattered debris of the Ottoman Empire, then about the English signs that now cover shop windows. I think about the conditions attached to International Monetary Fund loans that have reduced Turkey to a colony, about the corruption wreaking havoc with the Turkish economy, and about transnational corporations spoiling the land and the water in Anatolia. Then I notice that I am standing at attention, head bowed and eyes moist.

How to write about the Turkish War of Liberation without repeating patriotic clichés? How to talk about Mustafa Kemal without repeating the stock phrases in the myriad of pages already written about him?

A friend in Quebec City once said to me, "He turned himself into a demigod, didn't he?" And I thought then that my friend could never understand the gratitude Turks feel towards Kemal.

He suffered from kidney failure. While he led the desperate War of Liberation in a defeated, weary, and invaded country, he writhed from kidney pains. It was his vision, brilliance, steely will, and sense of mission that produced the miracle of victory. What does it matter that he was an alcoholic, overbearing, long-winded?

Creating a secular republic from the ruins of an Islamic empire was an awesome task. He accomplished it with astonishing diplomacy and grace, and with surprisingly little violence.

My parents weep when they talk about the sense of hope and purpose that filled this country during the first decade of the republic. Their experiences form a part of my own sense of identity and self-esteem. And so, yes, I feel a wrenching love for Mustafa Kemal Atatürk.

☾

In Anatolia's larger cities, modern buildings, avenues, billboards, traffic jams, supermarkets, and shopping centres resemble those in European cities. Theatres show mostly American movies. There is a McDonald's on the corner of our street. There are theatres, operas, orchestras, and chamber music concerts.

During our first winter in Ankara, Jean and I see Giuseppe Verdi's *Un Ballo in Maschera* at the State Opera, a modest pink building that I remember from my childhood. The production is respectable and impressive, even though the tickets only cost the equivalent of $5 Canadian. Young singers, all employees of the State Opera, pour their hearts out in a ritual of passion, loss, and betrayal. I feel as if I'm in a time warp — a fully subsidized opera company performing at a time when most public services are being privatized!

"I doubt they would ever privatize the State Opera," my brother, Semih, tells me later. "It wouldn't be viable."

After taking in *Un Ballo in Maschera*, Jean and I become addicted to the opera in Ankara. In the spring, we hear Pyotr Ilyich Tchaikovsky's *Eugene Onegin* performed in Russian (with surtitles in Turkish) — such a difficult work, sung exquisitely. *Eugene Onegin* is repeated in the fall, so we return and applaud until our palms burn. A week later I go to George Frideric Handel's *Deidamia*. I have never seen a Baroque opera before, and I rave to Jean, "I might have expected this quality of performance in a city like Prague or Paris, but in Ankara! For less then $5 Canadian ...?"

Culture is such a complex mix in Turkey. I see a stunning performance of Sophocles's *Antigone* at the Ankara State Theatre. The music of John Sebastian Bach is played at concerts and festivals, and most educated Turks have read the classics of Western literature. But the sources that have fed Turkish art and culture are different from the Judeo-Christian and Hellenic paradigms that have formed Western art and culture. The origins of the myths that suffuse Anatolian culture are in ancient Anatolian traditions, in a shamanist past in Central Asia, in Islam, and in the War of Liberation of the early twentieth century.

In Ankara I also see a play based on the Sumerian legend of Gilgamesh. Its characters are Ishtar, Gilgamesh, Enkidu, Ereshkigal — all mythical figures more ancient than Ulysses, Moses, Job, and Jesus. I realize with some surprise that Mesopotamian mythology, which has contributed so much to Judaism, Christianity, and Islam, is part of Anatolian culture.

But in the era of globalization the values and images of commercial American culture rise over and above all other myths, reach every corner of people's lives. The hills around the cities are covered with *gecekondu*s (squatters' houses). In shantytowns women wearing kerchiefs watch American soap operas on television in the afternoon, while children play barefoot on dirt roads. The loves and crimes of glamorous Americans in luxury mansions affect and at the same time alienate millions of people. Uneasy with the corruption of their own traditional values, many Turks turn to arabesque, a culture expressing the pain and longings of the villagers who have left their villages to find poverty in the city.

☾

I grew up just a couple of blocks away from the apartment where Jean and I now live in Bahçelievler, a name that means "houses with gardens." Forty years ago that was an accurate description of a neighbourhood where modest middle-class folk built small houses in large gardens. My parents had a pink stucco bungalow surrounded with apricot and cherry trees at the corner of Twenty-first Street and Seventh Avenue. From its open windows, Bach's two-part inventions and Mozart's piano sonatas spilled out onto the street every evening as my sister, Gülsün, practised the piano several hours a day. There were lilacs in front of our house. On summer nights, the sound of jazz drifted from the terrace of Akalın, a wedding hall kitty-corner from our house. Gülsün and I would lean against the windowpane of our bedroom and listen to the saxophone.

Music is my father's passion. His father forced him to abandon his dreams of a career as a musician, so my dad became a lawyer and worked for the government. He knows five languages: Greek, French, German, English, and Turkish. My affectionate, protective mother belonged to the first generation of university-educated Turkish women. On winter nights, she held small towels against the coal stove in our living room and wrapped the heated towels around our feet in our unheated bedroom.

Now it is my turn to comfort her. In Ankara my brother, Semih, and I visit my parents every afternoon. In a ritual that seems solidly established but

Three girls in a squatters' neighbourhood pose for a photograph in Ankara's Ulus district. (Semih Bilgen)

is actually extremely fragile, we have linden tea with them and eat the small cakes that my father buys every day from the bakery across the street.

Bahçelievler has become a crowded, noisy suburb full of apartment blocks. The bungalows and most of the fruit trees are gone. Akalın is still there, but it no longer has a terrace. And a bank — a five-storey block, all gleaming glass, steel, and concrete — sits on the corner where my family once had a pink stucco house in a garden full of cherry and apricot trees. Before my departure for Canada, my parents had moved to an apartment on the eighth floor of a star-shaped block.

Their apartment is unchanged since my adolescence. The dim entrance always smells faintly of floor wax, and the portmanteau that stood sentinel when I was a teenager is still there. The Siemens radio that sits on the piano is now an antique, and the plaster bust of Beethoven has turned yellow. The cupboards and shelves are cluttered with old sheets, old clothes, and old books. Nothing is ever thrown out. When I visit my parents, I enter a time warp where the past remains frozen — for now.

My parents are withering. Advanced osteoporosis severely limits my mother's movements. She walks with tiny, slow steps and is in pain all the time. Each day brings her new endings. Suddenly, one day, she can no longer lift her arms above her head. I begin to help her dress and undress, and to take baths. She is ashamed to be naked before me, even though she can't see her own shrunken body, her thin, stooped shoulders and loose skin. She stands in the bathtub and leans against the edge of the tub while I soap her curved back, which looks so diminished that I think about dry pods hanging from acacia branches in the fall — shells that have completed their task of seeding and await decay.

Later, one evening, as my brother and I have tea with our parents, my mother breaks into a ballad:

> *"Selanikte top atılır, gidim bakim kim vurulmuş*
> *Yarim vurulmuş, ince gömlek kan boyanmış*
> *Yolla yarim yıkayayım, gül dalında kurutayım ..."*

> "There are gunshots at Thessaloniki,
> Let me go and ask who has been shot.
> My love has been shot. His thin shirt is bloodstained.
> Send it to me, my love, so I can wash it and dry it on a
>   rose bush ..."

"My own mother used to sing that when I was a little girl," she tells us.

"Gunshots at Saloniki," I whisper to my brother. "That ballad dates from the Balkan Wars when the Ottomans retreated from Yugoslavia, northern Greece, and Bulgaria."

"When our mother was a little baby," my brother whispers back. "Almost a century ago ..."

My mother was born in Doyran (today on the border between Macedonia and Greece) to a Muslim Turkish family that fled to Anatolia in 1912 when the Ottomans lost the Balkan Wars. She heard stories of how her granny locked the door of their house in Doyran and carried the key for years. "We'll go back to our home one day," my grandmother told my mother.

They never did, of course. My mother grew up in Ankara. She lived in the most violent century in human history, in a region convulsed with war, yet her life was untouched by horror. She glows with pride at being a "Daughter of the Republic."

She remained single —and chaste — until age twenty-nine when she chose her own husband, also a lawyer, and stopped working only after I, her second child, was born. Her deepest fulfillment was in motherhood. Her presence during my childhood was like sunshine — warm and full of delight in us, her children.

My mother escaped the veil but not the conventions of Turkish society. She accepted middle-class restrictions and never rebelled against the role of wife and mother. In her long life, she has known only one man — my father.

But as the years passed, she regretted her fierce chastity. Her hazel eyes cloud with tears when she remembers her unexpressed, unlived love for a left-wing poet.

"I refused even to take a walk with him," she says. "I thought I was being virtuous. But life has never rewarded me for that sacrifice. It was foolishness."

Under her mattress, one day, my brother and I find newspaper clippings about the funeral of the poet. "Your dad would be jealous if he saw these," she tells us, and gazes at the face in the grainy, faded newspaper photo. "*Ah canım,* oh, my dear."

My parents' lucid minds retain the memories of an entire century — the century that depleted the world. My father sees the past in a glowing light. He frequently relives his youth, describing the images in his head, and is always puzzled that no one he knows shares them — and by sharing validates them — anymore.

"Do you remember the horse carts that stood in front of the railway station in Ankara during the 1920s?" he often asks my mother. "They used to line up in the little square where taxis are parked now." My father has grown deaf, which allows him to interrupt any conversation with descriptions of the world in his mind.

In his mind's eye, he sees horse carts in the large, treed avenues of the new city. As he speaks, I see them, too, and I regret the clutter, the debris of steel and concrete, that has filled Ankara.

The living memory of a century will be lost when my parents go, I think.

((

The October afternoon is mild, golden. Horse chestnuts drop their ripe fruits on the pavement. Plump seed pods hang from acacia branches. Beyond the hills of the city stretches the treeless, ochre-hued central Anatolian plateau. The clouds cast mauve shadows on slopes of ancient volcanic rocks, craters on a worn surface.

It is Thanksgiving weekend in Canada. I used to love Thanksgiving. I loved the scent of decaying leaves, the low angle of the sun, the screams of departing geese over the Saint Lawrence River. It felt right to me to express gratitude for the bounty of a harsh land, to mark the season of gold and russet before the onset of a dark winter. Our apartment in Old Quebec City had a loft whose dormer windows looked north at the Laurentian Mountains. From my desk, I could see the galvanized steel roofs of the houses across the street, and beyond them, the mountains that changed colour from season to season, even from day to day. At Thanksgiving the slopes became scarlet with blazing maples. Mornings were sharp with frost. Tourists strolled on Dufferin Terrace. An old man fiddled jigging tunes beside the railings of the terrace. Ash leaves sparkled in the sunlight as they fell, turning and drifting in the wind.

Before leaving Quebec City, I went for a walk with my camera. I peered through the lens at the facades of row houses with their steep, gleaming roofs; at the massive Catholic architecture of the seminary; at the Cathedral of Notre Dame (whose bells tolled heavily to announce the hours); at the old post office with its steel dome and blackened bronze statue of Monseigneur Laval and converted Indians standing in front; at the cast-iron cannons and streetlamps along the ramparts. How Nordic my neighbourhood was! Dufferin Terrace was spacious even crammed with tourists and buskers. Baskets of geraniums hung from lampposts on rue Saint-Jean. An accordion player stood at the foot of the stairs that wound up towards Château Frontenac. The smell of French-fried potatoes and bacon lingered in the air beside sidewalk bistros. The sky, the trees, the creamy Saint Lawrence were all crisply outlined, everything in clear focus.

During those days before our departure, I floated in Quebec City, resisting new attachments. I recognized a gentleman on rue Couillard, someone I frequently met on the street. His appearance, with shoulder-length white hair and a magnificent, thick, and long mustachio, was striking. He also recognized me. We looked at each other directly for a moment before passing.

A couple of days later I spotted him again, this time in the distance at a shopping mall — the downscale Maille Centre-Ville. I resolved to greet him, but he beat me to it, hailing me with a deliberate bow and a warm smile. The reciprocity of the friendly impulse filled me with happiness. A day later, when I saw him once more, this time on rue Saint-Jean, we both broke into big smiles. He slowed down, bowed, and said, *"Bonjour, madame."*

Suddenly, I was sad. He would not run into me again. *Perhaps I should talk to him. Introduce myself, tell him I'll be leaving.* As the thought formed itself, we had already passed each other and the gentleman had turned the corner of rue Saint-Famille.

This business of taking leave holds the secret of death. If people can learn to take leave — to grieve and let go — they might ultimately learn to die gracefully. Let go. Open the hand softly, sadly, but without resistance.

☾

These days the chorus of pigeons on the acacia branches outside the window wakes me at dawn. As soon as sunlight dapples the brick roof of the house across the street, a teenage boy struts along with a tray of sesame bagels on his head, crying *"Sıcaaaak simiiiit!"* A little later, as I drink coffee, another wail pierces the air. A man pushing a cart crowded with bottles of drinking water calls out, *"Suuuya!"* Tomato and onion sellers will come next.

Still later, when I rush past the janitor hosing the entrance of our apartment building, the hallway smells of wet stones. I pick up a newspaper, *Radikal*, on my way to the bus stop. When the bus comes, I sit at the back and stare at grey concrete apartment blocks and a stream of cars and trucks along the way. I get off the bus at METU's administration building and walk briskly between the horse chestnuts, pines, weeping willows, and oleasters on campus to the Department of Modern Languages. The tea that Dursunali, the mustachioed caretaker of the department, brings me in a glass has an acrid taste. The weeping willow outside my office window shines in the sunlight. Looking at it, I catch my breath because my ordinary mornings in Ankara seem so extraordinary.

Chapter Two
MATAR KUBILEYA,
MOUNTAIN MOTHER

"The goddess was born of blood." Dr. Reşit Ergener, the stocky, middle-aged, and mustachioed man who makes this statement, seems embarrassed when I ask him if he means menstrual blood. He looks down into his glass of cognac and begins to fidget.

Ergener knows things I want to learn. A retired economics professor and an amateur expert on archaeology and mythology, he wrote a slim book entitled *Anatolia, Land of the Mother Goddess* that I read in the 1980s while still living in Winnipeg. What astonished me in this book was the evidence Ergener presented for the continued worship of a great goddess in Anatolia long after the emergence of powerful male gods in ancient Egypt and Mesopotamia.

I called the publisher to get Ergener's number at the university, and the professor agreed to meet me in the posh lobby of the Conrad Hotel in the district of Beşiktaş on the Bosphorus. Now I eagerly question him, and he squirms, as if awkward to talk about sexual matters.

"In your book," I say, "you talk about the connections between women, early agriculture, blood, life, death, and the goddess. I just want to understand more clearly —"

"So you know," he says, "that for thousands of years God was a woman in Anatolia?"

"Yes. She had different names in different civilizations — Kubaba, Wurushemu, Cybele," I recite. "Or Kubileya — Mountain Mother in the

Phrygian language, which hasn't been deciphered beyond a few words. I thought the goddess was born of the mountainous landscape."

"Ah," Ergener says, "then you have made the connection between mountains and female breasts. [I hadn't.] Rivers flow from the mountains like the milk that flows from the breasts. Sumerian and Babylonian texts also refer to 'Mother Mountains' from which the sun rises and sets each day ..." He pauses, as if collecting his thoughts. "Anyway, the Phrygians came to Anatolia much later. They embraced the worship that was entrenched in the land."

This figurine of the Neolithic goddess of Çatalhöyük now resides in Ankara's Museum of Anatolian Civilizations. (Semih Bilgen)

"But what do you mean when you say she was born of blood?"

"Let's go way back in time, all the way to the end of the last ice age around the tenth millennium BC, to the beginning of agriculture. Very likely it was women who discovered agriculture, and in the earliest agricultural societies, called Neolithic, survival depended on two things — birth and a good harvest. Both of these things were fraught with risk, and both were in the hands of women. Those societies must have been woman-centred."

"Okay," I say. "So tell me about blood."

"Before the beginning of agriculture and the domestication of animals, people might not have known the role played by males in reproduction. Birth was a mysterious process for which the woman was responsible. From the mouth of the womb where a baby emerged, blood poured out for a few days each month, and blood flowed during birth, as well. Yet blood also meant death. When people or animals bled, they usually died. So in the primitive mind, birth was seen as a consequence of death. You see?"

I nod, commanding myself to be still. Imagine the dread of our human ancestors at the mercy of brutal, unpredictable nature — nature that died each year, that killed but that also returned to life and nurtured. Imagine their awe before female bodies that bled every month and that grew large. Female bodies that writhed and groaned and pushed out babies covered with slime and blood from between their legs. Blood, death, but also life. The power of blood. The dread of blood.

Imagine a world in which men hunted with weapons of stones and bones, and women picked berries and edible herbs. But then, by some fortuitous accident or shrewd intuition, women started agriculture after they realized seeds sprouted into plants. The children of such women had a greater chance of survival, and suddenly their power increased. I read about this in the first volume of Mircea Eliade's *A History of Religious Ideas*: "The fertility of the earth is bound up with feminine fecundity; hence women become responsible for the abundance of harvests, for they know the "mystery" of creation. It's a religious mystery, for it governs the origin of life, the food supply, and death. The soil is assimilated to woman."

My companion in the lobby of the Conrad orders another cognac and warms to his topic. "As you know, those early agricultural peoples of the periods we call Mesolithic and early Neolithic very likely saw a connection between the spilling of blood, death, and fertility. Menstrual blood was associated with the fertility of the land. Do you know, for example, that much later, the Roman writer Pliny believed that if menstruating women walked through the fields barefoot, their hair loose and their skirts lifted up to their thighs, harmful insects would be exterminated? To this day, all over the world, there are peoples who attribute tremendous power to menstruating women. Today's taboos are related to the vestiges of ancient fears. Fears related to life — and to death."

The professor goes on to explain that the shedding of blood in sacrifices is also associated with fertility and with the renewal of nature. "Sacrificial ceremonies can be interpreted as a simulation of menstruation," he says.

"But why," I ask, "were sacrificial animals mostly male?"

"Not *were*. To this day, even in Islam, sacrificial animals *are* male. Perhaps in some dark prehistoric age human males were sacrificed to ensure fertility and the revival of nature. Rites enacting the death and resurrection of a king or god might have been widespread in the eastern Mediterranean for thousands of years. And there's something else. This may seem bizarre, but men seem to have envied women's reproductive powers. They seem to have imagined they could become fertile by imitating women and bleeding from their genitals. There are many stories of castration and reproduction from severed genitals."

But what about the goddess? I almost ask him. Instead, I hear myself think out loud, "So all those people would have imagined the immense force of the universe, that creative and destructive force, as female. Of course …"

He puts down his glass of cognac as if to say the matter is resolved. "I have to rush to pick up my teenage son from my ex-wife's place. Let's talk again some other time."

Çatalhöyük

On a Thursday in early June, Jean and I ride to Çatalhöyük on the yellow BMW through the Konya Plain in south-central Anatolia, between sugar beet fields and concrete irrigation pipes running along the roadside. Nine kilometres after the town of Çumra, and across the road from the village of Küçük Köy, we turn right near a cluster of poplars and stop in front of a small white guardhouse on whose shady porch the guard, Sadettin Dural, drinks tea.

"Everyone is at the dig site," he says.

"Can we join them?" I ask.

He shakes his head. We will have to be accompanied. Excavation Director Shahina Farid is expecting us and would like us to wait. We accept the offer of tea and sit in the shade.

In front of the one-storey dig house, two village women from Küçük Köy, thirty-five-year-old Hatice and her sixteen-year-old daughter, Hülya, both in şalvars (loose, ballooning pants) and flowered head scarves, sit at a table before platefuls of soil, carefully extracting particles with tweezers.

Hatice has a round face with hazel eyes, and a gap between her two front teeth. "We're separating the pieces of obsidian, bone, and bead," she tells me. "We put each group of materials in a different plastic bag. The experts will analyze them in labs."

Before the recent excavations began in 1992, she and other villagers let their cows and sheep graze on the mound. "Our elders said spirits lay here. We all knew there was a city buried under the ground, but it was part of our village."

As we chat, another village woman from Küçük Köy prances out of the kitchen and grasps my hand with the spontaneity of a child. Twenty-four-year-old Mavili bubbles with talk and laughter. "I was the first one from our village to work here," she says. "And now half the village has joined me."

The job has changed Mavili's life. It allowed her to do something bold and dangerous for an Anatolian village woman: divorce an abusive husband and set herself and her nine-year-old son free.

"Here comes Shahina," Mavili says, "the boss."

A young, petite woman in loose overalls and a baseball cap appears in the yard of the dig house. Shahina Farid, an archaeologist from England's Museum of London and the site director at Çatalhöyük, looks like a teenager but exudes confidence and competence. Born of Pakistani parents in London, she speaks English with a British accent. "It's lunch break," she tells us. "You'll eat with us, and then I'll take you to the site."

((

"This is where women's groups perform goddess-worshipping ceremonies," Shahina says beside a white stone stuck in the ground to mark the highest point of the Neolithic mound being excavated.

From the top of the mound where Jean and I stand with her in the warm wind, we can see the village of Küçük Köy surrounded by poplars and willows across a dirt road. The mound is covered with tall, dry grass. Its southeast side is dug in layers, some sections going down twenty metres, and an international team of archaeologists is in the trenches. One of them, Charlie, lies on the ground facedown, scraping the earth with an instrument that reminds me of a small paintbrush. A round rust-coloured object pokes out of the ground. A piece of pottery? No, it's a 9,000-year-old human skull, Shahina tells us. Charlie is trying to uncover the skeleton without damaging it.

Çatalhöyük is one of the largest and earliest Neolithic settlements in the world. In 1961 English archaeologist James Mellaart started to excavate the southeastern wing of the seventeen-kilometre-high mound and found twelve layers of settlements, all from the Neolithic. Each layer is made up of at least 3,000 houses made of mud bricks.

The first known nature painting on the planet is on one of the mud-brick walls between layers of plaster. It depicts an erupting volcano and something resembling a city plan. Other wall paintings show hunting scenes, a leopard fight, and vultures above a headless human body.

Bulls obviously had some religious significance: the walls of many of the houses at Çatalhöyük are decorated with plastered bulls' skulls and horns. In his book *Çatal Hüyük: A Neolithic Town in Anatolia*, Mellaart suggests they represent the male element of the supernatural. Other writers, such as the late archaeologist Marija Gimbutas, associate bulls with male sexual energy and regenerative powers. In one of the rooms, above several bulls' skulls, there is a stylized figure resembling a woman whose arms and legs are spread as if she is giving birth. The dead were buried under the floors.

Dozens of clay figurines of voluptuous females have been found at Çatalhöyük, some holding a child, some even engaged in sexual intercourse. One figure, found in a grain bin, is particularly mysterious: a fat woman with pendulous breasts and a

Archaeologist Shahina Farid poses with a 9,000-year-old skull at Çatalhöyük.

hanging belly sitting on a throne between two leopards. An object resembling a head lies between her feet. Some researchers say she is shown in the act of giving birth.

There were no male figures among the finds, except an occasional man or child in a female's arms. Researchers first thought the female figurines might be associated with fertility magic or with some other cult use. But the enthroned woman with the wild cats suggests a goddess.

Soon the secret of the great discovery was out. Travel agents began to organize "Goddess Tours of Anatolia." The summit of the mound at Çatalhöyük became a sacred spot for contemporary devotees of the goddess.

"They tie ribbons on this low fence, they hold hands in a circle, they even chant in unison," Shahina informs us.

James Mellaart couldn't continue the excavations at Çatalhöyük because at the time there were no known techniques to preserve the excavated mud-brick walls. There are also reports that Mellaart was expelled from Turkey for alleged involvement in a scandal concerning lost Bronze Age artifacts. A committee of archaeologists later proved his innocence, but he never came back to the site. However, Cambridge University's Ian Hodder, one of Mellaart's students, returned in 1993 with an international team and resumed excavations.

In an email interview with me in 2001, Hodder said that he questions some of Mellaart's conclusions. "The female figurines may have represented a psychological process expressed in art as the people who lived in the settlement domesticated wild plants and animals," he wrote. "We certainly found nothing that indicates that women had higher status than men at Çatalhöyük." But Hodder found nothing that might indicate women had lower status, either.

Here I will say that I am neither a New Age spiritualist nor a follower of Wicca nor a goddess worshipper. I am simply a female researcher who is passionate about Anatolia's human past and who is fascinated with the likelihood that completely different societies than the ones we now take for granted once existed on this soil. On the trail of the Anatolian goddess, I have come to understand something striking, frustrating, and exciting about prehistoric archaeology: there are so many gaps in research, and so little proof about how prehistoric peoples viewed the universe, that ultimately we are left with one archaeologist's speculation pitted against another's.

But here is what I find mind-boggling about Çatalhöyük: the settlement had no fortifications and the site never suffered war. None of the human bones found there show any evidence of a violent death. No weapons likely to have been used against human beings have been discovered. A human society where war was unknown!

The people of Çatalhöyük lived extremely close together. They built layer upon layer on the ruins of the mud-brick houses on a gradually rising mound. The houses had adjoining rooms, with entrances from the roofs. There were no temples and no monuments among the remains of the settlement — in other words, no evidence of a hierarchy or central authority.

Riane Eisler argues in *The Chalice and the Blade* that the Neolithic was a period when societies conformed to a "partnership" model rather than a "domination" model introduced later by Indo-European peoples. She suggests that the opposite of "patriarchal" societies wasn't "matriarchal" societies, but societies in which both women and men had high status, and where diversity wasn't equated with inferiority or superiority. Eisler refers to Çatalhöyük as an example of a peaceful society where women likely had high status and where sexual relations were free of shame.

$$\mathbb{C}$$

The excavation team at Çatalhöyük works six days a week, ten hours a day, and takes Fridays off. On Thursday evenings, they have a soccer game. Men and women, Turks and foreigners, run together behind a ball at the foot of the Neolithic mound, while Hüseyin, the cook from Küçük Köy, prepares coals for a barbecue. The three village women don't play ball but watch at the edge of the field and cheer. I stand with them.

Mavili giggles and jumps. She confides to me that she is waiting for love. "*İçim kıpır kıpır.* Things are stirring in me. I don't know if it'll come, or when, but I'm waiting."

Later in the evening, Mavili tells me about a solitary, recent grave on the east side of the mound. It belongs to a *kötü yola düşmüş kadın,* a fallen woman, of Mavili's parents' generation. The villagers didn't want the body in their cemetery, so they buried the woman at Çatalhöyük. Mavili puts her arm through mine and leads me to the stone that marks the grave: "Güllü Aysa. 22-2-1933. *Ruhuna Fatiha*" — "A Prayer for Her Soul."

While we pause before the grave, a bunting perches on the granite gravestone and chirps. It seems fitting to me that Güllü Aysa, who was harshly judged even after death, now rests in the realm of Anatolia's first Mother Goddess, with the bones of an ancient people who might have found nothing wrong with her way of life.

After the football game, the cook hands everyone half a loaf of fresh bread stuffed with spicy lamb patties, *adana kebap*, with sliced onions, tomatoes, and a yogurt sauce. As the embers of the fire die, the village women and the foreign specialists skip rope together in the pebble-covered yard in front of the dig house. Their happy sounds rise in the Anatolian plain near the dug mound of ancient mud-brick walls and a half-uncovered human skeleton from 9,000 years ago.

That night, in Ian Hodder's room where Jean and I will sleep (Hodder won't come to the site until July), I reread sections of Mircea Eliade's *A History of Religious Ideas*. Eliade says women were the original owners of the earth and of the harvest. The working of the land, the sowing of seeds in the Great Mother's body, was a religious rite in itself.

The night advances. The archaeologists who will begin work at 7:00 a.m. have all turned in. Suddenly, a voice thunders outside the dig house. Jean and I scramble to the door.

"This is a world-class historic site!" Sadettin Dural, the guard, is chasing a herd of sheep away from the pasture beside the excavation covered with plastic sheets and sandbags. He waves his arms and yells at a human shadow between the poplars — a shepherd. "Don't let me catch you and your sheep near here again!"

The night is heavy with the chirping of crickets, and an owl hoots at regular intervals. The air outside has turned chilly and smells of wet grass.

☾

On a spring-like February night, I ride behind Jean on the motorcycle, staring at the thick smog that smothers Ankara — coal pollution. We weave between cars and trucks, slipping through streets crowded with concrete-block apartments. Neon signs and billboards advertising Levi's jeans, cellular phones, and Internet servers whip past us, and I think about the crisis of vision that is killing the Earth. The greenhouse effect. Droughts. Dioxins, PCBs, electromagnetic fields. Poverty. Corruption. Economic collapse. Wars fought over oil and gas in the Middle East and Central Asia.

At the dawn of the third millennium AD, greedy and warlike civilizations are destroying the world. We live in a fury of consumption as if our human nature condemns us to doom. But our human nature is constructed, imagined, under certain cultural, economic, and political circumstances. Is there still time to imagine differently, to build kinder societies? And what if, thousands of years ago, people did just that, *on this land*?

In *The Language of the Goddess*, Marija Gimbutas argues that peaceful, egalitarian, goddess-worshipping civilizations thrived in the Middle East and Europe for thousands of years before the arrival of nomadic, patriarchal, and warlike Indo-Europeans from the Russian steppes between 4500 and 2500 BC. Gimbutas says that goddess worship lasted about 20,000 years during the Paleolithic and Neolithic periods, and that we can't comprehend the classical Greek and Roman civilizations without understanding this "old" prehistoric religion. What she doesn't say (because her research was in Europe) is that the "old" religion continued in Anatolia for thousands of years, even after the invasions of patriarchal Indo-European tribes, and that it had a profound influence on Mesopotamian civilizations and monotheistic religions.

The theory of the "old" religion sounded appealing but abstract when I read Gimbutas's books in Canada. Gimbutas's methodology was later criticized by other archaeologists, but in Anatolia her theory resonates with meaning and mystery. Here I see the mountainous landscape out of which the goddess was born. I marvel at the frenzied renewal of life after the spring rains, and at the variety of flowers and fruits that burst out of the land.

"Do you know why you decorate bulls with garlands each spring?" I yearn to ask villagers astride donkeys on country roads. "Do you know why you call those bulls that inseminate your cows *damızlık*? Because here, on your lands, male breeding animals once represented the goddess's groom, Tammuz or Dumuzi."

I want to tell the farmers about the Amazons and about Minoan Crete: "Neolithic Anatolian colonists found their way to Crete around 6000 BC, bringing their knowledge of agriculture and their goddess with them. What if they were the ones who sowed the seeds of a legendary civilization that prospered for 4,000 years? Imagine!"

Pieces of the Puzzle — the Amazons

What happens after Çatalhöyük? Where does the Anatolian goddess emerge next? I am free to research and to strain my imagination on the missing pieces of the puzzle.

Historians describe a 2,000-year period of obscurity in Anatolia after Çatalhöyük was abandoned. They say that from the fifth millennium to the third millennium BC small agrarian communities continued to live in various regions of the peninsula, but they built no great monuments and left behind no remarkable objects.

I embark on a pilgrimage to the fortress hill in Ulus, a shabby district with medieval-looking shops on streets packed with dilapidated houses in the oldest quarter of Ankara. Walking up the hill, I note how surprisingly close the outer fortifications are. Stairs lead to a park, with acacias and lindens between the outer and inner walls of the fortress. From there I watch the city sprawl beneath me in a haze.

Across the street from the southern gate of the park there is a domed building in the Seljuk style that was once an inn and a *bedesten* or market. Today it is the Museum of Anatolian Civilizations. A massive falcon made of basalt, and a headless marble torso with the tight chest, firm belly, and modest testicles of a larger-than-life Roman warrior, sit in its courtyard. Hittite and Phrygian lions carved from marble, basalt, or limestone, and dozens of clay amphorae, are strewn about the garden between rose bushes. Blocks of stone with Latin and Greek inscriptions lie around as if part of the landscape. I recognize a classical statue: a headless

A dirt road winds up a hill in Ankara's Ulus district. (Semih Bilgen)

woman on a throne, her skirt draped over her knees and the remains of what might have been a lion beside her right foot. Cybele, the great Mother Goddess!

When this museum is empty of tourists, it can move me to tears. Daylight streams in from its glass-covered roof, and I stand before glass cases in which objects excavated at ancient sites bear silent testimony to a mysterious human past on this soil.

The fat goddess of Çatalhöyük lounges in a glass case, her haunches spread on a throne. Dozens of plump female figurines with large bellies, big hips, and pendulous breasts — reclining, sitting, and standing — fill the Neolithic displays. And then there are the huge bulls' heads and bulls' horns made of plaster, some of them stylized, and life-size bulls' heads found on walls.

The Stone Age gave way to the Bronze Age in the third millennium BC when metallurgy was developed and trade grew in importance. The fortified settlement at Alacahöyük flourished in central Anatolia during the Bronze Age. Magnificent artifacts — bronze stags and sun discs, gold jugs and jewellery, and all kinds of idols created from various metals and ivory — were discovered in richly furbished tombs at Alacahöyük. Now they all reside in glass cases at the Museum of Anatolian Civilizations.

The people who lived in Alacahöyük in the third millennium BC were the Hatti, who worshipped a splendid sun goddess. There she is! Her body is silver, her head is gold, and a large triangle represents her genitals. This slim figure replaced the fecund figurine of the late Stone Age. On display there are dozens of female-shaped ivory idols, golden twin idols in the shape of women, a stylized bronze woman nursing a baby, and several figurines of women cupping their breasts with hands as if offering sustenance to worshippers. As I stare at the goddess's many manifestations, passages from books I have read about Anatolian prehistory fall into place. In *The Creation of Patriarcy*, Gerda Lerner says the Hatti possessed a strong matrilineal tradition:

> Early Hatti governance was based on a system in which the right of succession lodged in the *tawananna*, the prince's sister…. A male ruler married his sister, who as *tawananna*, was a priestess with considerable economic and political power…. Her male child inherited the right of succession, not because his father was the king, but because the right of succession lodged in the *tawananna*.

Another book by a Turkish writer named Kürşat Başdemir argues that Anatolia experienced a longer matrilineal (or woman-centred) period than other ancient societies in the Middle East. He contends that the topography of Anatolia — the mountain ranges parallel to the northern and southern coasts, the mountainous eastern region, and the mountains that lie perpendicular to the sea in the Aegean region — effectively separated much of the peninsula from the rest of the region.

In Başdemir, who is also trying to fit together the pieces of the puzzle of the Anatolian goddess, I recognize a kindred spirit. I find his telephone number and call him at the engineering firm where he works.

"Oh, I think the Hattis were woman-centred, all right," he says. "They were the descendants of the goddess worshippers of Çatalhöyük. And what's more, at the end of the third millennium BC they fled from the waves of invading Indo-Europeans and established some sheltered communities. I think they became known as the legendary Amazons."

His theory is plausible and appealing. He explains that the topography of the Anatolian peninsula made it difficult in prehistoric times for a strong state to unite the various ethnic communities, which means that even after invasions and the collapse of states and empires in central Anatolia, small matrilineal societies continued to live in the mountainous regions to the north and south, and some of the original matrilineal tribes took refuge in the Pontus Mountains of the Black Sea region.

Donald J. Sobol in *The Amazons of Greek Mythology* describes two separate tribes of Amazons found in Greek myths. He says the first was a tribe of Libyan Amazons, natives of a lost island along the North African coast. The second tribe appeared later, along the southern shore of the Black Sea, and established an empire in Anatolia. This second tribe of Amazons also founded a great temple to the Greek goddess Artemis in Ephesus where Libyan refugees fled from the Greek god Dionysos. Sobol laments the absence of definitive proof of the historical existence of the Amazons, but he points out that there is no proof, either, that they didn't exist.

Başdemir is convinced that the legendary Amazons (who, according to the Greek historian Herodotus, lived in the Termessos region on the Black Sea coast of Anatolia) were tribes who continued to defend the Anatolian goddess and to spread the old religion. "Theirs," he says, "was the most ancient and the most powerful women's movement in history."

I find nothing in history books or archaeological reports to refute his theory.

In Mesopotamia, by the beginning of the third millennium BC, the Sumerians started to build city-states, and soon they invented cuneiform writing, thus initiating recorded history. Anatolians didn't write until the end of the third millennium BC. Sometime in that millennium nomadic, warlike Indo-European tribes arrived in the Middle East with metal weapons and horse-drawn chariots and subjugated the earlier peoples of the region. In Anatolia the invaders who conquered the Hatti lands came to be called the Hittites.

The Hittites eventually built a military kingdom in central and southeastern Anatolia. The carvings on their city walls are also housed in the Museum of Anatolian Civilizations. They show soldiers at war, and people being trampled under horse-pulled chariots. But they also illustrate a procession led by the goddess Kubaba on her throne, followed by priests and priestesses carrying sacrificial animals and sheaves of wheat.

Kubaba's throne sits on a lion, and the goddess holds a pomegranate in her hand — a symbol of fertility. As I stare at that procession, another piece of the puzzle falls into place.

The Goddess of a Military Empire?

In late May, Jean and I rent a car to take Normand, Jacques, and Lucie, three friends visiting from Quebec City, to Hattuşaş, the capital of the Hittite Empire. We head towards Ulus and then turn north through shanty-filled hills dotted with poplars and acacias. Soon we are in the Central Anatolian Highlands, heading towards the town of Sungurlu in the province of Çorum.

The hills are lush green and resplendent with poppies, wild mustard, and birds. Storks are in flight, and bee-eaters cross the road, doing their strange fluttery dance.

By the time we arrive at Boğazkale, the village near the ruins of the Hittite capital, the sky has turned dark with charcoal clouds, and we hear thunder. Families of white geese waddle on the dirt roads of the village. Under the pines in the courtyard of the Aşıkoğlu Motel, we drink cold beer and eat fried eggplant with yogurt sauce, dried beans with tomatoes, and grilled chicken breasts.

We take rooms for the night and set out on foot to visit the ruins.

"It's going to rain," the motel owner warns.

"We don't care," we answer, in English, Turkish, and French.

Large, heavy drops of rain fall as we climb the rocky hill where the ruins stand. The valley and the brick-tiled roofs of village houses lie like toys below us as the glowering sky closes in. The long, winding uphill road is deserted, except for a shepherd and his flock of sheep. There are no tourists.

The stone foundations of the ruins of Hattuşaş form regular rectangles on the hillside. To our right are the remains of the temple of Teshub, the storm god. We stroke the rectangular block of bluish stone at the centre of the ruins. It has black-and-cream veins and is slick from the rain.

"Perhaps it's a meteorite," I say, "the most ancient form of the goddess, according to Mircea Eliade."

"But you said this was a temple of the storm god," Normand says.

"The first use of the name Hittite is found in the Old Testament," I explain. "It refers to an Indo-European people who arrived in Anatolia during the second millennium BC and conquered the lands of a peaceful agrarian people called the Hattis. The Hattis worshipped a sun goddess. The warlike, patriarchal Hittites brought their storm god to Anatolia. But goddess worship was so entrenched in Anatolia that even the Hittites ended up embracing her cult. There's a great deal of evidence that they adopted Hatti traditions and beliefs."

"If the Indo-Europeans were warlike and patriarchal," Jacques says, "isn't it a little far-fetched to jump to the conclusion that they embraced the cult of the goddess?"

"Wait until I take you to Yazılıkaya, fifteen kilometres from here," I answer. "There, at a stunning open-air sanctuary, the entire pantheon of Hittite goddesses and gods are on perpetual parade on rugged cliffs. You know which event dominates that pantheon? The sacred wedding ceremony of Teshub, the Hittite storm god, and Hepat, the sun goddess of the conquered Hatti people. It's carved on the rocks right there. Hepat is standing on a lion and has a pomegranate in her hand, and Teshub is holding lightning rods. The Hittites found a great way to reconcile the goddess cult with the storm god. They joined them in holy matrimony."

Then we speculate about whether such a sacred wedding ceremony was enacted in real life between a Hittite king and a Hatti priestess who stood in for the goddess. I have read that Hittite texts mention Hittite queens in close relationship to the sun goddess. To be accepted by the conquered population, perhaps, as Merlin Stone suggests in *When God Was a Woman*, Hittite rulers had to enact a sacred union symbolically by marrying Hattian princesses or priest-esses. And that may well be how the great fertility goddess, now called Kubaba, came to grace Hittite city walls.

I tell my friends that historians, such as Ekrem Akurgal in *A Cultural History of Anatolia*, comment on the surprisingly high status of women in Hittite socie-ty. At a time in Mesopotamia when male domination was already established, Hittite queens held as much power as kings, and women were equal to men in every area of life.

"So this could have been a temple where both the storm god and the sun goddess were worshipped," Normand says.

We'll never know for sure, I think. *All that remains are the stones of the temple's foun-dations and the mysterious bluish block at the centre.*

At the southeastern end of the summit of the hill, we stand before the mon-umental arched gates of massive ramparts. The snout and paws of one of the two lion sphinxes guarding the city are broken from 4,000 years of wind and rain.

Below the ramparts we pass through an arched stone tunnel. When we come out to glowing daylight at the other end, we stand below a flight of stone stairs, looking out on a forest of dwarf oaks.

"Was there a city here after the Hittites?" Jacques asks me.

"Oh, yes. Waves of different people kept settling in the cities of earlier peoples, and they blended with one another for thousands of years."

Then I tell Jacques that something catastrophic happened to Hittite cities around 1200 BC. Waves of new warrior tribes coming from Thrace and the Balkans destroyed the late Hittite Kingdom. Archaeologists have found evi-dence of devastating fires at some Hittite cities. They say Anatolia entered another period of chaos around that time.

The one-room museum at Boğazkale is still open when we return to town that evening. The attendant turns on the lights for us and watches as we wan-der between the cases displaying Hittite, Phrygian, and Byzantine artifacts. The backyard of the museum is full of tombstones with Byzantine crosses on them.

Later we drink *rakı* (an anise-flavoured alcoholic drink) and eat crisp *börek* (a savoury cheese-filled pastry) on the terrace of the motel. The air smells of wet soil and wild roses. *"Le bonheur n'est pas loin,"* Normand says. "Happiness isn't far away."

"Hittite tablets, Phrygian bowls, and Byzantine coins and tombstones, all in one tiny museum," Jacques notes. "What a country!"

"A statue of the Phrygian goddess Cybele was found in the ruins of Hattuşaş," I announce to my friends, "which means that around 800 BC, long after the Hittites, the Phrygians captured the city."

Tipsy on *rakı*, I then launch into a gory Hittite myth of castration and regeneration: "Once upon a time, a god named Kummarbi bit off the genitals of Anu, an older god. You may think this is outlandish, but a tribe called the Hurrians in Upper Mesopotamia passed this myth on to the Hittites in Anatolia, and Hittite tablets tell the story in cuneiform. What's more, other eastern Mediterranean people tell similar myths. Anyway, Kummarbi castrated Anu, but Anu warned him that he, Kummarbi, might conceive from the severed genitals and give birth to monstrous gods. Kummarbi then spit off Anu's genitals, and the earth conceived from them."

"Great tale for a summer night at Boğazkale," Normand says.

I am warming up. "Look," I continue, "the details of the rest of the story are lost because of damage to the tablets, but the myth does describe how Teshub, the storm god, eventually replaced Anu. Now this is important because the themes of castration and conception from the seeds of severed genitals keep reappearing in the mythology of this land. Anatolian peoples seem to be obsessed with the flow of blood as in menstruation, as if they believe men might become fertile like women, if only their genitals are cut off …"

By now Jacques and Normand are impatient. They look at each other and cast downward glances at their own genitals. The conversation deteriorates, and I give up. My Québécois friends have missed the juiciest part of the story. I haven't even come to the Phrygians, and to the myth of Cybele and Attis …

This statue of the Phrygian Cybele flanked by two musicians was found in Hattuşaş near Çorum and is now in Ankara's Museum of Anatolian Civilizations. (Semih Bilgen)

49

((

For several hundred years after the arrival of new warrior tribes from Thrace and the Balkans around 1200 BC, and after the collapse of the Hittite Kingdom, Anatolia remained in darkness. Several Neo-Hittite states survived in southern and southeastern Anatolia, but in central Anatolia no remains of new cities or monuments date from that period. By the early Iron Age (800 BC), the Phrygians established a new kingdom by uniting the peoples who had settled inside the arc of the Halys River in central Anatolia. Gordion became their capital under legendary King Midas.

And now I come to the myth that my Québécois friends were too squeamish to hear. Once upon a time, the sky spilled its seed on the earth and the earth gave birth to a hermaphrodite monster. Jealous spirits (or gods, according to the ancient Greeks) castrated the monster. His severed genitals fell to the ground and an almond tree grew from them. A river nymph ate an almond from that tree and became pregnant. The castrated monster became a goddess served by bulls, guarded by lions, and counselled by serpents. She could make nature burst with life or wither in death. Then she fell in love with a shepherd who happened to be the son born to the river nymph, the son whom the goddess herself had engendered from her own severed male genitals.

The shepherd was about to marry a princess. The jealous goddess appeared to him and drove him crazy. He castrated himself and died beside a fir tree. Bright flowers grew from his blood. The goddess then mourned her loss, repented her own fury, and travelled to the realm of the dead to bring her beloved back to life.

The goddess came to be known as Cybele. And the name of her son/lover was Attis.

Ancient Greek scholars tell us that according to Phrygian mythology Cybele was born from the earth on which Zeus had spilled his sperm. Originally, she was a hermaphrodite named Angdistis, but other gods, jealous of her power, castrated Angdistis and she became the goddess Cybele. An almond tree (or pomegranate in some versions of the myth) sprang from the severed genitals of Angdistis. Nana, the daughter of the River Sangarios, ate an almond from that tree (or put a pomegranate against her breast) and conceived a child named Attis, who became the goddess's beloved.

The Greek historian and geographer Pausanias and the early Christian polemicist Arnobius tell slightly different versions of this myth to explain the Phrygian rites. But both writers lived several centuries after the collapse of the Phrygian Kingdom, and both of them Hellenized the myth.

How savage, how bizarre, all this jealousy, castration, and conception from severed genitals seems! The story of the great goddess and her dying and rising lover/child is one of the earliest myths in the eastern Mediterranean — now pushed beyond memory or rendered unrecognizable by Judeo-Christian trimmings. Before the dawn of history, it was this story that explained the mysterious cycles of nature to people whose survival depended on those cycles. The rites performed in connection with this story marked the yearly decay and revival of life, regulated the seasons, and ensured the fruitfulness of the earth and its creatures.

Variations of this theme emerged in Egyptian, Mesopotamian, pre-classical Greek, and even Norse mythology. At some dark prehistoric age, people enacting this myth, with a priestess or queen who stood in for the goddess and who celebrated a yearly sacred marriage, might well have sacrificed a young man personifying the lover. As time went by, perhaps the sacrifice of virility (and the sacrifice of bulls or rams, which symbolized male virility) replaced the sacrifice of life.

In Greek mythology, it is Chronos who severs his father Uranos's genitals and throws them into the sea. Uranos's sperm engenders Aphrodite, and his drops of blood spawn giants.

Pessinus

> These unsexed beings, in their Oriental costume, with little images suspended on their breasts, appear to have been a familiar sight in the streets of Rome, which they traversed in procession, carrying the image of the goddess and chanting their hymns to the music of cymbals and tambourines, flutes and horns, while the people, impressed by the fantastic show and moved by the wild strains, flung alms to them in abundance, and buried the image and its bearers under showers of roses.
>
> — Sir James George Frazer, *The Golden Bough*

As a university student, when I read Sir James George Frazer's description of "these unsexed beings," I had no idea that the British anthropologist was describing the eunuch priests of the great Anatolian goddess Cybele. I remember reading about Pessinus in *The Golden Bough*. Many years passed before I realized that Pessinus, the centre of goddess worship from time immemorial, was in Anatolia. It is found at a sleepy village named Ballıhisar, about 140 kilometres west of Ankara.

Jean and I ride there in May. On our way, we see storks perched in fields, and larks, doves, and magpies flying and chattering between poplars. Spring rains have splashed the plains with a riot of colours. The ditches are full of poppies. Wild mustard and thistle flowers ripple in yellow and purple waves. Gophers dart through the tall grass and disappear in holes in the damp earth. I smell thyme on the wind, and imagine the distant past.

Ecstatic, savage spring rites. The din of cymbals, flutes, and drums. Eunuch priests wearing lavish robes, and scented with perfumed oils. A sacrificial bull adorned with garlands. Blood spilt in sacred caves. A black stone — a meteorite. The faceless Cybele . . .

A modest yellow sign on the highway points left: "Pessinus Harabeleri 13 Kilometres." The ruins of the ancient sacred city are under a village surrounded with oleasters, apricot orchards, and sugar beet fields. A winding road descends towards a valley. We stop beside a mound overlooking the village and walk on pieces of marble and columns jutting out of the ground between the weeds. With each step, we raise clouds of white butterflies.

A rooster's call blares through the village. White geese stroll over dirt roads between pieces of marble columns. Blocks of marble lie beside barn doors, near the village fountain, and under bales of hay. Marble columns stick out of barn fences and the walls of whitewashed village houses with red tile roofs.

The ruins of a temple rise beside the mosque in the middle of the village, separated from the dirt road by a wire fence whose gate swings open. Nothing identifies the place — no plaque, no tourist stand, no pay booth. The stone fences around the village houses look so similar to the stone walls of the temple that I wonder where the temple ends and the village begins.

On this Sunday morning in spring, the village appears deserted. A woman saunters past on the dirt road, carrying a tray of hot flat bread on her head. She stops to offer us a loaf.

"My cousin is getting engaged today," she says. "Theirs is the white house across from these old stones. You've come all the way from Ankara to see these stones? They tore down some village houses to uncover them."

Garlands and naked bodies are carved on some of the pieces of marble strewn on the ground. The inner part of the temple consists of massive blocks forming corridors as in a labyrinth. I wind my way through them and stand at the centre of the labyrinth where eunuch priests in long robes once kept the most ancient and the most sacred form of the goddess: a piece of black stone — a meteorite.

☾

Pierre Lambrachts, the Belgian archaeologist who excavated the temple at Pessinus during the 1960s, only found the Roman temple — a relatively recent structure that had replaced the earlier ones that are assumed to have been there. Excavations were extremely difficult because the village sat on the ruins. A plaque on the wall of the tiny museum at Pessinus says that Lambrachts believed the Phrygians had inherited the cult of Cybele from earlier Anatolian civilizations. The image of *Matar* in Pessinus was said to be so ancient that it was not made by human hands but had fallen from the sky.

We owe everything we know about Cybele's rites to ancient Greek and Roman historians such as Polybius, Strabo, and Pausanias, who described in their writings the "barbaric" Anatolian festivals that eventually spread to their lands. These writers tell us that the Romans borrowed the cult of Cybele from the Phrygians. Strabo says in his *Geographia* that Pessinus was financially self-sufficient and independent of political interference. When warrior tribes (such as the Phrygians and the Cimmerians) invaded Anatolia, not only did they leave Pessinus untouched, but they also embraced its cult.

Lynn Roller, an expert on ancient religion, says in her book *In Search of God the Mother: The Cult of Anatolian Cybele* that there is no evidence to prove that the orgiastic rites described in detail by classical historians were performed in Anatolia before the cult appeared in Rome. But once again, Roller has no proof at all that those rites weren't performed in Anatolia. It is documented that the worship of *Magna Mater* (Great Mother) was imported to Rome from the Phrygians in Anatolia. Yet faced with a culture whose writing is not deciphered, one expert's speculation is as good as another's.

Frazer writes in *The Golden Bough* that in Pessinus the drama of self-mutilation, death, and resurrection told in the Cybele and Attis myth was re-enacted again and again in wild, orgiastic rites at the spring equinox each year.

Festivals of blood and ecstasy commemorating Attis's death and resurrection lasted thirteen days.

On March 15, the brotherhood of reed bearers brought cut reeds to the temple and worshippers mourned the death of Attis. Seven days later the brotherhood of tree bearers brought a decorated fir branch representing the dead god and carried it through the streets, chanting lamentations. March 24 was *dies sanguinis*, the day of blood. On that day, an orchestra of flutes, cymbals, and drums played wild music while people danced in a mounting delirium, and while Cybele's eunuch priests, called the *Galli*, flagellated themselves with whips and slashed their own skins to make blood flow.

A young man in an ecstatic trance would let out a wild scream and cut off his own genitals with a sacred dagger. He would then run like a madman, blood streaming down his legs as he waved the severed organ like a precious trophy until he finally hurled it into a house. Someone in the house would bring out a woman's garments to the bleeding man. From then on, having offered his manhood to the goddess for the fecundity of the earth, he would become one of the *Galli* and live in a woman's clothes.

The Roman poet Catullus wrote a poem in a metre called Galliambic because its rhythm imitates the wild music of the rites of Attis. The poem, in C.H. Sisson's translation, begins by describing the madness that causes a devotee of Cybele to castrate himself:

> Carried in a fast ship over profound seas
> Attis, eager and hurried, reached the Phrygian grove,
> The goddess's dark places, crowned with woodland.
> And there, exalted by amorous rage, his mind gone,
> He cut off his testicles with a sharp flint.

The worshipper, symbolically named Attis, later regrets his self-mutilation, but the irreversible act has forever enslaved him to Cybele. Catullus ends the poem with a plea:

> Great Goddess, Goddess Cybele, Goddess Lady of Dindymus,
> May all your fury be far from my house.
> Incite the others, go. Drive other men mad.

The night of March 24/25 was filled with funeral lamentations, but on the morning of March 25, *hilaria*, the day of joy, Attis's resurrection was celebrated with joyful dances. On March 28, a gory initiation rite called *taurobolium* sanctified the neophytes. Eunuch priests would hold down a bull decorated with garlands of flowers. One of the priests would raise a sacred knife to the beast's throat. The initiate would enter the hole beneath the grille of the sacrificial altar and wash in the blood of the animal as it was slaughtered. Mircea Eliade, in *A History of Religious Ideas*, says this sacrifice might have taken the place of self-mutilation, "for he offered the victim's genital organs to the goddess. He was admitted to the 'nuptial chamber' (*pastos, cubiculum*), as a mystical husband of Cybele, just like the Gallos, who entered this sacrosanct place to offer the Mother the fruits of his mutilation."

As the music mounted to a crescendo, those purified by the hot blood spurting from the dying bull would dance with renewed ardour, celebrating their communion with Cybele. Thus, as the initiates were reborn for eternity, the earth and its people would be washed with the blood of the sacrificed bull, the powerful masculine animal (another symbol of Attis) lying lifeless on the grille of the altar.

☾

While I walk across the stones of the Roman temple in Pessinus, a gaggle of turkeys, cackling loudly, waddles down the marble steps, which form a semicircle like a small amphitheatre outside the labyrinth. To the right is a rectangular structure labelled "Altar." I close my eyes to imagine the din of cymbals, tambourines, and flutes rising in the wind, with a sudden intimation: *the origins of theatre might have been here in those barbaric rituals. The origins of Bacchic festivals were probably here!*

I glance up from the ruins of the altar and see the minaret of the village mosque. Across the dirt road are pomegranate trees covered with flame-coloured flowers. A couple of villagers hoe sugar beet fields in the distance. At the tiny museum in Pessinus, a collection of bones and human skulls resides in a cardboard box. "Are these real?" I ask the attendant.

"Of course," he answers. "There was a necropolis in Pessinus. These are bones the villagers found when they were farming or building their houses."

I have a wild fantasy. I wonder if the people of this village hear the clang of cymbals, tambourines, and flutes in the night, if they are visited by ghosts of bleeding priests, or by a wild goddess offering a pomegranate. If a village youth had such hallucinations, he would think himself possessed. Yet it seems unthinkable to me that someone might live beside the remains of the stone labyrinth and not have such visions.

The City of Midas

"Make a wish and say a prayer as the train crosses the Sakarya River," my mother says.

I called her to say goodbye before taking the train to İstanbul.

"That crossing is sacred," she adds.

Sakarya, the ancient Sangarios, on whose banks Cybele first met Attis, I think. "That's because the Sakarya is sacred to Cybele," I tell her.

She pauses. "Still," she says, "pray."

It is dusk by the time the train reaches the Sakarya (Sangarios) Valley. The brownish river rushes and gurgles in a canyon between majestic cliffs.

I have prepared my wish and hold my breath, waiting for the crossing. But then I notice something that makes my heart sink: blue and white plastic bags hang on the reeds and on willow branches along the river. It is an ominous sight, ordinary and horrifying at the same time. The debris of the twenty-first century pollutes the banks of the sacred river. The train clunks onto the wooden bridge, and with a heavy heart I make my wish.

The Sakarya cuts an arch through northwestern Anatolia and empties into the Black Sea at the village of Karasu. The highlands inside that arch are Cybele's lands. The countryside between Afyon and Eskişehir is dotted with her sanctuaries. I am on my way to İstanbul to meet Jean, who is riding his motorcycle there. When I hook up with him, we set out together on his bike to explore forgotten shrines.

We ride south towards Afyon and enter a dreamworld of fields with sugar beets and white and mauve opium poppies beside cliffs and bizarre rock formations. Whenever we halt to peer at a map, villagers straighten their backs and come to shake our hands. Women wearing colourful *şalvar*s and carrying old-fashioned hoes pass on the backs of donkeys and greet us with broad smiles and "*Hoşgeldiniz*, welcome."

Local people know about the goddess shrines.

"You should see Aslan Kaya, Lion's Rock," says Şerife Karagöz, an elderly woman on her way to her potato fields. She describes a giant boulder on which a bride stands between two lions. "Just keep going between the cedars," she adds.

Our motorcycle dives into the sand between oak trees, its wheels spinning and digging in. We advance slowly and eventually reach a grotesquely shaped boulder on our right. It is eroded and covered with lichen, but there is no mistaking the rearing lion carved on its southern surface. The shrine is on the boulder's western surface: a square niche with a temple roof, and Cybele, the *bride*, between two rearing lions.

Speechless, Jean and I circle the boulder, linger across from it, then climb onto the stones beside it to touch the rock. Then, suddenly, we both spy something strange: there are hollows where Cybele's and the lions' genitals should be. Has the rock been worn down from being rubbed by worshippers? Jean finds this explanation implausible, but he can't come up with a better one.

A goddess whose priests castrated themselves, and whose creatures and whose own image on rocks have hollowed-out genitals! Perhaps all our explanations will be implausible. Perhaps the mystery will remain impenetrable ...

I remember Reşit Ergener's observations about blood, sacrifice, and fertility. I think about the Romans who later embraced the cult of Cybele and who considered her priests, the *Galli*, women. (They used the female pronoun to describe them.) Roman writers referred to "the licentious behaviour" of the *Galli*, who roamed the streets with their long hair and in their extravagant robes begging alms for *Matar* in high-pitched voices.

Lynn Roller, in her book *In Search of the Mother: The Cult of Anatolian Cybele*, remarks that the *Galli* removed their testicles, but not their entire sexual organs, and that their castrated status made it impossible for them to reproduce but didn't appear to inhibit their sexual appetites. Roller reports that numerous anecdotes described the *Galli* as purveyors of offbeat sexual activities — clearly titillating to respectable people — and that Cybele's priests entered erotic liaisons with both men and women. "Thyillos," Roller tells us, "writes of Aristion, who once tossed her hair to Cybele, but is now dead from excesses of heavy drinking and all-night festivals of love."

The ambiguous sexual status of the *Galli*, Roller goes on to say, was precisely the thing that made them covertly attractive. The element of sexual ambiguity, the feminine quality of the priests, suggested that the male participants in the cult of Cybele could toy with transvestitism, bisexuality, and emotional release. "Small wonder that men kept returning to mistress Cybele," Roller writes.

☾

"Which way to Midas City?" I call out from the motorcycle to villagers in the fields after we leave Lion's Rock.

"*Dosdoğru,* straight ahead," they answer back. Driving south towards Eskişehir, we pass through a forest of Mediterranean pine, then enter a barren countryside marked only by strange rock formations. As we approach a village, we wonder if we are still on the correct road, but then, suddenly, know we have arrived.

A reddish monument carved into the face of some rocks towers behind the village. It has a temple-shaped facade with geometric designs, and a square niche that once housed a statue of Cybele. On the temple-shaped gable, there is some writing. Researchers have deciphered only one word — "Midas," the name of the most famous Phrygian king — so they refer to this monument, erroneously, as the Tomb of Midas. It is actually a shrine to Cybele.

Here, just as in Cappadocia, volcanic turf has formed wild shapes and people have chiselled caves, shrines, altars, and ceremonial sites into the rocks. It is hard to distinguish man-made caves from natural ones. The Phrygian *Matar* reigned particularly in places where nature was savage and magnificent, where the crust of the earth was full of peaks, cracks, and crevasses.

In *A History of Religious Ideas,* Mircea Eliade explains why that was so. He says the development of iron metallurgy suddenly rendered the earth sacred: "Metals 'grow' in the bosom of the earth. Caves and mines are assimilated to the womb of Mother Earth. The ores extracted from mines are in some sort 'embryos.'"

On the eastern side of the cliffs, there is a sharp descent from an acropolis, with steep, worn steps leading to two gaping caves — a sacred pitch-black womb. Jean and I stand before it. I imagine a procession of gaudy, perfumed eunuch priests descending those stairs. Did they carry torches? Did they play wild music? Cymbals and flutes — said to have been invented by the Phrygians — were Cybele's favourite instruments. They are still the most common instruments in Anatolia.

In the second century AD, Clement of Alexandria, as reported by Eliade in *A History of Religious Ideas*, wrote a mysterious sentence about the rites of Cybele. "From the tambourine I have eaten; from the cymbal I have drunk; I have become the *kernos*; the room I have entered." He was referring to an initiation rite. Was it in such forbidding chambers that the initiates drank from the cymbal and ate from the drum?

Like many archaeological sites in Anatolia, this wild place was also used by earlier and later civilizations. Hittite reliefs on some of the cliffs show that the Phrygians inherited this sanctuary from the earlier peoples of Anatolia and passed it on to the later ones. Byzantine tombs stood beside the Phrygian shrines.

Stairs lead to a cave at the Cybele sanctuary in Midas City.

Hürü Kara

In his book about the Anatolian goddess, Reşit Ergener describes a wild, remote place in central Anatolia where some villagers found a relief of the goddess carved on the rocky cliffs on the banks of the Scylax (İncesu) River. The spot was unrecorded, he says, practically unknown to experts or tourists.

On an October afternoon, my brother, Semih, and I set out in his Polo in search of the village of İncesu. We drive northeast from Ankara through treeless mountains that resemble giant sand dunes, turn on dirt roads whose bumps hit the undercarriage of the car, descend into valleys where villagers harvest wheat, ask for directions, and finally reach a verdant oasis of poplars, willows, and figs surrounded by crimson cliffs.

A group of women sits on the banks of the river, sorting sheaves of rice. "Oh, yes, the lady on the rocks," they say when we tell them what we are looking for. "This is the right place." Then they look us up and down and ask if we have a change of clothes.

One of the women, a regal-looking elderly matron wearing a black head-dress, approaches us. "You'll have to wade in the water up to your chest," she says. "There's no other way."

One and a half kilometres of wading in the water! It is late October, and a cold wind blows from the mountains.

Disappointed, we walk around the village in the canyon. The land is sliced as if a violent cosmic event broke the crust of the earth, forming crags and cre-vasses. We strain to look beyond the bend where the cliffs on both sides of the river turn west. "Is there no mountain path?" we ask people we encounter. "Can't we follow the banks?" No, we are told. The woman on the rocks is unreachable except through the water.

We return to the group of ladies on the banks of the river. The face of the old woman with the black headdress is full of wrinkles, and she has wisps of henna-dyed hair at her temples. "Hürü Kara," she introduces herself, "widow and grandmother." She kisses my cheeks and holds my hands as if I am a long-lost friend. "That's my house," she says, pointing at a pink house among wal-nut trees. "Come, drink some tea. I'll recite verses for you."

My brother and I walk up the slope to a small house with a balcony fac-ing the river. We leave our shoes on the porch and enter a room furnished with embroidered cushions. Hürü's married daughter serves us blood-red tea in glasses with slender waists.

"You promised us verses," I remind Hürü.

She lifts her head, closes her eyes, and begins in a low, slightly hoarse voice:

> "Gel ağlayarak bacım Hürü,
> Kuru yerden yer istiyor,
> Oğlu yok, yüreği yangın,
> Çobanlardan kar istiyor ..."

> "Come weeping, my sister Hürü,
> She wants a dry place.
> Her son is gone, her heart's on fire.
> She wants snow from shepherds to extinguish it ..."

Taken aback by the beauty and sadness of the verse, we stop sipping tea. Hürü opens her eyes. "My son, Garip, was killed in a blood feud ten years ago," she tells us. Then she gets up, takes a photo out of the Arborite cupboard in the corner, and shows us a smiling young man with sideburns and high cheekbones.

After many hugs and good wishes, Semih and I finally make our way back to the old Polo. "Wait!" Hürü shouts before we can start the car's engine. She disappears for a couple of minutes, then returns to thrust an armful of rice stalks through the window. A parting gift.

"Write to me," she says. "I'll write, too. I'll send you verses."

Back in Ankara, I dry the rice stalks and put them in a copper jug on my windowsill.

Eight months later, in July, Semih and I make a second trip to İncesu, once again getting lost between the mountains and wondering if the place exists at all. We are on the verge of giving up when my brother recognizes the cluster of walnut trees near the village and the cliffs on the banks of the river.

It is high summer. Most villagers are away in their sugar beet fields, but we find Hürü Kara beside a wood stove in a hovel, making flat bread with a toothless old woman. This time we bring her some gifts: a box of *lokum* (Turkish delight) and some soap. We accept her invitation to eat at her house after our expedition upstream.

We set out with a teenage boy as a guide, wading in the river up to our waists, fording it from time to time. Our guide advances with a fast and sure gait while we slip on sticky mud and hurt our feet on rough stones. The cliffs surrounding us are red from ferrous oxide and are full of fissures. Oak, fig, and walnut trees grow wild on the banks. The river winds west, and as we turn to follow it, the sky grows darker as if the bluffs are hiding the sun. Then the wind picks up.

While we stare at the sky and at the red-and-mauve cliffs soaring above us, our guide stops and raises a hand towards the right bank. "There she is!"

At that remote place, on the steep surface of the canyon facing the river, behind a fig tree, is a life-size carving of Cybele. Wind and rain have eroded the features of her face, but the folds of her tunic are still visible. Across the water from where she stands, there is a gaping black hole at the bottom of the cliffs — an underground cave with steps descending 300 metres into the bowels of the earth. Reşit Ergener, in *Anatolia, Land of the Mother Goddess*, says the carving was made between 280 and 264 BC during the Pontus Roman Kingdom.

After our adventure, Semih and I change our clothes in the car and head to Hürü Kara's one-room house. Her granddaughters are folding flat bread and pouring yogurt into a tin-lined copper pot when we arrive. Hürü is making us tea on a wood stove on the front porch. We eat broad beans in olive oil, fried eggs, yogurt, and bread. Hürü brings us a tray full of freshly picked walnuts, peels off the green coating on the nuts, staining her hands black, and offers us the tender white kernels.

Later, as we get into the car to leave, Hürü runs out to give us a plastic bag full of sugar. "I can't let you go without a gift," she says. "Take this. Don't forget me."

I write Hürü a thank-you note from Ankara and send her copies of the pictures I took at her house. On a winter morning, when the air has a hint of frost, I receive a letter from my new friend.

Widow, grandmother, and poet Hürü Kara appears pensive in her ometown of İncesu.

"I send you greetings, my lady daughter," she writes. "Greetings to my gentleman son. [She means my brother.] I kiss your eyes. I hope you are well. Your letter made my heart glad. I'm sending this to you hoping that you'll receive it and it will make you glad." Then she breaks into rhyming verses in an oral tradition that dates back to the Middle Ages:

> The birds of this village fly high
> To drink from open waters in wide spaces.
> Misty mountains, give passage
> To end separations.
> Weep, my eyes, in longing.
> Hürü woman sits alone, no one hears her voice.
> Give passage, smoky mountains.
> No one protects the one who has no kin.
> I alone wear the rough shirt of separation.
> Give passage, smoky mountains.

She ends her letter with: "Forgive me. This is the best I could do. I kiss your eyes and wait for your speedy reply."

I write back to her: "Dear Hürü *Abla* [Older Sister]. Your verses have made me glad. I think often of your village. I, too, kiss your eyes. Be well."

By the end of the third century BC, the Romans embraced the worship of Cybele. During the reign of King Attalus 1 of Pergamon, an oracle prophesied that the only way to end the war between Rome and Carthage was to bring the great Phrygian goddess to Rome. The Romans asked the Phrygians for the sacred black meteorite, and in 204 BC they transported it from Pessinus to Rome by boat. They placed it in a temple built for her on the Palatine Hill. From then on, the Anatolian goddess called *Magna Mater*, her chariot pulled by lions, and her orgiastic rituals became a part of Roman life.

Artemis of Ephesus

In June, apricots as large as eggs ripen in the garden of my parents' summerhouse on the Aegean coast. Flame-coloured flowers adorn pomegranate trees. The red bougainvillea I planted during a visit from Canada years ago has trailed up the garden wall and is full of flowers. Oleanders bloom on the roadside. Early in the morning, thyme, oregano, and rosemary release their scents, and the sea is cool, its surface creamy.

Half asleep, I walk into the water before breakfast. I shiver, dive in, and begin to stroke. Lines of light move in the sea — blue-green jelly, rippling, jiggling. Goat bells tinkle on the hills. I lie on my back, thinking about the Amazons. In the early morning, their world doesn't seem so far away.

The ruins of the ancient Ionian city of Ephesus are sixty kilometres to the south — a forty-five-minute motorcycle ride. Ephesus is where Saint Paul preached the gospel, and where Saint John and the Virgin Mary are said to have taken refuge after Jesus Christ's crucifixion. But the city is best known for its great goddess Artemis whose turreted crown, Eastern dress, and the bees, bulls, and sea creatures swarming on her skirts belie her Hellenic name.

I have seen the statues of the Ephesian Artemis perhaps a hundred times. With the dozens of breasts (or eggs or bulls' testicles) protruding on her chest, wild creatures on her skirts, moons behind her head, and lions on her arms, I have always known that she wasn't the Hellenic virgin goddess of the hunt. But I didn't know what to make of her until I began to solve the mystery of Cybele. Now I know that the Ephesian Artemis is none other than the great and ancient Anatolian goddess. Now I understand Pausanias who says that long before the arrival of the Ionians, she was the goddess of the Amazons, who erected her statue under a beech tree and who danced wildly around it, clanging their shields.

Pausanias also says that it was the Amazons who first built many of the cities (such as Priene, Myrina, Kyme, Symrna, and Ephesus) on the Aegean coast of Anatolia, and who established the cult of the goddess who came to be known as the Ephesian Artemis.

On a marble frieze in the museum of Selçuk, the town near the ruins of Ephesus, the Amazons stand in perpetual motion. Their short tunics fly, wisps of hair fall over their faces, and they hold their shields as if in a war dance. Homer, in *The Iliad*, refers to them as "The peers of men." He says they fought to defend Troy against the Achaeans.

In Greek mythology, the Amazons are the daughters of Ares, the god of war, and Harmonia, the goddess of love (the counterpart of Aphrodite). One of their weapons, in addition to the bow and arrow, is the double-bladed axe, a weapon associated with goddess worship and familiar from wall carvings found in Hittite cities and in Crete.

Were the Amazons a figment of the mythical imagination, or were they, as Turkish writer Kürşat Başdemir suggests, Anatolian warrior women defending and spreading the land's ancient way of life and its old religion — the heroic warriors of the Anatolian goddess?

The word *Amazon* has several possible roots. According to Herodotus in *Histories*, it may have some relationship to the word *oior-pata*, which means "man-slayers" in the Scythian language. That's one possibility. The second is that it may have been derived from the Greek *a-mazos*, which means "breastless," to describe the tribe of women who cut off their right breasts for the sake of archery. A third explanation connects their name to the word *amissa* (*amissawana*), which in the Luwite language means "land of the holy mother," and which became the name of a town on the Black Sea coast of Anatolia (today's Samsun) where the Amazons lived.

They have left no written documents, and the legends that refer to their feats have always been interpreted through a patriarchal prism. Ancient historians tell us anecdotes and legends about them, viewing them sometimes with admiration, sometimes with astonishment, sometimes with awe, and sometimes with contempt.

In *Histories*, Herodotus describes the young Scythian men who found an enemy corpse after a battle with the Amazons and who thus discovered that their enemies were female. He says the Scythians advanced and pitched their camps near the enemy "on account of their strong desire to obtain children from so notable a race," and that the Amazons accepted to make love with the Scythians but refused to live in their country, saying, "we could not live with your women — our customs are quite different from theirs. To draw the bow, to hurl the javelin, to bestride the horse, these are our arts of womanly employments. Your women, on the contrary, do none of these things, but stay at home in their wagons, engaged in womanish tasks, and never go out to hunt, or to do anything."

Such anecdotes, always shaded with the patriarchal biases of the writers, seem to refer to the last stages of the existence of the Amazons. Amissa and Themiskyra on the Black Sea coast were their lands.

If the Amazons were the original peoples of Anatolia, the descendants of the people of Çatalhöyük and of the Hattis, they would have moved northwards in the third millennium BC to flee the Indo-European Hittites. Sheltered by the Pontus Mountains, they would have continued their woman-centred existence until the arrival of sea-faring tribes from Thrace and the Balkans around 1200 BC, and the fall of Troy to the Achaeans around the same time.

This hypothesis is exciting.

British writer George Thomson remarks in *Studies in Ancient Greek Society: The Prehistoric Aegean* that prehistoric societies in the Aegean region of Anatolia were matriarchal or matrilineal. Perhaps this observation (based on Herodotus and other ancient historians) is not surprising; after all, the Amazons and their goddess seem to have been rooted in ancient Anatolian traditions.

☾

A billboard at the ruins of Ephesus says the Ionian city was founded early in the first millennium BC. According to Greek legend, Androclos, the son of an Athenian king, set sail for the Anatolian coast after the oracle at Delphi told him that a fish and a wild boar would lead him to a spot where he would found a new city. One day, while Androclos was frying fish, a fish fell out of the pan and disturbed a wild boar in the bush. Androclos hunted the boar and decided that the oracle had been fulfilled.

The Ionians were among the Hellenic tribes who invaded the Aegean coast of Anatolia during the late second millennium BC. But the city that became Ephesus was much older than the Ionian city. Greek myths, as related by Herodotus, tell us that Amazon Queens Marpesia and Hippo established Ephesus, built a wooden statue of their goddess Artemis under a date tree, and danced around it noisily, singing and clashing their shields. Recent excavations demonstrate that the myths may well be historically accurate: more than 1,000 years before the arrival of the Ionians, a Bronze Age settlement named Apasas existed on the same site. When the Hellenic tribes arrived, they found the region populated and the ancient Anatolian religion entrenched on the Aegean coast, just as it was in the interior of the peninsula. At Apasas various Anatolian peoples were living around the temple of the great Anatolian goddess.

For several centuries, the Anatolian states resisted the Hellenic invaders. Homer's *Iliad* tells the story of the siege and fall of Troy, one of those states on the northern Aegean coast. Apasas was another state, farther south. The Ionians finally captured Apasas during the first millennium BC and built a new city, which they named Ephesus. They adopted the goddess of the land and gave her the name of their own virgin, the hunting goddess Artemis.

But the Cybele shrines found in Ionian cities show that the cult of Cybele lived on along with the worship of Artemis. It appears that the indigenous population continued to call the goddess Cybele, and continued to worship her in the ancient way, while the ruling classes preferred the Hellenic name of Artemis.

Selçuk

In summer, storks nest on top of the columns of the Roman aqueduct in Selçuk, the town that now stands near the ruins of Ephesus. On a hot day in June, a dozen storks fly between the columns and the red-tiled roofs overlooking the little square where old men play backgammon and drink tea. Before venturing out to walk three kilometres to the ruins of Ephesus, I eat a meal of green beans and tomatoes in olive oil with a side dish of yogurt at a small restaurant on the square.

I am sipping Turkish coffee and contemplating the storks when suddenly a wild cry issues from the square. A woman is screaming, and her voice fills me with dread. Old men continue to play backgammon, and the waiter who served me calmly leans against the door, looking towards the benches under the aqueduct. I follow his gaze and see a middle-aged woman with long, unkempt hair and a suntanned face with strong features.

Wearing a loose, flounced skirt and a colourful vest over a cotton blouse, the woman stands beside a bench and shouts, "A curse on this town, on all of you!" She shakes a finger at the town as she curses it, and her voice almost breaks. "You hypocrites. You infidels. May you all rot in your own dirt and your own tears!" After each phrase, she lets out a horrible wail.

"She is hurting," I say to the waiter. "Someone should go to her."

"Don't," he says. "She'll curse you, too. That's Şerife."

I press my hands to my ears to shut out the anguished voice.

"Years ago," the waiter says, "this Şerife became the mistress of a married man, and when he left her, she fell into a bad life, *kötü yola düştü*. She worked at the bars around here, prostituted herself, got into drugs. Now she goes around cursing the town, and then we don't see her for a while. People are used to her, but we don't want her to disturb the tourists."

Şerife suddenly grows quiet. Two police officers appear beside her. One speaks to her while the second holds her arm. At first she pulls her arm away and looks as if she is arguing with them. Then she picks up a bundle from a bench and begins to shuffle down the road, stopping from time to time to continue to curse, but her voice has lost its strength.

I pay for my lunch and stroll towards the mulberry-lined road leading to Ephesus, Şerife's cries ringing in my ears. *A defeated Amazon*, I mutter to myself.

The Artemision

Half a kilometre from Selçuk, a sign points to the Artemision, the great temple of Artemis, which once was one of the Seven Wonders of the World. It was this temple that spread the city's fame across the Ancient World and made it a place of pilgrimage and refuge. Now it is a swampy hole surrounded by huge eucalyptus trees. White geese swim in puddles, and lizards dart between the cracks of massive stones where once stood the altar of the Ephesian Artemis.

Pausanias says the first priestesses of Artemis were the Amazons, and they were called *Melissae* (bees). The whole organization of the sanctuary, even in classical times, seems to have rested on the symbolic analogy of a beehive, with swarms of priestesses called bees, *Melissae*, and numerous eunuch priests named *Essenes* or "drones."

In the seventh century BC, the Ionians built a majestic new temple in Ephesus to honour Artemis. It was destroyed several times by wars and fires, but they rebuilt it in the sixth century BC using the finest marble they could find. Their best artists made brass and silver sculptures for the temple, and they gilded the columns with gold and silver.

The hierarchy in the temple of Artemis was different from that in other temples in Greece. Her priests, called *Magabysos*, or *Curetes*, were castrated like the priests of Cybele, and the Artemision was not only a place of worship but also a centre of social and economic activity.

The worship of the Ephesian Artemis was noisy and frenzied just like that of Cybele. Classical writers talk about howling and clashing noises, shrill flutes, and whirling dances in her honour. The Greek poet Callimachus, in his *Hymn to Jove* of 260 BC, says the *Curetes* danced vigorously, "rattling their arms." The Roman poet Virgil adds, "They clash the cymbals of the Great Mother to imitate the noise made by swarming bees."

Today two large statues of the Ephesian Artemis stand in the Hall of Artemis in Selçuk's small museum. They were both found buried in sand (almost hidden for protection) under the Prytaneion (the administrative building) in the ruins of Ephesus in an excellent state of preservation. The three-metre-tall Great Artemis that graces the west side of the hall was made during the first century AD. She wears a crown that looks like an Ionic temple whose columns are supported by griffins and sphinxes. Behind her head there is a moon, with lions and griffins on each side. The lions that stood beside Cybele are now on the goddess's arms.

On the east side of the hall is the 1.74-metre-tall statue known as the Beautiful Artemis. It was made about fifty years later than the Great Artemis. Its marble is of better quality, and the bits of gold that remain in its cracks reveal that it was gilded.

The reign of Artemis of Ephesus continued well into Christianity. The Bible tells us that when Saint Paul arrived at Ephesus in the summer of 54 AD, preaching that gods made by human hands were no gods at all, thousands of rioting Ephesians filled the great amphitheatre, shouting, "Great is the Artemis of Ephesians!"

Even after Christianity became the official religion of the Eastern Roman Empire, the rites of the goddess continued. In 431 AD, the third ecumenical council of the Christian church met in Ephesus. Unable to get rid of the worship of the great goddess, the church doctors declared that the Virgin Mary had spent the last days of her life in Ephesus and died there.

The Byzantines destroyed the Temple of Artemis. In the second century AD, they used some of its magnificent marbles to build a church for Saint John on a hill a couple of kilometres from the Artemision. During the sixth century, Emperor Justinian started to construct the church called Hagia Sophia in Constantinople. He ordered his men to transport huge blocks of marble from the Church of Saint John and from the ruined Temple of Artemis in Ephesus for his own marvel of architecture.

In the eighteenth and nineteenth centuries, archaeologists from the British Museum in London transferred many of the treasures from the Temple of Artemis to Britain. The pillage of the temple was complete.

In the fourth and fifth centuries AD, despite the rise of Christianity in Anatolia, the cult of Artemis was still alive. An inscription found near the Celsus Library in Ephesus describes how a Christian named Demeas destroyed a statue of the goddess and replaced it with a cross. In 401 AD, Bishop John Chrysostomos dismissed four priests in Ephesus because they didn't fight hard enough against the cult of Artemis.

Behind the remains of Ephesus is a hill called Bülbül Dağı or Nightingale Mountain, which is covered with forests and has a sacred spring. In the eighteenth century, a saintly German nun named Anne Catherine Emmerich had visions in which she saw the house of the Virgin Mary on the hill beside the sacred spring. The nun (who also suffered from a bleeding skin disease that devout Catholics interpreted as stigmata) described her visions to a writer named Clement Brentano. After the death of the nun, Brentano wrote a book relating the description.

Years later, towards the end of the nineteenth century, a French team came to Bülbül Dağı, desperately searching for the Virgin Mary's house. Near the spring, they came across the remnants of some ancient walls. Ethnic Greeks from the nearby village of Kırkıca (today's Şirince) said the spring was sacred (each year on August 15, people still perform special rites at that spot).

"Enough evidence," the explorers said. "This is where the Virgin Mary spent her last days and died." The Catholic Church accepted the conclusion and bought the land surrounding the ruins. Then, in a last-ditch effort to wipe out the memory of the worship of Artemis, the Vatican erected the first church dedicated to Mary at that sacred place, setting up a shrine in Ephesus for the chaste mother of Christ.

On the way to the "Virgin Mary's House," the paved road winds towards the summit of Bülbül Dağı. The mountain is so beautiful, the vistas below it are so wide, and the light is so magical that there is no mistaking the place: this is Mountain Mother territory. As you drive, you come upon a statue of the Virgin Mary holding her arms out at breast level, palms open, just like the Artemis of Ephesus.

☾

So now I know the secret. From time immemorial, God was a woman in Anatolia. This sunny, mountainous peninsula — the colour of whose soil ranges from eggshell-white to brick-red, and in whose villages, women covered from head to toe walk timidly, eyes cast down — was the realm of a great goddess. I cradle the secret, dwell on it, and appreciate this land in a new light. I watch sunlight and cloud shadows move over the wine-dark Anatolian hills and feel as if *Matar* might still be breathing over the moist earth to burst open the seeds in the spring.

The Phrygians and the Romans worshipped the goddess with flutes and tambourines. Her priests castrated themselves in ecstatic trances, flung their severed genitals into caves as offerings to her, and ran like madmen, blood streaming down their legs the way blood flows from menstruating women. They donned gaudy, embroidered robes, swirled ecstatically to a frenzied beat, tossing their long, perfumed hair, and washed in the hot blood of sacrificial bulls. Torch-lit processions of her worshippers wound up towards rock sanctuaries on the mountains in the night, chanting hymns.

I strain to imagine their music, to guess the hypnotic beat of the hymns to *Matar*. I wonder if the people who came after the Phrygians might have borrowed their modes or rhythms, and if the land remembers. Might a lingering Phrygian spirit recognize a turn in the flute's lament or the drum's frenzy, say, at a village wedding today?

No ceremony I have ever witnessed has had the fever, the ecstasy and the horror, of those rites. I want to understand them, as if to tap the source of some repressed collective memories.

The goddess's shrines and sanctuaries are all over Anatolia. I have seen her figure on cliffs and on pieces of granite beside fields of white and purple opium poppies. I have stood before her altar at a sanctuary now called Midas City, stared at steep marble stairs leading to a gaping black cavern, and longed for visions. But Cybele, the Great Mother of mountains and caverns and wild creatures, is now worn and crumbled. She hoards her mysteries, and the stones stand mute.

More than 7,000 years of unbroken worship of a Mother Goddess on Anatolian soil and in the Middle East is now pushed beyond memory. The secret is buried so deeply that I look at the stones of the Artemision with awe, trying to imagine the people who laid them. Theirs was a savage world, too, as cruel as ours but different.

No other deity in any pantheon has as many different names as she has. In Anatolia she was Hepat, Kubaba, Kubele, Matar, Cybele, Agdistis, Leto, and Ephesian Artemis. The Sumerians called her Ma, Marienna, Inanna. Babylonians knew her as Ishtar, Astarte, Ashtoreth. In Egypt her name was Isis. In Crete she was Gaia or Rhea. Her dying and rising lover was Attis, Dumuzi, Tammuz, Baal, Osiris, Adonis ...

The goddess's cult had an immense influence on Western religion and culture. The relics of her worship are rich and significant. The battered, eroded, collapsed remains of her carvings, statues, shrines, and caves are all over Anatolia. Yet no cultural tradition that I know of (except fringe groups such as transsexuals and paganists) has claimed them.

The Cybele that emerges through the mists of time, the goddess with the pomegranate, falcon, and lions, is a far cry from the trendy New Age goddess my feminist friends in Canada long to invoke at the dawn of the twenty-first century. She is all the more fascinating for her dark side, for the sexual mysteries of her rites.

There is evidence that in goddess-worshipping societies women had high status, that they were sexually free, able to own property and pass it on to their children, able to display feats of physical and mental strength, and able to govern. Herodotus and Strabo tell us that in many areas of Anatolia, ancient sexual customs were followed in the worship of the goddess. Even married women lived in temples from time to time and made love to strangers. Strabo also wrote that in his travels he witnessed that the children who were born to temple women were considered legitimate and respectable and simply given the name

The Roman temple of Cybele and Zeus at Aizanoi stands in all its ruined glory near the city of Uşak.

and social status of the mother. He added, as Merlin Stone recounts in *When God Was a Woman*, that the name and title were then proudly used in all official inscriptions. Strabo further comments, as related by Stone, that in the Anatolia of his period, "the unmarried mother seems to be worshipped.... An inscription from Tralles in western Anatolia, carved there as late as 200 AD by a woman named Aurelia Aemilias, proudly announced that she had served in the temple by taking part in the sexual customs, as had her mother and all their female ancestors before them."

☾

Today, in the twenty-first century, the call of the *muezzin* spills from the minarets of mosques five times a day in Anatolia. A paternal god rules supreme and deems femaleness sinful. Yet even the pre-Islamic Arabs worshipped a triple goddess called Al Uzza, Al Lat, and Al Menat. The Prophet Mohammad's first wife, Hatice, was a wealthy businesswoman, and she proposed marriage to the young Mohammad before he became a holy emissary. One of the representations of the goddess in the Arab world was a sacred black stone, a meteorite, called Kaab'a, which is still a revered place of pilgrimage for Muslims, who pray in the direction of something named Kible. Kaab'a, Kible, Kybele, Cybele — is there a connection?

In the ancient religion of the goddess, the snake was the guardian of the goddess's mysteries and a symbol of her sexuality and regenerative powers. The snake was associated with immortality. In the Mesopotamian legend of Gilgamesh, it is the snake who steals the secret of immortality from Gilgamesh. But in Assyrian mythology, the god Marduk crushes the head of Tiamat, the ancient goddess who takes the shape of a dragon. Crushing the head of a serpent — killing a dragon — is so widespread in legends and myths around the world that it probably represents the destruction of the power and the memory of the worship of the goddess.

I try to imagine a world in which the supreme deity is female. On this land, I want to discern the traces of superstitions handed down from people who feared and adored the lusty goddess holding a pomegranate and guarded by lions. I stand in a wild grotto, gazing at the huge carving of Cybele on cliffs, attempting to comprehend a time when femaleness might have been shame-free. Today, in Anatolia and in the West, the Mother Goddess is absent from mainstream culture — from poems, plays, novels, operas — as if her rites never shaped our collective past. So I trace the pieces of the ancient puzzle to challenge and restore my own imagination.

I am not advocating the revival of the blood-smeared rites of castrated priests, slaughtered bulls, and temple women, nor am I about to worship the statue of a woman in flowing robes flanked by leopards and counselled by serpents. Yet that statue excites me. I journey from archaeological site to archaeological site, from museum to museum, and recognize her: Mountain Mother, Earth Mother, born of blood, whose breath still revives nature in Anatolia every spring.

Chapter Three
SACRED WOMEN

In their licentious intercourse at the temples the women, whether maidens or matrons or professional harlots, imitated the licentious conduct of a great goddess of fertility for the purpose of ensuring the fruitfulness of fields and trees, or man and beast; and in discharging this sacred and important function the women were probably supposed … to be actually possessed by the goddess.

— James George Frazer, *The Golden Bough*

In the dingy lounge of Zührevi Hastalıklar Hastanesi (Municipal Hospital for Venereal Diseases) in Ankara's remote Dışkapı district, I meet Hacer, a haughty young prostitute, indignant at having to stay three days because she had gonorrhea.

"I promise I'm not going to work. Let me go home," she argues with the doctor.

"Sorry, I don't make the rules," replies the doctor, a thin middle-aged man. "Three days in hospital, that's the law."

It is a hot day in June. Thursday. Checkup day for women whose brothel licences have even numbers. Outside, the air is brown with exhaust fumes from the cars and trucks crawling bumper to bumper on the throughway beside the green three-storey hospital.

The doctor has tired eyes and tells me he longs for retirement. "What we do here is *hamallık* [drudgery]," he says to me. He and his assistant will spend the afternoon staring through a microscope, looking for the gonorrhea or the syphilis bacilli.

The dimly lit corridors of the hospital swarm with women dressed in skirts and T-shirts. Most wear no makeup — ordinary folk anxious to return to work. Standing in line in front of the examination room, a heavyset older woman complains of rheumatism and swollen legs.

With her pendant of zircon, her rows of gold bracelets, and gold rings on each of her fingers, Hacer looks too regal to grace the torn vinyl chairs of the fluorescent-lit lounge. She has the slim, flat-chested body of a child. Her permed bangs fall over almond eyes with heavy lids. A cigarette case in one hand and a cell phone in the other, she pouts before a black-and-white television whose screen is covered with "snow."

"Hundreds of men come to my workplace every day to walk around and look at us," she tells me. "Some decide to pay for a visit. The rest are only interested in sightseeing. Still, I make a living."

Hacer's workplace is an Ankara *genelev*, or municipally regulated brothel.

On a postcard showing the rugged fortress hill in the centre of Ankara, you can see the *genelev*s at the bottom of the hill in Bent Deresi, a cluster of run-down, cream-coloured houses with blue windowsills. Three hundred women are sequestered there, working full-time under police guard.

Bent Deresi, a shabby part of Ankara, sits on the ruins of layers of civilizations. It was in Hittite territory during the second millennium BC, but the first people who built a city there during the eighth century BC were the Phrygians. Towards the end of the first millennium BC, a Galatian tribe called the Tektosags arrived in Anatolia, and according to ancient geographer Strabo, they were the ones who built the fortress on the hill. The Romans and the Byzantines came next.

To the left of the road going up to the fortress is a ruined Roman theatre whose stone seats and tumbled columns are covered with plastic bags and Coke bottles like any old empty lot in any old run-down neighbourhood. The hillsides are filled with shanties.

The alley that leads to the brothels is lined with cheap restaurants and stores selling shoeshine kits, camouflage outfits, plastic lighters, and trinkets. There is a mosque on the corner of the street, also cream-coloured like the

Ankara's fortress ridge features a ruined Roman theatre, shanties, cheap restaurants, a mosque, and the city's brothels, the buildings at the foot of the hill.

brothels. Mustachioed men mill around from morning till night in the din of the violins and the tambourines of arabesque music spilling from a *kebapçı* (seller of grilled meat) nearby. A tin partition hides the entrance of the brothels from the view of passersby. A policeman guards the entrance, checks men for weapons, drugs, or alcohol, and prevents ordinary women from entering.

One afternoon I stroll in that alley, the only woman in sight, a tourist gone astray. As I approach the police checkpoint, some men call out, "Madam, madam, this way!" pointing to the exit from the alley. A woman can't enter the brothels unless she has a prostitute's certificate recording the obligatory weekly checkups for sexually transmitted diseases and stating her place of residence and her place of work. Brothel women aren't allowed to live with a man or move to another location without special permission.

I walk up to the fortress park on the hill and linger at the edge of the park to watch the cream-coloured houses from above. Men move in a steady stream like a column of ants through the courtyard and out through the back door. A blonde woman leans against the railing of a balcony at the back, smoking a cigarette. The wailing voice of a female singer rises faintly all the way up to the park. The air is sweet with the scent of acacias, and a buttery haze clings to the hills around Ankara.

I have come out of the Museum of Anatolian Civilizations across from the park. At the museum I stood before a small stone carving showing two images side by side: a naked man and a woman embracing, and a woman holding a child. A sign below the carving said it was probably the very first depiction of *hieros gamos*, sacred sexual union, and that it was found at Çatalhöyük in central Anatolia.

Hieros gamos was the sexual union between a goddess and a god — a sacred rite performed all over prehistoric Anatolia, Mesopotamia, and the eastern Mediterranean. Each spring a priestess who stood in for the goddess lay with a king who represented the demigod (Attis, Dumuzi, or Adonis), while in temples, women coupled with unknown men. People believed that their embraces would make nature burst with abundance.

In a book entitled *Sacred Pleasure*, Riane Eisler describes a time, now pushed beyond memory, when people celebrated life and pleasure, and when the giving and receiving of sexual pleasure were religious rites. There was no prostitution in prehistoric civilizations of the Middle East. There were *hierodules*, or *qadishtus*, sacred women who took part in celebrations of fertility and regeneration. Highly respected women engaged in sex with strangers in the temples to please the goddess and to ensure the fruitfulness of the earth.

Temple women were honoured in society. Boys went to the temples to lose their virginity, and in return for sexual bliss, men made offerings to the temple to benefit the goddess and the community. Temple women often came from wealthy families; they were looked after well and were free to get married.

Anatolians didn't use writing until the second millennium BC, but the Sumerians have left many tablets that were deciphered during the twentieth century, describing the annual marriage of the goddess Inanna, "the sacred whore of the universe," and her lover, the shepherd-king Dumuzi. Sumerian tablets contain erotic poems that Inanna's high priestess and the king, who represented Dumuzi, sang to each other during the ceremony where sacred prostitutes would pass before the couple in a procession. In *History Begins at Sumer*, Samuel Noah Kramer records one of these erotic poems:

Dumuzi:	Oh, Inanna, you will find joy with my caresses, with my love.
Inanna:	As for me, my vulva, For me, the piled-high hillock,

Me, the maid — who will plow it for me?
My vulva, the watered ground — for me,
Me, the Queen, who will station his ox
there?

Dumuzi: Oh, Lordly Lady, the king will plow it
for you,
The king, Dumuzi, will plow it for you.

Inanna: Plow my vulva, man of my heart!
The man of honey who makes my honey
flow.
My groom, the lover of my heart,
Your joy is sweet as honey,
You have charmed me. I tremble before you
Come, our bed is ready.
It's sweet to sleep hand to hand and heart
to heart.

The sexual rites were so deeply entrenched in the Middle East that these erotic verses later found their way into the Old Testament. Kramer, in *History Begins at Sumer*, says a major part of the Bible's Song of Solomon very likely "is a modified form of an ancient Hebrew liturgy celebrating the marriage of a Hebrew king — a Solomon for example — with a goddess of fertility, a Sacred Marriage rite that had been part of a fertility cult that the early nomadic Hebrews took over from their urbanized Canaanite neighbors, who in turn had borrowed from the Tammuz-Ishtar cult of the Semitic Akkadians, and which was itself but a modified version of the Dumuzi-Inanna cult of the Sumerians."

☾

According to a law passed in 1930 in Turkey, anyone can open a brothel and run it as a business in any city or town where there is a police force, a municipal health centre, and prostitutes. Brothels have to be located in an enclave apart from residential neighbourhoods, away from immediate view. Women who want to work there apply to a special commission called Fuhuşla Mücadele

Komisyonu, or Commission to Fight Against Immorality, whose main purpose is to prevent the spread of sexually transmitted diseases. The commission consists of a municipal official, a doctor, and a high-ranking police officer

The municipal police department has a morality desk that regulates the brothels. When I phone the commanding officer at Ankara's morality desk to ask for an interview, he refuses. "The administration of brothels," he says, "constitutes a state secret."

Under Turkish law, prostitution is not illegal, but introducing someone to the trade is. Forcing a child under fifteen to work as a prostitute is punishable with a two-year prison term. The sentence goes down to six months for introducing a twenty-one-year-old to the occupation.

To work in a brothel, a woman has to be over twenty-one, unmarried, and a Turkish citizen, and she has to convince the commission at a board interview that she is already a prostitute. If she does, she is given a certificate that marks her for life.

In small towns, the women live in the brothel. In large cities, they can apply for a special permit to sleep at home. Twice a week they have to submit to a routine checkup for gonorrhea and syphilis. Close to 4,000 women are registered to work full-time in more than 600 brothels across the country.

I finally get special permission from Ankara's director of health to witness a session of admissions to the brothel. On a hot summer day, the three members of the all-male commission sit in black leather chairs in the office of the director of health, the noise of traffic rolling in through the open windows. One by one the prostitutes enter and answer questions about why they want to be in the brothel.

Aysel, the first woman who comes in, is crippled. She wears a flowered summer dress and leans on crutches. "Childhood polio," she tells the director of health. A friend of her older brother seduced her years ago and left her with a baby, a son who is now eight years old. She informs the commission that she is working illegally, is scared of violence, and desires the "security" of a brothel. Aysel has spoken to a brothel owner and has been offered a job.

When the policeman asks if she is ashamed of what she does for a living and worries that her son will find out, she replies that she intends to leave the occupation "before he grows old enough to understand." Then the municipal official asks why she doesn't do some other job, and she begins to cry. "I have sunk to this," she says between sobs, "because life has left me no alternatives."

"Don't you think your handicap will be a problem?" the municipal official inquires.

"So far," Aysel answers, "it has never prevented me from finding customers."

At the end of her interview she thanks the board and stands. The commission members watch her limp to the door, her crutches making a rhythmic sound on the linoleum floor. They unanimously decide to grant her a certificate.

After that the applicants come in one after the other. Most of them speak deferentially and are ready to weep and plead with the men in the room. Two of the women say they are from the village of Germencik near the city of Aydın. Both are swarthy and have a defiant manner. Neither sheds any tears. One says she is married and wants to earn some money so she and her husband can build a house. The other says she has two sons in the village with her mother and that she sends them money. The commission members seem more contemptuous of these two.

"Aren't you ashamed of doing this job and not even looking for other work?" the policeman asks one of them.

"There's no other work that gives me as much money as I can earn at the *genelev,*" the woman replies. She is young and thin and wears jeans.

After she leaves the room, the commission chairman whispers to the policeman, "These are Gypsies. Many have settled in that village. The most common occupation for women is prostitution. Their husbands accept it. They look after the kids."

That afternoon six applicants are granted brothel certificates.

((

At the municipal hospital Hacer tells me she received her brothel certificate at age eighteen. Her life story repeats the clichés of the child prostitute. A Muslim from the mountain village of Hacı Hamza in central Anatolia, she was forced to marry at fourteen and had a child at sixteen. Hacer's mother-in-law beat her, so she left the family and found herself on the streets. Her parents told her she belonged to her husband's family. She worked in a clothing factory and even slept there, but the boss made advances, so she left. Her husband got a court order to keep their child.

Hacer became a bus attendant and met Ümit, a married man in his thirties and the son of the bus line's owner. "The moment I met him the room was charged with an electric current. It was a great, desperate love."

After a period of bliss with her lover, Hacer met one of Ümit's friends, who happened to own a brothel and who told her she could be rich. Ümit "reluctantly" encouraged her to work, then took all her money and began to beat her.

"How I loved the man who pushed me into this life!" she tells me. "No one can love like I loved him." Hacer put up with Ümit's cruelty for a long time, but when he faked some documents to steal an apartment she had bought for them, she left him and kidnapped her son, Mustafa, who now lives with her.

Hacer is a primary school dropout, but as a little girl she memorized the Koran. "They called me *hafız* ['she or he who knows the Koran by heart']," she says. "I still read the Koran some nights when I feel clean."

"At the brothel the day starts at noon," Hacer tells me. Half-naked women sit in a semicircle in the waiting room, drinking tea and smoking. The boss is an administrator called a *vekil* (representative), who works for the owner. Men crowd at the entrance, staring and strolling.

A client approaches a woman and asks, "What's your room number?"

She tells him and adds, "You go on up and undress. I'm coming up." In the room, the customer pays before sex. Afterwards, he is expected to give a tip. If the woman takes more than fifteen minutes with a client, there will be a knock on the door. The *vekil* will tell her to hurry up.

Between clients the women talk. They often complain to one another about lovers who haven't called. Some women weep, others take amphetamines. Frequently, shouts rise from behind closed doors as women swear at clients who make unusual demands or who skimp on the tip. When that happens, the *vekil* rushes upstairs to prevent trouble.

The houses have three floors, with three bedrooms and one bathroom on each floor. Each woman has her own room with a bed, a closet, and a chair. She is free to decorate her room as she chooses — some put lace curtains on the windows, others boast that they change bed sheets after every customer.

One day I visit the municipal hospital at 9:00 a.m. and find a plump, middle-aged woman who wears sweats and seems too old and too carelessly groomed to be a prostitute. She smokes and watches cartoons on the television. Her face is worn, and her greying hair is short and straight.

"Why are you interested in these women?" she asks me.

"Because their lives are so invisible," I say.

"I'm one. Have been for thirty years." Her name is Naciye. "I retired last year," she adds, "but I couldn't live on my retirement pension, so I went back to work."

"Do you still get customers?"

"Sure." She laughs, revealing nicotine-stained teeth. "If you treat them right, you'll always get customers."

Naciye reminds me of someone. I feel as though I've seen her round belly, hanging breasts, and coarse features, heard her laughter, somewhere before. She says she promised herself one more year of income and then she'll "repent, quit this sinful life, and turn to God."

"You're religious?" I ask.

"I didn't go to school, but I learned the Koran."

"Do you think of your work as sinful?"

"Society does. *Orospu.* Whore. Would you want your daughter to associate with a whore?"

Naciye tells me she sometimes runs into her regular clients walking on the street with their wives. "It's strange to walk past them as if I've never seen them."

She says she lives alone in a middle-class neighbourhood and that she has had boyfriends in the past, but not anymore. "They're trouble. Now I'm the only person allowed to enter my home."

"What about the need for love?"

"I bury it."

Naciye grew up in a village near the Black Sea. At fifteen her parents arranged a marriage for her with someone much older. She had two children, now estranged. Naciye fell in love at eighteen and eloped with a man who brought her to an Istanbul brothel. The hardest thing in her life, she says, is loneliness. "My family of origin has cut all ties with me. My children consider me dead."

Each night, as soon as she leaves the brothel, Naciye changes her name and assumes a different identity. She tells people she works as a cleaner in a hospital. "You know something strange?" She chuckles. "I believe my own lie."

But the lie isolates her. "I have to stay away from neighbours. Their husbands might be clients. Even the corner grocer might be a client. Like a leper, you avoid everyone. You impose a quarantine on yourself."

As we chat, two other women come into the lounge. One of them, Songül, is twenty-five and attractive. "I don't find the job so hard," she tells me. "I avoid pimps, and I don't worry about anyone's judgment. I have boyfriends from time to time. I want to save some money and quit in a couple of years."

The third woman, Arzu, is older and fatter than Naciye. She sports dark-rimmed glasses. Arzu nudges Naciye. "The young ones don't know now much harder it gets as you get older. I'm fifty. What do I need gonorrhea for? It gets harder and harder to lift my skirt for some stranger." Arzu says her adult son is doing his military service in eastern Turkey. "As soon as he returns, I'll retire and go back to my parents' village on the Black Sea coast."

"It's easy to dream," Naciye snickers. "In this profession, everyone talks about retirement, but no one retires."

Suddenly, I know who Naciye reminds me of. It's Nanabush, the trickster in Ojibwa mythology, as she was portrayed in Tomson Highway's play *Dry Lips Oughta Move to Kapuskasing*. Fat, worn, bitter, and wise — a joker who knows sorrow.

☾

When I was growing up in Ankara, I hardly knew what a brothel was, or what exactly happened there. But I knew that it was the unspeakable Sword of Damocles dangling over females, the most degrading place imaginable, and that all women, including myself, were in danger of "falling" inside one. My mother hinted at this whenever she feared I might be attracted to a boy. As an educated republican, my mother accepted the dominant Judeo-Christian (and Muslim) notions about sex as if they were natural and inescapable. *Unless it happens between a man and wife wanting children, it shames and degrades females. Males have a natural need for it. They can't help wanting to use female bodies.* I understood at puberty that I had to protect my virginity fiercely and seek safety in a respectable marriage.

So, at middle age, I stalk some of the women who work in Ankara's brothels as if to dispel a childhood fear. They are ordinary people. Some of them are kind, some are mean, but most are terribly, horribly sad. Most of them seem to accept society's harshest judgments and view themselves as sinners. Their jobs are legal. In fact, the municipal governments that regulate their workplaces and receive taxes from them share the role of pimp with the brothel owners. Yet from the policemen to the clients, from the doctors to the women themselves, everyone regards brothel women with scorn.

Is it natural to sell sex? Is shame inescapable for *hayat kadınları*, "women of life"? How did temple women lose their honoured status? How did sex become a commercial exchange that degrades only the seller? Were the Canaanites who practised the ancient sexual customs as "immoral" as the Old Testament judged them to be?

What happened in Mesopotamia at the dawn of history?

The Sumerians have left us some tablets that describe the social changes that still affect our lives and that explain some important developments that took place in Mesopotamia more than 5,000 years ago. The first was the emergence of city-states. The second was the discovery of cuneiform writing. Rivalry between different city-states led to a third development — militarism. Militarism, in turn, strengthened the position of males in society and weakened the status of females. People began to accept that women were "lesser" creatures because any man could penetrate their bodies without their consent.

As the city-states warred with one another, people started to accept that the tribes they conquered could also be made into "lesser" creatures, otherwise known as slaves. They accepted as natural that some people were lower in rank than others. They began to expect women of subordinate classes (slaves and serfs) to serve men of the upper classes sexually, whether the women wanted to or not. Class divisions and slave trading became acceptable.

These developments took place gradually over hundreds of years. The Sumerian civilization gave way to the Babylonian and Assyrian ones. By the second millennium BC, Assyrian men wanted a family structure that would allow them to pass their wealth on to their sons. That meant they wanted to be certain of their own paternity, and the only way they could do that was by controlling female bodies. And so virginity became a moral and economic value, and that was when commercial prostitution appeared.

By the late second millennium BC, the social rules on sex were so completely reversed that Assyrian laws passed in 1200 BC allowed men to use concubines and prostitutes but called for the death penalty for unfaithful wives. Written records from Mesopotamia tell us that Babylonian brothels were staffed with slave women — the dregs of society. People now made a distinction between respectable women whose sexuality and fertility belonged to one man and commercial whores whose sexuality belonged to all men.

The wearing of a veil, which has become a symbol of political Islam today in Anatolia, developed into an important mark separating respectable women from prostitutes. In early Sumer, temple women wore veils as symbols of distinction. But as patriarchy strengthened its hold on Mesopotamia, women who were married to upper-class men also started to wear veils. Finally, between 900 and 600 BC, Middle Assyrian Law 40 completely reversed the meaning of the veil. The law forbade temple harlots to cover themselves and dictated that respectable women, women belonging to men, had to veil themselves when they went out. The social transformation was complete. From then on "public women" would be shamed.

☾

Hacer invites me to her home. "My workplace closes at 10:00 p.m.," she says. "I'll pick you up at 10:30."

I wait for her in front of the Bulka Pastanesi on Seventh Avenue in Bahçelievler. The street is noisy and crowded like a fairground.

Hacer waves at me from across the street, her short, curly hair lifted with a comb behind her right ear, a snake bracelet high on her arm. As I greet her with a kiss on both cheeks, I recognize her perfume — Cabotine.

Together we walk towards the gas station where she parked her car. She thanks the young attendant, who looks at her with a grin. If only he knew that he could buy her the next day at the city's brothel for a pittance.

Hacer's car is a BMW with cream leather seats, air-conditioning, and a stereo CD system.

"Yıkılmadım. Ayaktayım. Dertlerimle baş başa," sings Mahsun Kırmızıgül from the stereo. He's the hottest arabesque star in the country.

Hacer sings along. "I'm not destroyed. Still standing up, though all alone with my pain.... Not defeated by cruelty and evil."

"That's your theme song," I say.

She turns up the volume, and the car shakes with drums and violins. "I'm still standing. Yeah, let them see." City lights stream outside the car windows as Hacer sings and smokes.

"Do you still miss Ümit?" I ask her.

"He calls, but I hang up on him." She turns the music down. "But there's emptiness in my life."

"One of these days you'll meet someone else."

"I'm seeing someone now, someone who treats me with respect."

She says her current boyfriend is only twenty-one and is the son of a sunflower oil factory owner. He knows about her job and seems to accept it.

"But it's strange. We've been seeing each other for eight months, yet we don't make love. He hasn't even kissed me yet."

She parks the BMW beside a streetlamp in front of an apartment block in Küçük Esat, one of Ankara's residential neighbourhoods. A child and a young woman wave from a second-floor window. "I told my son, Mustafa, and the Kazakh maid, Gül, that I work as a receptionist at a contracting company and that I have to work overtime every night," Hacer informs me.

The child, a thin boy of nine, and the young woman with Oriental features come outside to greet us. We walk up a flight of stairs and enter Hacer's apartment, taking off our shoes before stepping on the imitation Oriental rug. A brown Chihuahua puppy prances out of the hallway and begins to yelp. "Down, Lady!" Hacer shouts. She guides me into the living room, which is lit with a Tiffany lamp and furnished with four navy-and-cream-striped wingback chairs and a cream sofa. An aquarium bubbles on a shelf beside silk flower arrangements and large framed portraits of Hacer. High on the wall there is a plaque with writing in Arabic.

"It's a prayer for protection against evil," Hacer says. "I told you I'm religious."

Newspapers are spread over the living-room floor to train Lady. Mustafa throws a pencil across the room and giggles as the puppy scampers after it, barking excitedly. Hacer turns to her son in a sudden rage. "You idiot!" she shouts. "Stop getting that dog excited, or I'll teach you a lesson."

Mustafa stares at the floor, and the pup whimpers.

Gül, the Kazakh maid, prepares dinner. "A clandestine immigrant," Hacer whispers to me. At 11:30 Hacer

Hacer smiles for the camera with Lady, her pet Chihuahua. (Hacer)

invites me to the table. We sit across from each other and eat lentil soup, rice, and salad.

"What's the matter with Mustafa?" Hacer asks Gül. "He seems distant."

"He's been waiting for you at the window since nine o'clock," Gül replies.

"You're not very close to your son," I observe.

Hacer shrugs. "I didn't even know him when he was little."

After supper Mustafa politely kisses his mother and goes to bed. Gül makes us Turkish coffee while Hacer brings me piles of photographs. My interest in her life appears to please her. "This is the first time someone like you, someone from the *ordinary* world, has come to my house," she tells me.

In one photo she looks like a school kid. In another she appears to be a fashion model. Her hair is blonde and long in one photo, black, short, and sleek in another. In yet another photo, she is laughing in a kitchen. "That's in Bursa," she says, "when I was running a brothel myself. It was a happy time. And that's Ümit. I didn't know then that he was cheating on me." Ümit, her first pimp and the love of her life, is a middle-aged man with a moustache and a beer belly.

Hacer hesitates to show me photos where she isn't wearing makeup. She also dislikes her flat chest and says she is going to get silicone implants.

Then she reveals some secrets about her emotional world. "Gigolos hover around brothel women," she says. "Not just pimps, but gigolos. Dangerous men, skilled lovers who know how to make a woman feel good. You get hooked on one and you go crazy. You also have to pay through the nose."

It has happened to her.

"I fell for a man who really turned me on. The way he touched my face made me melt. He was like a drug. I needed him and felt insecure all the time. When I told him what I did for a living, he said he already knew. He was a gigolo. I knew then that he wanted money, so I forced myself to leave him. If he called today, I wouldn't turn him down, but I won't call him.

"A couple of days ago I heard he was seen with Sibel, a Romanian girl who also works at the brothel. I was hurt all over again. You see, we have unwritten rules here. We never go out with another girl's gigolo or boyfriend. A client is different. You can take any client, any time. But someone's boyfriend, no. Even after a relationship is over, there are such strong feelings. We all know this."

The fear of disease haunts Hacer. She complains that her clients refuse to use condoms. "The laws are bad," she says. "To protect the clients, they force us to get checkups, but there's no law to force the clients to use condoms. If a woman asks for one, the man wants his money back."

"And birth control?" I ask.

"Strictly the woman's problem."

Like most girls in the brothel, Hacer is on the pill. She says IUDs are also popular.

Being twenty-six and attractive, Hacer sees at least fifteen clients a day. She hopes to leave work one day as soon as she can buy herself an apartment and save enough money to live on the interest. "But in this line of work the money just melts away," she says. "All the girls dream of a saviour. If my new boyfriend wants to support me, if he offers me an apartment and a living, I'll stop working. There would be no love between us, but there would be kindness and respect."

I ask her if she enjoys sex with her clients. "I like sex," she answers. "If I didn't have a boyfriend at the moment, I might enjoy it with a client, but it's rare. It's a job."

At 2:00 a.m. I begin to yawn. I want to call a taxi, but Hacer won't hear of it. "I can't let you go out at this time of the night," she says. "You'll sleep here." She offers me her bedroom and says she'll sleep on the sofa. I protest, but she says she wants to watch a movie on television, anyway. "Here, I'll change the sheets."

I settle in the narrow single bed in her small bedroom, beside the dresser on which stand tubes of cream, a bottle of Cabotine perfume, and a box of vitamins. A small tree-shaped night lamp behind the door casts red light. The sliding door of a closet full of folded sheets and towels is open, and several books line a shelf over the bed.

I toss and turn in Hacer's bed, unable to sleep. When the sky starts to lighten, I sit up and examine the bookcase. There are two photos of Hacer in a pewter frame, and a couple of books — a volume of Muslim prayers, a book about the day of last judgment, a selection of verses from the Koran, and a book entitled *Sevdaya Sevdalıyım,* or *In Love with Love: Memoirs of a Prostitute.* I pick up the last and read the first chapter about life in a small-town brothel.

Then it is morning. I know that Hacer will sleep until 9:30 and go to work at noon, so I tiptoe into the living room. She is asleep on the sofa in her purple cotton nightgown, one thin arm thrown over the pillow. *I have a son her age,* I think. I leave a note on the coffee table: "Have a good day, Hacer. Thanks for your bed."

Quietly, I let myself out and hail a cab on the sunny street. From the taxi window, I can see the fortress hill lit by the early-morning sun, the ancient ramparts against a whitish sky.

Two weeks later I meet a lonely, aging American writer named Sandy in the lobby of a modest hotel across from Hagia Sophia in İstanbul's Sultanahmet district. While we chat about books, I tell him I'm writing about prostitutes, and he says he has an interest in them, too.

"Have you interviewed any men who use prostitutes?" he asks.

"No," I say. "I'm more interested in the women."

"I've visited prostitutes in Turkey. I'm not a private person. I'll tell you about my experiences. First of all, men often feel nervous and anxious with a prostitute. She's the one who's in control, and she can judge him where he's most vulnerable because she's more experienced than he is. She can compare him to others. Before meeting a prostitute, I shake like a leaf inside."

"Perhaps not Turkish men," I say. "I get the impression they're contemptuous of prostitutes."

"But contempt is a way to hide insecurity," Sandy says. "The macho manner can mask fear. When I see a prostitute, I want to pretend it's a relationship, at least for that moment. The exchange of money demeans both of us, but I want to pretend it's human contact."

He goes on to tell me that he once hired a brothel woman outside her working hours. "We sat beside the pool at my hotel, and this girl peeled pistachio nuts and fed them to me. She actually put them in my mouth. For a moment, I felt as if she was my wife, and that was a moment of happiness."

He is fascinated with *genelevs*, thinks of the women there as slaves, but is drawn to them, anyway. "They're mysterious for me," he says.

☾

Among the Arabic tribes of the seventh century AD, Islam allowed men to gratify their sexual urges with four wives and with as many female slaves — *cariye* (concubines) — as they could afford. Sex with slave women served to protect the chastity of free women. If a slave girl became pregnant from her master and gave birth to a son, she would have to be set free after the master's death, and the son would inherit a portion of the master's wealth. To protect the man's property, the religion that forbade contraception in marriage allowed men to ejaculate outside the vagina during sexual intercourse with slave girls.

The origins of the famous belly dance were in parlours where half-naked concubines danced to arouse their masters. In many upper-class Muslim households, long after slavery was abolished, the master continued to demand sexual services from servants, just as feudal lords in Christian Europe exercised *les droits des seigneur*, the right to take the virginity of their female servants.

☾

At the municipal hospital, Nuray runs after me as I descend the stairs. "*Doktor Hanım*, I also would like to talk to you."

"I'm not a doctor, just a writer," I say. We go into the dusty boardroom where the remains of someone's lunch, a tray with a half-eaten plate of tomato salad and a bowl of yogurt, lie on the table.

Nuray exudes warmth. Her dark eyes gaze directly into mine. She has short platinum hair and tawny skin. "Thank you for being interested in me. I'll tell you everything about my life. You might help change people's attitudes towards women like me."

An adopted child who was regularly beaten by her adoptive parents, Nuray fell in love at eighteen. "He took me to the brothel in İstanbul," she tells me. "I didn't know the first thing about life."

Nuray wants me to understand that her work is no different from a nurse's or a bank teller's. "A nurse pokes around the bodies of strangers because they need care. I work with another part of my body, but it's honest work. I'm a whore, yes. But I'm a whore for my bread." She then invites me to her place and insists, "I have an orderly family life. You'll see."

A week later, on a rainy night, I walk up and down Niğde Sokak, a street in a middle-class neighbourhood. I find Nuray's apartment and ring the doorbell. A handsome, mustachioed young man wearing a black leather vest opens the door, then retreats inside to get Nuray.

"I forgot that you were coming," Nuray says after she rushes forward to hug me in her Adidas sweats. "Come in. This is Bülent."

Bülent returns to the spacious living room, settles on the couch in front of the television, and picks up his lit cigarette. Two children, a teenage girl and a preteen boy, come in to shake my hand.

"This is Eray, my son," Nuray tells me. "And this is Damla, my almost daughter. And this is my sister, Sultan. Not a sister by birth, but a sister in life."

Sultan's body is severely deformed by polio. We shake hands.

Nuray orders the children to finish their homework and go to bed. She then tells Bülent that we'll chat in the bedroom so he can continue watching television in peace. We sit cross-legged on peach satin cushions tossed onto the floor beside peach flounced satin curtains and a matching bedspread. A poster-size portrait of Nuray hangs on the wall. Sultan brings us coffee.

Lowering her voice to a whisper, Nuray explains her relationship with Sultan. Many years ago the deformed woman was left on the street with a baby, Damla, so Nuray took them in. "I look after her and she helps me at home. We're a family. I love Damla as if she were my own daughter." Ten-year-old Eray is Nuray's own son from a man she lived with. "The children know nothing about my work. I tell them I work at a contracting company." Bülent is the son of the owner of the brothel in the central Anatolian town of Çorum where Nuray worked five years ago. "He left his wife to come to Ankara with me. He's good to me. He drives me to and from work every day."

When I ask what Bülent does for a living, Nuray changes the subject. And as for the law forbidding a man in her home, she says she fought to bend the rules. She knows many cops by name and calls them *abi*, or "elder brother."

"They did raid me one night while Bülent was in the shower. I was worried about the kids. The cops took Bülent and me to the police station, took away my home permit, and said I had to stay at the brothel. I asked to see their commander. 'Look, Recep *Abi*,' I said. 'My commander, I'm providing a handicapped woman and two children with a living. This man is part of my family. He's not exploiting me. Not beating me. Can't you leave my family alone and pursue criminals?'"

Nuray says the commander was impressed. In the end, the police didn't give back her home permit, but she found an old one and managed to come home. "They haven't bothered us since then," she says. "I hope they never will."

Her most unforgettable lover was a gangster. "When I was in love with Selami Şahin, I lived in a house with his family. You wouldn't believe the sense of belonging that I had with them. I knew they'd be behind me all the way. I called Selami Şahin *abi* and I respected him profoundly. What a man!"

But there was trouble and she had to leave. "They all went to jail for murder. Those were men who would kill to protect their own."

Nuray offered to tell my fortune from the sediment in the Turkish coffee cup. Solemnly, she turned the cup in her palm. "You are worried about a sick person. This is likely to be a rough winter for you." My mother was ill. Her age and sickness were partly why I was in Turkey.

"Are you religious?" Nuray asks.

"Well ... no."

"There's the shrine of a female saint in Samanpazarı district. Go there, pray, make a wish. And when your wish comes true, you have to clothe a poor child."

"Do you do that?"

"Regularly. I make the rounds of all the shrines. I clothe many poor children. I want God's forgiveness."

At 1:30 a.m. I ask Nuray to call a cab, but she insists that Bülent will drive me. Their car is parked in the street — another BMW! From the conversation between Bülent and Nuray in the car, I understand that he spent that day at the police station.

"They dragged him in because someone said he had an unregistered gun," Nuray explains.

Bülent is irritated with Nuray because she went to see the station commander on his behalf. "You don't have to meddle in my affairs," he snaps at her.

In front of my apartment block, Nuray gets out of the car and hugs me. As I run towards the door, she calls after me, "*Allaha emanet ol.* Rest in the care of God."

☾

In *Anatolia, Land of the Mother Goddess*, Reşit Ergener writes: "Prostitutes were known as *charis* (or *caritas* in Latin) since they combined beauty and goodness. Hesiod described how the spell of prostitutes 'moderated the behaviour of men.' Ishtar, the goddess and supreme prostitute of Babylon, declared, 'I am a prostitute. I am compassionate.'"

None of the women I encounter at the desolate municipal hospital seem as sad as soft-spoken, middle-aged Zeynep, who tells me that distaste for her work and anxiety about her adult children gnaw at her soul. Small, with dark hair and delicate features, dressed in a black skirt and a white cotton blouse, she could easily be mistaken for a bank teller.

She says she is thirty-eight. When I ask for her phone number, she recoils in horror. "No," she says. "My daughter would suspect something. No one ever phones us."

Zeynep agrees to meet me in a pastry shop. When she arrives, she is jumpy and frequently glances over her shoulder. I buy her a cup of tea.

"Some days I don't get any customers," she says. "Some days I might get ten, other days just one. By the time I pay for the room, I end up owing money to the boss. I have to work at this filthy job another fifteen years in order to receive a small pension. I'm so sick of it that it must show on my face."

Zeynep has two adult children: a twenty-year-old son doing his military service, and a twenty-four-year-old daughter, divorced, living with Zeynep, and dependent on her. She aches from fear that her children might find out about her work.

Born in Konya, the centre of Islamic fundamentalism, Zeynep, at fifteen, married a boy she loved. She gave birth to three children one after another. One of them died as a baby. Zeynep still believes that he died "from the evil eye."

"Then I sank into this," she tells me. "We never had enough money. We went to İzmir, where my husband tried to run a coffee shop, but it didn't work. He said I should work." Zeynep was twenty years old. When her husband took her to the brothel in İstanbul, she thought she would work as a maid. "I saw the women sitting in their underwear. I sat there. A customer came and asked me, 'What's your room number?' I said I didn't have a room number. He said, 'Let's go upstairs.' I said, 'No I'll sit here.' Then someone came and said, 'Look, you'll go in a room and you'll do with the customer what you do with your husband.' I told my husband, 'I can't do this job.' But I did go back to the brothel. I did the job, but I left my husband. 'If I'm going to lie under strange men,' I said, 'I don't want you.'"

Since then her days and years have been shapeless and meaningless. "You try to wipe out each day that's lived. It's a life that leaves you with nothing. No place in society, no savings, no friends, and worst of all, no memories."

Over the years the clients' faces, voices, and bodies have blended with one another to form a dull mass, Zeynep says. "Some are gentlemen. Some aren't."

She lives in dread of two scenarios. The first one is a police raid on her home. "What would I tell my children?"

The second scenario is more nightmarish. "One of my son's friends, or even my son himself, could come to the brothel one day ..." Ever since her son became an adolescent, this fear has poisoned Zeynep's days. "Do you now understand why nothing can ever make me happy?"

She stirs her tea but doesn't drink it. "I brought up my children doing this filthy work. But imagine lying all the time to the only people you love. The lie has lasted so long that the truth would destroy us all. I'm already destroyed, but my children …"

"Have you considered other work?"

"Once you enter a brothel, you're marked. No other employer will take you." We sit silently for a while, then Zeynep suddenly gets up. "I'd better go back to work. Thanks for the tea."

☾

Hacer calls me one evening. "I want English lessons," she says. "I'll pay the going rate. Will you teach me?"

I don't have the time, but to encourage her I mumble something about not wanting money and end up agreeing to teach her for half the going rate. She insists that I take a taxi to her house on Saturday morning and offers to pay my cab fare. I accept.

At 10:00 a.m. the following Saturday I ring Hacer's doorbell. Gül, the maid, answers and says her mistress is in the shower. The Kazakh brings me tea, and I wait.

Eventually, Hacer emerges and greets me. Then she sits at the table before a lavish breakfast of toast, cheese, fruits, and an omelette that Gül has prepared for her. I remind Hacer that we agreed to start at 10:00.

"Why don't you join me at breakfast?" she suggests. "It won't be long."

I tell her that I have already eaten. Privately, I think, *Here I am, the personal tutor of a prostitute who works at the brothel. I'm spending my precious Saturday morning waiting in her living room while a maid serves her breakfast. She's making no effort to hurry. She's not embarrassed to keep me waiting. I'm the one who's uncomfortable and confused. She's in control.*

When we finally begin the lesson, it is painful. Hacer has bought a textbook, but she can't concentrate and doesn't understand even the simplest grammatical concepts such as tense and case, because she has never studied her own language.

As I explain the difference between singular and plural, she suddenly shouts at Gül, "You thick-headed idiot! Didn't I tell you not to put the dog's bowl near the shoes?"

Gül is sitting on the couch staring at a magazine in her hand. I stop talking. The anger rising from Hacer fills the room like smoke, hot and choking.

At noon, when Hacer thanks me and pays me, I feel awful accepting her money and dread another lesson with her.

Later, during the next week, she calls to postpone our next lesson. "Instead of coming Saturday, how about late Monday night? You can come and stay here."

"I can't Hacer. I'm sorry."

I never see her again.

Months later I find myself wondering about Hacer. She seemed so ready to open her life to me, so willing to answer my questions, so frank. Yet she eludes me. What is at her centre? Was she ever authentic?

Motherhood certainly isn't her strong suit. I saw no tenderness in her towards Mustafa. When she spoke about wanting a life outside the brothel, her words were empty of longing or hope. Even the music in her car seemed staged, perhaps selected to impress me. Is it rage that keeps her going? Is transformation still possible for Hacer, or has her crust hardened? Perhaps her appetite for material goods — the jewels, the BMW, the apartment — define her.

Then, suddenly, it comes to me.

"I'm scared," Hacer said when we talked about the dangers of her occupation. "AIDS — that's no joke. It means death. I'm only twenty-six." Her eyes, wide open, looked straight into mine in terror. That was when Hacer was most genuine. She was most truthful in fear.

☾

"What becomes of prostitutes when they get old?" I ask Naciye and Arzu at the municipal hospital one day.

Naciye bursts into laughter. "They die."

Nanabush, the trickster, I think.

"You mean when they no longer get clients?" Arzu asks me.

Before I can answer, she says, "Some stay in the brothel and work as cleaners or tea makers. Some go back to their relatives in their villages. What happens to most? I don't know. They're people, like everyone else. Who knows what happens to them? I don't like to think about it. As for me, I'll retire in a year and go back to my village."

When you look up the hill from Bent Deresi, from below the ruins of the Roman theatre, you see that the worn, rocky surface of the hill is covered with the remains of ancient turrets and walls as if some miracle of geology formed such a crust. The cream houses with blue windowsills are directly below those remains. Some of the windows have lace curtains that move in the summer wind.

The women who are sequestered there — while they take tea, snipe at clients, swallow amphetamines, swig from liquor bottles, and fill their days with sexual acts — are not likely to know that the soil under the foundations of the brothels holds shards of Phrygian pottery and bones from Galatian burial sites.

On a summer morning, I sit still on a rock on the shanty-covered hillside facing the brothels of Ankara. Closing my eyes, I feel the sun on my face and imagine Hacer, Nuray, Zeynep, Naciye, Arzu, Songül, and the others in a different world. In my absurd vision, they rise to the music of flutes and cymbals, open their arms, and begin a slow dance, tossing their hair and twirling their skirts. The peeling plaster and blue windowsills of the cream houses dissolve.

I open my eyes, take a photograph of the fortress hill with the houses clinging to the hillside above parked minibuses, then walk away.

Chapter Four
GILDED ICONS WRAPPED IN FINE CLOTH

losing my eyes, I invite a ghost. I conjure up a face I know only from photographs — thin, with a wide forehead and high cheekbones, her head slightly bent to the side. My grandmother. Her eyes are almond-shaped, intelligent. I wait, longing to hear her voice, but the phantom recedes.

As I might rewind a cassette to hear the music at the beginning of a tape, I try to reverse my sense of time. More than ninety years ago, in 1908, my grandmother was twenty-one years old in Constantinople, İstanbul. I rewind my image of the city, too, and attempt to glimpse giant plane trees and wooden houses in lush gardens. I imagine her alive in that city, wanting, hoping, sometimes grieving, filling a string of days with ordinary motions.

Her mother tongue was Greek, a language that's impenetrable for me. In her head and in her heart, she held images and values of a culture that's foreign to me. If she had seen me as a baby, which she never did, she would have cooed *yezmoritcha*, "little face," in Greek.

My grandmother's first name was an operatic one — Leonora. Her friends preferred her second name, Lemonya, which means "lemon tree" in Greek. But I didn't know those names until I became an adult. I didn't know that my grandmother was *Rum* (Anatolian Greek). While my sister, my brother, and I were growing up in Ankara, her ethnic identity was kept secret because my mother feared it would "taint" us somehow.

Taint us with the heritage of Byzantium — the military aristocracy of the Eastern Roman Empire, the bastion of the Eastern Christian Church

Young Lemonya, my grandmother, holds her fancy shawl as though it might give her wings.

1,000 years ago, with its pomp and glitter. My mind holds fragments of images associated with that doomed, decaying empire devastated by crusading Venetians in 1204: torch-lit palaces hung with silk tapestries, crimson-clad emperors wearing jewelled scarves, the domed ceiling of Hagia Sophia (lit by forty windows) floating in holy space, gilded icons of saviour and saints surrounded by almond-shaped fields of radiance, priests in embroidered robes filling marble halls with their chants and incense.

The Western world still mourns the fall of Constantinople to the hated Turks. I am a Turk, but when I walk inside Hagia Sophia, I, too, mourn.

☾

On a wet October morning, while a brownish light filters through the sky and İstanbul broods in the sepia hues that remind me of old photographs, I hunch my shoulders and walk without an umbrella along the remains of the massive Byzantine walls at Edirnekapı at the northwestern end of what was once Constantinople. The streets are deserted, and I am on my own to find Blachernae Palace, the only remaining Byzantine palace in the world. First, I go in the wrong direction and find myself outside the ramparts. There, I come upon a large plaque that says: "It was through a hole in the city walls here that the army of Sultan Mehmet II entered the city in 1453."

The city. The picture-postcard image mesmerizes me during each boat trip from the Asian side of the Bosphorus to the European side: the peninsula jutting between the Sea of Marmara and the Golden Horn, domes and minarets glowing under a rosy sky at sunset. İstanbul. Constantinople.

In 312, on the eve of a battle, Roman Emperor Constantine the Great had a vision. A cross appeared to him with the words: "You shall win by this sign." He converted to Christianity, won the battle, and decided to move the capital of his empire from Rome to the provincial city of Byzance on the Bosphorus. Eighteen years later he turned Byzance into a sumptuous city, renamed it Constantinople, and made it the new capital of the Roman Empire.

In 395, when Emperor Theodosius divided the Roman Empire between his two sons, Constantinople became the centre of the Eastern Roman Empire — Byzantium, where Latin-speaking pagan Romans were gradually transformed into Greek-speaking Christians, and Anatolia came to be known as the land of *Rum* (Rome).

The Byzantine Empire was in full splendour during the Dark Ages, while Europe reeled from barbaric invasions of Goths, Vandals, and Franks. Later, waves of Persian, Slav, and Arab armies invaded Byzantine territory, and the empire began to shrink. But Constantinople remained the centre of Orthodox Christianity until the arrival of the Turks in 1453.

On the outskirts of İstanbul, just outside the ramparts of Edirnekapı, hills covered with concrete blocks fill the grey-brown horizon. Traffic hums below me. I hold still under the rain in memory of the siege and fall of Constantinople …

In the late medieval world of the early fifteenth century, Emperor Constantine Dragases (XI) Paleologos of Byzantium, resplendent in robes of velvet crimson, defended his throne against his brothers' claims in a diminished Byzantium after the brutal plunder of the Venetians on the fourth crusade in 1204. The Ottomans and Turkomans spread throughout Anatolia, conquering weak Byzantine provinces, and a new twenty-three-year-old sultan, the ambitious and brilliant Mehmet II, was on the Ottoman throne.

Europe was blind and deaf to everything east of the Adriatic and Aegean seas. Venice, France, and Catalonia knew almost nothing about the military potential, ambitions, and resources of Mehmet II, while John Hunyadi of Hungary signed a peace treaty with him. Alphonse V, the king of Naples, was busy with battles in Italy, and the Genoese across the Golden Horn from Constantinople wanted to trade with the Turks. No one took the Turkish threat to Constantinople seriously.

Rome pressured Constantinople to unite with the Latin Church, and despite fierce opposition from the Patriarch of Constantinople, a "union" was proclaimed in Florence in 1439. The Byzantines were more upset about this issue than they were about the Ottoman army at their gates.

In 1451, Mehmet built a fortress on the European side of the Bosphorus at the strait's narrowest point to cut communication and supplies from the Black Sea to Constantinople and to isolate the city. Constantine sent a representative to Italy, asking for money and arms to defend his realm. There was no response.

From a foundry in Hungary, Mehmet ordered the largest cannons ever used until then. He anchored a flotilla of more than 150 warships in the Sea of Marmara and called on Constantine to surrender. "No civilians will be harmed," Mehmet said. "The city will not be damaged." Lucas Notaras, a shrewd and ambitious Byzantine official, advised Constantine to negotiate with Mehmet, but the Byzantine king refused.

By September 1452, Constantinople was under siege.

The Byzantine city walls were the strongest in the world, but in places they were damaged from earthquakes. Constantine had fewer than 5,000 Byzantine soldiers and some Italian mercenaries. At its hour of peril Constantinople had no more than 8,000 defenders against more than 150,000 powerfully armed Ottomans led by an exceptional strategist. The morale of the Byzantine troops sagged as they faced a fateful battle, abandoned by Christian Europe.

The bombardment began on April 12, 1453. The cannons fired day and night, battering the weakest points in the walls. On the morning of April 18, at dawn, to the sound of drums, pipes, and war cries, Ottoman soldiers threw themselves at the walls with long ladders, only to be repulsed with the boiling oil, arrows, and stones of the Byzantines. Inside the city walls, panic reigned. "The Antichrist is here!" people shouted. "Where are the saints who protect our city?"

Mehmet ordered his fleet transported overland. Seventy ships descended the 4.4 kilometres across the hill and ravines of the Bosphorus on greased wooden toboggans, appearing one morning inside the Golden Horn. The Greeks were stupefied.

After a dismal failure to repulse the Ottoman fleet, the Genoese and Venetian sailors in the harbour bickered among themselves. The bombardment continued as Mehmet tightened the vise, and the Byzantine walls started to collapse.

Within the walls the people looked to the sky for hope and saw bad omens. During a procession, the statue of the Virgin Mary fell from the hands of the people holding it. Then a storm broke out. Food became scarce. Disorder and fear gripped the defenders on the ramparts.

The last Byzantine emperor continued to fight with a handful of men, praying for help from the West. There were rumours of a Venetian fleet on its way, but the horizon remained empty. Constantine's advisers told him to flee to Albania, but after thinking long and hard, he decided to die for his city.

Meanwhile the Turks dug tunnels under the walls and placed mines to shatter them.

As Ottoman campfires burned outside the walls and cannons continued to pound the ramparts, a procession of priests, nobles, women, and children carrying torches, icons, and purple silk flags gilded with the double-headed eagle wound its way around the city walls, chanting "Kyrie eleison." The flames of their torches trembled, and the roar of explosions drowned their voices. "Kyrie eleison" — more a dirge than a plea.

By dawn of May 29, fires broke out, a thick smoke covered the city, and the toll of church bells mingled with the din of cannons. The terrified Byzantines took refuge in churches, praying for a last-minute miracle to save the city they thought was protected by God and the saints.

The Turkish army threw itself against Constantinople "like a single man." A horrible scene of fury and rage ensued. An Italian named Pavros turned to his brother Troilus and said, "Tremble sun. Weep earth. The city is vanquished. Nothing is left to defend."

The Turks pushed on like madmen. A prominent Byzantine leader named Giustiniani was wounded and left the ramparts. Now, in total disarray, Byzantine soldiers fled towards the ships in the harbour. They were defeated, but the last emperor and a handful of men continued to fight.

By noon the city was conquered. Hagia Sophia, where a huge crowd of Byzantines sought refuge, was surrounded by the Ottomans. Mehmet entered the city on a white stallion and dismounted in the yard of the great church to kiss the earth.

He ordered his men to find the emperor. No one knew the fate of forty-nine-year-old Constantine Dragases. Some wondered if he had escaped. Ottoman soldiers searched among the heaps of Byzantine and Turkish corpses, washing the heads of the bodies in order to recognize the emperor. Finally, they found a corpse wearing a pair of stockings on which the double-headed eagle was embroidered in gold. They knew by those regal stockings that it was Constantine. Mehmet granted the dead emperor a royal Christian funeral.

The Turks pillaged Constantinople, but unlike the Venetians of the fourth crusade, they didn't destroy the city that was now theirs ...

Imagining the din of cannons and church bells, I retreat inside the city walls to find Blachernae Palace, a massive rectangular structure with marble columns and geometric mosaics adorning arched windows. Its roof has collapsed, and weeds have sprouted from the cracks on its marble floors. In the rain, I sit on a column lying near the entrance and stare at the pigeons flying between broken walls and galleries. The walls of the palace are cracked. The hallways are full of plastic bags and Coke tins. In the hall covered with weeds, I bow my head in memory of the last stand of Constantinople's heroic last emperor.

Ruined Blachernae Palace in İstanbul stands as a doleful reminder of the once-great glory of the Byzantine Empire.

((

More than 450 years after the fall of Constantinople, towards the end of the first decade of the twentieth century, it was in Hagia Sophia that my grandmother,

Lemonya, bowed her head before a *hodja* and whispered a few prayers in Arabic to convert to Islam. The Ottomans had turned the great Byzantine church into a mosque. My grandmother changed her religion and her identity there. To marry the man she loved, she became Seniye *Hanım* (Lady), wore a chador, and accepted the restrictions of Muslim Ottoman society.

A half-hour boat ride from the concrete heaps and exhaust fumes of İstanbul, miniature islands dot the Sea of Marmara. In English they are called Princes' Islands. The largest one is Büyükada in Turkish, which means "Large Island," or Prinkipo in Greek. Once it was a place of exile for princes banished from the Byzantine court. Today it is a Mediterranean paradise where 200-year-old houses still stand in overgrown gardens. Cars are not allowed on its cobbled streets — just horse carts and bicycles. The air smells faintly of horse manure. Near the harbour a row of restaurants and tea gardens stretch along the coast, facing a promenade lined with oleanders. On summer evenings, people flock to that promenade to stroll, to drink tea, to meet other people, to watch the sea and the boats that come and go. On the north side of the island, a pine forest descends towards the sea, all the way to a sandy beach.

I have a childhood memory from when I was about ten years old. We were on holiday at nearby Burgazada, staying at the house of a family friend. One morning there was a commotion at the door. My father's voice and unknown women's voices were raised in a language I didn't understand. At the doorway a middle-aged woman embraced my father, laughed, waved her hands, then hugged him again. Beside her a young girl giggled. I think she also embraced my father. They all spoke at once in a language I guessed to be Greek. I knew my father could speak Greek but never wondered why because he also spoke several other languages.

Did he seem unusually animated that morning, a little tense, or am I embellishing the memory? No one introduced my sister, my little brother and me to the two women. I don't know if they were invited in. We, the children, went outside to play. Later I asked my mother who they were. She said they were people my father knew from way back.

In 1988, while my home was in Winnipeg, my father's younger brother died of cancer in İstanbul. I happened to be in Turkey and went to the funeral in the yard of a large mosque on the Asian side of the city. The coffin, wrapped in green cloth, stood on a pedestal-like stone called a *musalla taşı*, while a turbaned *hoca* in a green robe led a special prayer. I stood at the back and noticed someone else standing there — an old woman wearing a black head scarf. We glanced at each other and nodded in polite greeting.

As people filed out of the mosque yard, the old woman came towards me. "I'm your Aunt Eleni," she said in accented Turkish. "You look like your grandmother. She was my aunt."

"Who? Excuse me …?"

"Your father's mother … Samim's mother."

I looked at her, speechless, while she explained our relationship.

"Well, I'm really your grandmother's cousin's daughter, but we were very close. I and your father were like brother and sister."

I don't remember what I mumbled in response. She asked after my father, I think, and I said he hadn't been able to come to the funeral because he was sick himself in Ankara. Before we said goodbye I did get her telephone number.

Over the years, I dwelt on that encounter. On many a bitterly cold winter morning in Winnipeg, when even exhaust fumes froze and hung in the air, I thought about Büyükada and tried to conjure up details from the discarded memory of the two women at the door — not much to go on. It took me three years to muster up the courage to call Eleni. Finally, in the summer of 1991, I did.

Eleni's daughter, Eftalya, answered the phone. "Oh, yes, of course I know who you are, Üstün. You're the one in Canada." She invited me to tea at their house on the island for the next day.

On the top deck of the boat to Büyükada that Sunday, a Gypsy man played the violin while a little boy beside him accompanied on a tambourine and sang. The boy's thin, wailing voice floated over the sea. When the song was finished, the man and the boy walked between the rows of passengers, solemnly holding out a hat.

At the island's dock the ship spewed out its load of passengers onto the quay and the newcomers blended with the crowds milling outside the gates. This was a summer place. Women were dressed in revealing, flamboyant things: backless tops, shorts in hot colours, flowing sheer skirts, and straw hats. Stores displayed beach toys, ceramics, funky jewellery. The smoke that drifted from restaurants smelled of grilled lamb — *döner kebap* rotating on spits. People ate and drank at tables scattered on the cobblestoned road. To the left of a little square with the clock tower was a lineup for horse carts. I got a cart within a couple of minutes.

We clip-clopped through narrow streets past the Splendid Palas, an ornate turn-of-the-century hotel, past villas in gardens with bougainvillea, roses, and fig trees, and stopped in front of a triplex. Two women waved at me from the third-floor balcony. While I paid the cab driver, they rushed down the stairs to greet me at the door. The toothless, shrunken Eleni, then eighty-two, hugged me, wept, and said, "Your chin, just like hers. Oh, my dear!"

Eftalya, a plain middle-aged woman, held my arm. We said nothing about not having known each other ... and why.

Eleni asked after my father. "Tell him to come and see me before it's too late," she said.

I promised I would. I wanted to talk about my grandmother. So did they. But first Eleni cursed my dead grandfather. "That Mehmet Emin! May his bones never rot and mix with the earth."

My grandmother, they told me, was born in 1887 during the dying days of the Ottoman Empire in the repressive reign of Sultan Abdulhamit. Constantinople was a sumptuous, decadent old city at that time, domes and minarets crowding the sky (the mosaics of Byzantine churches long smeared with white paint), tall ships waiting in its ancient harbour, rowboats swaying in front of villas on the Bosphorus, horse-drawn carriages rushing through narrow streets in the light of gas lamps.

Veiled Muslim women who weren't allowed to walk outside with men (not even with their husbands or their brothers), women whose place was in carpeted parlours with other women and children, and in the beds of their husbands and masters late at night, would have timidly, surreptitiously, watched the outside world from behind latticed shutters while the voice of the night guard patrolling residential neighbourhoods on foot every night would ring in the distance from time to time: "All quiet."

Quiet perhaps but blighted. The empire was bankrupt. A revolutionary movement called Ittihat ve Terakki (Union and Progress) was fomenting in Constantinople. Europe was in the throes of nationalism; the Bulgarians in the Balkans and the Armenians in Anatolia were rebelling.

Muslim women were excluded from public life. Most of them weren't educated. An Islamic education meant the teaching of the Koran in Arabic. The Turks were then using the Arabic script, which didn't suit the Turkish language and which was difficult to learn, so most people were illiterate. Only 5 percent of the entire Muslim population was educated to university level; almost none were women. Christian and Jewish women were free to study in their own schools, free to socialize, to dance and sing. All female actresses and singers in Constantinople were non-Muslim.

The Ottoman society was cosmopolitan, especially in Constantinople. It included Greek and Slavic Orthodox communities, Armenian Catholics, Jews, and Muslim Turks. People were free to practise their religions, to speak and be educated in their own languages, and to resolve civil disputes under their own church authorities.

Büyükada, the playground of the rich, was a place of sunshine and freedom even then. That was where Lemonya, my grandmother, grew up. She was an only child; her mother had died when she was young. Her father, Niccoli Efendi, was a farm manager in Karamürsel in northern Anatolia. Lemonya lived on the island with her aunt and her aunt's daughter. Niccoli Efendi came once a month to see them. The family worshipped at the small Greek Orthodox church that still stands on a slope overlooking the sea, its door usually open, candles flickering in its cool, dark hall.

Twenty-year-old Lemonya lounges in the garden of the house in Büyükada.

Every summer Lemonya's aunt rented a couple of rooms in her house to wealthy holidayers. Lemonya was a bright, gregarious girl. She began to pick up French and Russian from people she met on the island. She went to chamber music concerts at the houses of Europeans, sang in church, and even danced at garden parties.

In the summer of 1905, a medical student named Mehmet Emin came to the island with his mother and his brother and stayed at the rooming house of Lemonya's aunt. His upper-class Ottoman family owned land and vineyards near Kilis in the southeastern corner of Anatolia. Mehmet's older brother was a prominent doctor who had been instrumental in establishing the Red Crescent in the empire. His family lived and travelled with a retinue of servants. Handsome and self-assured, Mehmet was used to the attention of women. But Lemonya must have seemed far more interesting than Muslim girls who were covered from head to toe, and much more innocent than the "loose" women he knew. By the end of the summer, the medical student and the Greek girl were in love.

Mehmet returned to medical school and wrote love letters to Lemonya in Greek syllabics. I saw those letters, now in the bottom drawer of my father's mahogany desk, and marvelled at the love that made Mehmet learn Greek script.

Within a couple of years, Mehmet became a surgeon. He was offered a post at the large hospital in Salonika, and he proposed marriage to Lemonya. A Christian girl couldn't marry a Muslim man unless she converted to Islam.

At this point in the story my Aunt Eleni covered her cheeks with her hands to describe a catastrophe. "Mehmet Emin took her to Hagia Sophia and converted her to Islam. She did it. Converted for love."

Lemonya, she said, became Seniye *Hanım*, moved into a house with servants, and hid her gilded icons in a trunk.

Meanwhile, a revolution was gathering force in Russia, ethnic nationalism was spreading in Europe, unrest was rampant in the Ottoman army, Bulgarians were rioting in Macedonia, and a second parliamentary monarchy had just been established in Constantinople.

In Salonika my grandmother gave birth to a daughter, Reşika, who died from diphtheria when she was two and a half. Seniye *Hanım* grieved bitterly and burned with rage. Why rage? Because ... while the little girl had been lying in her deathbed, my grandfather was having sex with a female servant. That was how it was.

My mother told me this long after I told her that I knew who my grandmother really was. "I think that memory burned inside her like a red-hot coal," my mother said. "The memory of Reşika on her deathbed and ..."

My grandmother couldn't have been much older than twenty-two — so young to feel the darkness closing in. How did she continue to live in that hothouse atmosphere? How did she face the servants day after day knowing what she knew? Did she blame herself for the death of her child and the betrayal of her husband?

After Reşika's death, she gave birth to two sons. The elder one, Samim, born in Salonika in 1910, is my father.

In 1911 the Italians declared war on the Ottoman Empire over Tripoli. My grandfather was sent to the front as an army doctor. Between 1911 and 1913 he kept journals in which he described how hostile the Arabs were to the Turks and how he was shocked by the lack of hygiene in the desert. He wrote vividly and articulately, as though he knew that as an Ottoman surgeon witnessing a war in the last days of the empire, he owed this account to his own descendants. "Letters travel slowly," he recorded. "I miss my wife and my baby boy." My father has transcribed those journals from the Arabic script and has typed them in modern Turkish. They are now in a black folder in my father's bookcase in Ankara, behind his law books.

In that folder, I also found a photo of my grandfather, taken around the beginning of the twentieth century. With a thin moustache, an astrakhan fez slightly tilted to the left, an ascot, a striped vest, and a smoking jacket, he looks handsome, invulnerable.

And she? In Salonika, Lemonya took piano lessons. During the evenings, she played Muzio Clementi sonatinas on the piano — an upright one with two candle holders, the one that was in our house when I was a child. When she practised, my father used to lean his ear against the wood of the piano to listen to the chords resonating inside. Lemonya learned French, Russian, and Arabic in addition to Greek and Turkish. She had a knack for striking up conversations with people she met at a park or a shop. She made friends easily and frequently drank coffee with her Turkish, Armenian, and Greek neighbours.

After the Ottoman defeat in Tripoli, my grandfather returned to Salonika. Soon he was assigned to a new hospital in Kayseri in the interior of Anatolia. The family piled up their furniture in horse carts and hired a convoy of carriages to take them and their servants to Kayseri. There Mehmet Emin became the hospital's director and made a fine reputation as a doctor. My grandparents had a second baby in Kayseri. They remained there through World War I and through the Russian invasion and Armenian uprising in eastern Turkey, which led to the displacement and slaughter of hundreds of thousands of Armenians.

My grandmother's health was poor. She lost weight. Her doctor husband brought home potions and vitamins saying, "Seniye, here is a new syrup to fatten you."

"It was all useless," she told Eleni's mother. "None of those remedies made any difference. I couldn't gain weight. And he loved plump, voluptuous women." So he tired of his thin wife and helped himself to other women. All the young female servants in the house became his concubines.

All his life Samim Bilgen, my father, remembered the summer day in 1914 when his father, Mehmet Emin, took him to the hills of Çamlica and wrapped him in the Turkish flag for this photograph.

At the end of the war, when my father was eight, the family returned to Constantinople. The Ottomans had been defeated along with the Germans, and Allied troops occupied the city. On February 8, 1919, French General Franchet d'Esperey entered Constantinople on a white horse, mimicking the Ottoman Sultan Mehmet II, who had taken the city 466 years earlier. An Ottoman *mehter takımı*, "imperial band," provided fanfare for the parade, but the general silenced the music with a motion of his whip.

My father still talks about the sense of doom that hung in the air. "British warships filled the horizon," he says. "An entire fleet was anchored in the Bosphorus, and foreign soldiers patrolled the streets." The Royal Ghurkas in turbans left a strong impression on my father. He also remembers "the Carabinieri," Italian soldiers in three-cornered hats. His parents grabbed his hand and walked faster when they came across foreign troops.

The Greek government believed in what its politicians called the *megalo idea*, or "great idea," of reconquering former Byzantine territories from the Turks. The Greek king dreamed of sitting on the throne of a re-established Byzantine Empire, and the victorious Allies, especially Britain, encouraged him, urging the Greek army to invade western Anatolia and promising the Greeks the spoils after a Turkish defeat.

On May 15, 1919, the Greek army entered İzmir and began to advance towards the interior of Anatolia. The Ottoman Greek population welcomed the Greek army and joined its ranks. In Russia the Bolshevik Revolution was shaking the world, and people in Constantinople whispered to one another that an extraordinary soldier named Mustafa Kemal was putting together a ragtag army for a War of Liberation against the Ottoman aristocracy and the invading Allies.

Kemal arrived in Samsun on the Black Sea coast on May 19, 1919, to organize a Turkish resistance to the invaders. Neither the European invaders nor their Ottoman collaborators were prepared for the War of Liberation that ensued. Less than a year later, Kemal's National Assembly gathered in Ankara, and in late June 1920, Kemal's forces launched an offensive against the Greek army, which had invaded several large cities in western Anatolia.

My grandparents were passionate supporters of Mustafa Kemal. My grandmother admired his secular, progressive views.

My grandfather worked long hours and travelled frequently. Whenever he was away, my grandmother would take her children and go to Büyükada. My father called his mother's old aunt *Yaya* ("Granny" in Greek) and played with Eleni, her granddaughter.

Eleni remembered a peculiar incident from that time. She said one day, as my grandfather was preparing for one of his trips to Kilis, my grandmother looked in his suitcase and found a brand-new woman's umbrella and a negligee. She went wild. Servants were one thing, but a mistress! He said those things were gifts for his brother's wife. But my grandmother grabbed an open razor and shredded the gifts. She wept, screamed, and wore herself out.

It was soon after that incident, during the last year of the War of Liberation, when my father was about twelve years old, that my grandfather was offered a glamorous job as head surgeon of a large new hospital in Kilis, where he was well-known. Kilis was a pious town. The townsfolk had stoned the house of a dentist who lived there because he had dared to go out on the street with his wife. My grandmother refused to go there. But my grandfather, Dr. Mehmet Emin, accepted the job, anyway, and moved to Kilis, leaving my grandmother and their two sons in İstanbul in a house in Kadıköy on the Anatolian side.

With the Treaty of Sèvres on August 10, 1920, the victorious Allies carved up the former Ottoman Empire between themselves. The treaty created an independent Armenia in eastern Anatolia and a Kurdistan in southeastern Anatolia. It gave Thrace and the Aegean coast of Anatolia to Greece, central and south-central provinces to France, and the Mediterranean coast to the Italians. The Europeans also extracted economic privileges that reduced Turkey to the status of a colony. Only a small region in arid central Anatolia was left to the Turks.

The provisional government in Ankara refused to recognize the Treaty of Sèvres. By the end of 1920, the rebels defeated the Ottoman administration and were engaged in fierce battles on every front in Anatolia. In July 1921, Kemal's Turks launched a major offensive against the much larger and better armed Greek forces. The Battle of Sakarya lasted twenty-two days. On September 10, 1921, the Greek army began to abandon its positions near Afyon. Retreating Greek soldiers told the Anatolian Greeks to flee.

Caught in the wheels of history, the Anatolian Turks and Greeks, former "brothers and sisters," became enemies. As the Turkish army advanced and its victory appeared imminent, the retreating Greeks set fire to towns and cities that the Greek population was now vacating. It was a time of horrible violence. And afterwards, in the climate of pride and nationalism that swept the new republic, the Turks harboured tremendous resentment towards ethnic Greeks.

Mustafa Kemal, the victor of the War of Liberation, proceeded to sign separate peace treaties with each of the countries that had invaded Anatolia. At Lausanne, Switzerland, on January 30, 1923, the Turks and Greeks signed a treaty agreeing on a protocol for the exchange of ethnic Turkish and Greek populations. All of the Greek Orthodox citizens of Turkey except those living in İstanbul were to move to Greece. In exchange, all of the Muslim citizens of Greece except those living in western Thrace would come to Anatolia.

Huge waves of refugees had already fled from Anatolia to Greece and from Greece to Anatolia during the war. Crowds of hungry, sick, and weary people waited for boats, trains, and horse and ox carts. On October 20, 1922, a reporter named Ernest Hemingway filed the following report with the *Toronto Star*:

> In a never-ending, staggering march the Christian population of Eastern Thrace is jamming the roads to Macedonia. The main column crossing the Maritza River at Adrianople is twenty miles long. Twenty miles of carts drawn by cows, bullocks and muddy-flanked water buffalo, with exhausted, staggering men, women and children, blankets over their heads, walking blindly along in the rain beside their worldly goods.... A husband spreads a blanket over a woman in labor in one of the carts to keep off the driving rain. She is the only person making a sound. Her little daughter looks at her in horror and begins to cry. And the procession keeps moving ...

More than a million Anatolian Greeks left for Greece, leaving more than 100,000 houses empty, while close to half a million ethnic Turks (Muslim citizens of Greece) were forced to migrate from Europe to Anatolia. In all, almost two million people were displaced. No one knows how many people died from malnourishment, exhaustion, and epidemic diseases such as malaria during the upheaval. Entire villages became ghost towns.

The Treaty of Lausanne had simply formalized a process that was already taking place and established a joint commission to oversee it. The refugees were permitted to take their movable possessions, but their houses, shops, orchards, vineyards, and lands were left behind. The real estate, equipment, furniture, and land abandoned by departing refugees were allocated to arriving ones.

During that time, did Lemonya hide behind her Muslim identity, secretly glad to be in the mainstream and escape from the hatred? Did she celebrate the Turkish victory when the Greek army was pushed into the Aegean Sea, or did she mourn? Or did she repress a mixture of bitter feelings that threatened to corrode her?

Mustafa Kemal, now named Atatürk (Father of the Turks), outlawed the veil and set women free to participate in public life. My grandmother shed her chador and her turbans. On summer evenings, she walked to the quarter called Moda at the tip of the Kadıköy Peninsula, drank coffee at a table overlooking the sea under giant plane trees, and chatted with her neighbours and friends. Constantinople was now İstanbul, and the city was full of Russian refugees fleeing the Bolshevik Revolution. Many of them became her friends. On Sunday afternoons, a small orchestra conducted by a Russian émigré named Popoff played Viennese tunes in the tea garden beside the sea.

But Lemonya's health was deteriorating. In her mid-thirties, she had an operation to remove her ovaries. While she was recovering in the hospital, she received a brief letter from her husband in Kilis — an announcement. He told her he was divorcing her, giving her a lump sum of money, and delegating the responsibility of the bringing up of his sons to his brother, also a surgeon, in İstanbul. At the time, under *sheri'a* (Islamic law), marriage and divorce were matters that depended entirely on the whim of the man. There were rumours that Atatürk was repealing *sheri'a* and reforming the legal system. My grandfather must have rushed to get his divorce in the nick of time — he was getting remarried in Kilis.

Eleni was an adolescent at the time, but she told me, "Your grandmother was still weak from the operation. She read that letter and began to scream and call out his name: 'Mehmeeet, Mehmeeet!' It was as if she had gone mad. Then she got out of the hospital, and the next thing you know, she drank a bottle of cleanser called Sublime.

"My mother, her cousin, ran across a field full of huge turtles. She ran, stepping on the turtles as if they were stones, to get to the house of a doctor who lived across that field. My mother never forgot that day. Turtles like this [Eleni showed her arm up to her elbows]. She stumbled, but she kept running and stepping on those turtles. Lemonya was unconscious, her mouth was foaming. They rushed her to the hospital."

The medical staff pumped her stomach, and Lemonya survived. But soon after that she began to spit blood. A bad odour hung on her breath, hardly masked by the camphor in the medicines she had to take day in and day out.

My grandfather took the upbringing of his sons seriously. He regularly sent them money and instructions through his brother. The two boys went to a private boarding school to learn German and French. They saw their mother only on weekends. All decisions about their upbringing were made by their uncle.

After the divorce, my grandmother invested the settlement she received from her husband. She rented an apartment and took in boarders. Then she opened a beauty salon, styled women's hair, and did manicures. But her business didn't last long. She didn't have the savvy to build up a clientele. Gradually, she was reduced to poverty. Some nights she went to bed hungry. On weekends, when she expected her sons, she scrounged to get food for them. Sometimes Eleni's mother sent her bread.

And so, during the late 1920s, my father played the piano at silent movies and the violin at engagement parties and weddings. He had inherited his mother's love of music, and now he tried to support her with music. An earnest law student, he spent evenings and weekends at vaudevilles and nightclubs in İstanbul and brought his earnings to his mother.

One day, years after the divorce, Lemonya saw Mehmet Emin in İstanbul sitting on a park bench beside a walnut tree. She went up to him. "The father of my children," she said. "The father of my children.... How are you doing?" My grandfather got up and walked away without a word. As he left, my grandmother collapsed on the same park bench and wept.

When my mother and my father got married, Seniye/Lemonya confessed to my mother that she had always loved her husband, that she still loved him. She said she often dreamed about going to Kilis and throwing acid in his face.

When I was about eight, my grandfather, a stern old man who suffered from diabetes, heart disease, and chronic depression, finally returned from Kilis to Ankara with his second wife. He was tall. I remember his mouth, thin like a line. We, the children, were taught to kiss his hand and touch it to our foreheads as a sign of respect. We performed that little ritual whenever we saw him, but I always had a strange feeling that my grandfather didn't really see me. I don't remember him ever speaking to me.

He prayed five times a day, but towards the end of his life he had ugly attacks of depression. I once saw him pace up and down in the living room of his apartment in an expensive neighbourhood of Ankara. He paced, wept, and asked my father again and again, "What am I to do?" My father tried to comfort the old man with predictable words, but Mehmet Emin didn't seem to hear. He just kept sobbing and repeating, "What am I to do?" He died suddenly from a heart attack in 1965 at the age of eighty-two.

And did Lemonya/Seniye, who passed for a Turkish woman, who spoke Turkish always with an accent, whose sons were brought up to become upstanding Turkish men, feel marginal? Did she wonder about her place in the only society she knew? Did she miss the musty smell of the little church on the island?

Her conversion was a sham. "They say I converted to Islam," she often said. "If anyone tells you they're converting to another religion for love, don't believe them. No one would really abandon the religion of their childhood and their parents." All her life she clung to the icons of Jesus and Mary wrapped in fine cloth and hidden in her trunk.

On a late afternoon in November when my father was ninety, we drank linden tea in my parents' living room and my father suddenly began to talk about the grief that descended on Turkey when Atatürk died in November 1938. "My mother and I lived in a third-floor apartment in Ankara at the time," he said. "We saw the long cortège of foreign troops and heads of state who arrived to honour him. The cortège wound its way down Ulus and towards the train station. My mother sat on the balcony of our apartment, quietly watching. A band played Chopin's funeral march, and my mother remained still as a statue. I can still see her in my mind's eye."

I can, too. I imagine the Ankara of the late 1930s on a grey autumn day, its wide avenues lined with young acacias, and the ancient, rugged hills of Ulus with the fortress rising in the background. I picture the cannon cart carrying a coffin wrapped in the flag, the statesmen in formal clothes, the honour troops from various armies in ceremonial uniforms, and the thousands and thousands of Turkish mourners, all slowly advancing to the falling chords of the funeral march, repeated again and again by the trumpets and the horns. My grandmother, a thin woman in her early fifties, watches the parade from her balcony. What does she feel?

One day during the 1930s she went to the Greek Orthodox church in Kadıköy. She waited in the hall until the priest was alone, walked up to him, told him her story, and asked if he would give her communion. The priest was sympathetic but replied with a firm no. It couldn't be done. She went from

Lemonya poses in a Christian cemetery in Istanbul beside a relief of Saint George slaying the dragon.

church to church until a Russian Orthodox priest took pity on her and agreed to do it once a year in secret. Lemonya told this to her cousin and to no one else.

She was consumptive, Eleni said to me. A coal stove burned in the corner of her room. She tore pieces of cloth from an old sheet, coughed into them, and threw the bloodstained strips into the burning stove. Her husband had given strict orders to keep their boys away from her for fear they might catch her disease. "How she suffered!" Eleni said. "How he made her suffer."

In my mind's eye, I conjure up scenes from the early married days of my parents. World War II devastates Europe. The Germans have invaded Bulgaria and Greece. Turkey is in a state of emergency, its army on alert. My father has been called to military duty and leaves his young wife with his mother. Every night the two women cover their windows with black cloth and huddle around a large Siemens radio. Through the hiss and the crackle they get news of the war, hear Marlene Dietrich singing "Lili Marlene." The older woman's sleep is broken. She gets up in the middle of the night, makes herself coffee, and sits in the dark hallway, her arms crossed at her chest, holding herself. Sometimes she confides in her daughter-in-law. "I love my son, Samim, like a lover," she says once. And she demonstrates it bitterly. On a Sunday morning, Samim comes home on a weekend leave. The young couple is in bed; their door closed. The mother bangs on the door. She can't stand the intimacy between her son and his wife. Mother and son shout at each other.

Such scenes recurred. Eventually my grandmother moved out of my parents' apartment and went back to Istanbul. A couple of years later she died alone in a rented room in a rooming house.

My father was amazed at the crowds of people who came to her funeral. The cortège was so long that it was like the funeral of a celebrity. Even Mehmet

Emin's cousins showed up to pay their respects to the dead woman. Her long hair hadn't turned white. A tuft of it had spilled from the coffin, and a bystander said, "This must be the funeral of a young girl. How sad!"

Lemonya had asked my father to bury her in a Greek Orthodox cemetery. He tried. He went from church to church in Istanbul looking for a compassionate priest. But no church would accept the remains of a woman who had converted to Islam. My father didn't know about the Russian Orthodox priest who used to give her communion. Who knows if that priest might have given her a burial? My father failed to fulfill his promise. My grandmother, Leonore Lemonya, the daughter of Niccoli Efendi, lies in the Karacaahmet Muslim Cemetery in Istanbul under a tombstone that identifies her with a Muslim name: Seniye Bilgen.

After visiting Eleni and Eftalya that time in the early 1990s, I told my parents I had been to the house on Büyükada. My father was speechless — so stunned that he appeared awkward. I think he was relieved, even grateful, that he could now talk truthfully about his mother who had been betrayed repeatedly in life and in death. Even my mother seemed glad to remember her mother-in-law and to set the record straight. "She showed me her icons," my mother said. "She clung to them all her life." But when I told my father that Eleni wanted to see him, he was evasive, as if he didn't want to open a curtain he had already closed. I understood that he had no intention of visiting her.

Now, when I go to Istanbul, I visit Eleni and Eftalya. They have no relatives left in the city. Most of them immigrated to Greece during the 1920s. Eleni says their relatives in Athens have invited them to visit, but she doesn't want to go. Both she and Eftalya are afraid. They have heard that cars with Turkish licence plates have been stoned in Athens.

I wonder about culture and identity. The heritage of Byzantium and the Greek Orthodox Church are "other" to me, mysterious, alien. Yet I have discovered in middle age that I am, in some way, formed by them. I grew up surrounded by Turkish values and embraced a Turkish identity, but my family was somehow different from the mainstream. I now know that it was Lemonya, my long-dead grandmother — her secret identity, her secret roots, her secret love for a religion that is foreign to me and to most Turks — that made my father different, made us different.

I know a sentence in Greek: *Meto afto kinito, fagame Cerkes tavugu.* I don't know how to write it in Greek syllabics. It means: "We got into a car and went to eat

Circassian chicken." Circassian chicken, a dish with a walnut-and-garlic sauce, was my grandmother's favourite food. She taught my mother this sentence one day during the 1940s when the two of them took a taxi to a restaurant in Ankara to feast on Circassian chicken. *Meto afto kinito . . .*

On the summit of Büyükada, there is a small Greek church named Hagia Yorgi (Saint George), surrounded with Mediterranean pines, laurel, and myrtle bushes. It is a heartbreakingly beautiful place. To get there, you take a horse cart to a clearing from where a cobblestone footpath takes you uphill for about a kilometre. When you reach the summit, the tolling of a large church bell greets you. The small white church overlooks the pine forest and the Sea of Marmara as far as the eye can see. The air is fragrant, and only birdsong and the rustling of pine branches break the silence.

In the churchyard, there is a little-known, inexpensive restaurant that serves heady local wine, succulent grilled chicken, eggplant fried in olive oil, and a salad of tomatoes, cucumbers, and onions in olive oil. The restaurant is usually half-empty even on holidays.

I think about Lemonya, my grandmother, at Hagia Yorgi. I stare at the sea and raise my glass of wine to greet her. *Kalimera Lemonitchamou. Posise?*

She joins me. We listen together to the wind in the pine branches, to the crested lark in the myrtle bushes. We sit still together, cradling our regrets until sadness dissolves in the white light rising from the sea.

Chapter Five
ONE GREAT GOD

At dusk Ankara surrenders to a chaos of traffic. Pedestrians rush home in semi-darkness, weaving between cars parked on the sidewalk and cars crawling and honking in the streets. At a major intersection where drivers ignore the lights, a traffic policeman stands on the road, the conductor of a wild orchestra as he waves his arms and blows his whistle. Over the din of traffic rings the evening *ezan* or prayer call: "*Allahüekber Allahüekbe.... Eşhedüenlailahe illallah* ... God is great. God is great.... There is no idol but God ..."

When I was a child, the distant call of the *muezzin* five times a day was a reassuring marker of daily rhythms. There were no loudspeakers on minarets then. My mother taught me to say *Aziz Allah* (God is holy) when I heard it. She encouraged me to grow quiet and to listen. My mother loved the *ezan*, and I loved my mother.

Closely related to my love for my mother was my love for Allah, and I secretly believed that Allah loved me. My mother gave me a prayer book in which Arabic verses were written in Turkish script. I memorized the most important ones and repeated them at bedtime before starting my personal entreaties in Turkish. Sitting in bed, holding my two palms open at chest level, I recited *Elhamdülillahi rabbil alemin, Irrahmani rahim* in a language probably unrecognizable to Arab ears.

My mother was cheerful in her faith. She prayed five times a day, never went to the mosque, and never emphasized the notions of sin or Hell. My mother told us the god of our religion was the same as the god of the other two great religions, Judaism and Christianity, but ours was the most recent of the great religions and the most perfect. Muslims had no visual image of god because *It* defied description. Allah had no gender. My mother said that people who used the term *Allah Baba*, "God the Father," were making a mistake, borrowing a fallacy from other religions. Allah knew everything. *It* was everywhere at once, heard every voice, knew every thought, and was loving and merciful.

My father never spoke about religion. On a shelf in our house, I found a book about Michelangelo with a reproduction of the painting on the Sistine Chapel ceiling. The book was in English, and I couldn't read that language at the time, but somehow I had a feeling that the bearded old man at the centre of the picture was God. I said nothing to my mother about my discovery, but from then on, whenever I thought about Allah, I imagined that bearded old man with muscular thighs and a forefinger pointing towards a naked young man.

During the month of Ramadan, my mother let me fast for three days. The rituals around the fast connected us. She prepared a special meal in the middle of the night, and her voice, when she woke me up, was full of tenderness. My mother prepared foods I liked for *iftar*, the meal at dusk. The holiest moment of the fast was the twenty-sixth day of Ramadan. That night the sky opened up to all prayers in memory of Mohammad's first communication with God's angels. How I celebrated that special access! How I anticipated that night!

My mother witnessed her country's transition from a crumbling Islamic empire to a secular republic, where the Constitution clearly and firmly separated religion from the state. Her sister, two years older, was forced to wear a veil at fourteen and to marry at fifteen. My mother was thirteen when the Republic of Turkey was proclaimed and the veil outlawed. She pleaded with her father for permission to go to university, registered for law school, became a proud member of the first generation of university-educated Turkish women, and worked as a reporting clerk at the Department of Justice, managing to remain single until she was twenty-nine. After I, her second child, was born, she left her job to look after our family. My mother never covered her head. She dressed fashionably and wore Molyneux perfume. I used to dab some on my wrists when she was away.

My childhood world had only one religion, Islam, and only one god, Allah. But it was the urban world of the young Turkish republic, open to Western culture and lifestyles. The contradictions inherent in this mix didn't become apparent to me until I was at university in Winnipeg. There I realized that Fyodor Dostoyevsky, whose novels I had devoured as an adolescent, and Johann Sebastian Bach, whose preludes and two-part inventions my sister played night after night, were both steeped in Christianity, and that without knowing it, I had absorbed some of the values of that alien religion.

Today religion still binds my mother to her long-dead father, and to the soil from which she sprung in Doyran, Macedonia, more than ninety years ago. Her faith exacts prayers, charity, and decency from her and offers peace. She doesn't pressure us, her own children, to believe what she believes. But she prays, secretly, regularly, lovingly, five times a day. Her solitary ritual needs no intermediary. When her agnostic husband and children pronounce judgments about religion, she changes the subject.

The *ezan's* last words, *"La Ilahe Illallah,"* ring through the sky and silence falls. People carry loaves of bread for supper as they scurry home through dark streets. Smoke rises from the chimneys, filling the air with the faint smell of sulphur. Satellite dishes on the roofs of concrete blocks. City lights. *La Ilahe Illallah.* The only idol is Allah.

((

"The word *Muslim* means 'one who has surrendered,'" Şerife Katırcı, a born-again Muslim writer, tells me in the tiny lobby of her one-room day-care centre called Altın Nesil (Golden Generation) in a former squatter neighbourhood of Ankara, now full of apartment blocks.

Şerife has dark eyes in a stern face with no trace of makeup, and her slow movements exude authority. She is covered in an Islamic hijab (a draping kerchief or turban that covers the neck and forehead) and jilbab (a loose floor-length gown that hides the lines of the body), which makes me think of a mother superior at a Montreal convent. Şerife has written books about women's lives. Her first work, an autobiographical novel, describes a woman's search for meaning, her repeated failures in life, and her discovery of a true identity in Islam.

"Obedience to the will of God means total surrender," she says. "It brings us inner peace, trust, and salvation." Şerife's slender teenage daughter, also covered from head to toe, takes a break from the pre-school children to whom she is teaching English and serves me tea and butter biscuits.

Şerife was born in Kayseri (ancient Roman Caesarea) to a traditional family and was married at seventeen. She gave birth to three children who died from crib deaths, one after the other. "I felt hopeless," she tells me. "I collapsed spiritually and emotionally."

In that state of despair, she came across an interpretation of the Koran — a flicker of light. "I bought a Turkish version of the Koran next, and I was flooded with light. I felt it was written for me." She speaks softly and slowly, pausing from time to time as if to assess my reaction. I sense she is wondering about my own religious beliefs, but she doesn't ask.

Now she finds secular activities meaningless. "Women's superficial talk about clothes, shopping, or TV programs is unbearable to me. Islamic cover makes me feel clean, free of men's attentions."

It is late afternoon on a sunny spring day. While we speak, mothers, none of whom wear Islamic garb, arrive to pick up their children. They all warmly thank Şerife while they help their children put on their shoes and coats.

"Do you teach religion here?" I ask.

"We start all activities with the name of God, but we leave religious education to the families."

"But how can an intelligent woman accept Islamic restrictions?"

"What restrictions? Islamic laws set women free to be true to their natures. I am free to be creative and I am free to run a business. Islam shelters me from competition with men, and from games of seduction. I am grateful for that protection."

She then describes the world of justice, security, and certainties that she longs for. No hunger, no violence, no immorality. "Some people say it sounds unreal, like a myth. But it's the material world with all its suffering and strife that's fleeting and unreal. We have no choice but to submit to the will of God. Isn't the pain that we inflict on each other the result of a mistake in vision?"

"Is there room for non-believers in such a world?" I ask. "Is tolerance for differences possible?"

Şerife pauses, then says, "We, the believers, have to work harder to show unbelievers the truth."

It is getting dark, and the children are gone. Şerife's daughter has finished tidying up and is waiting for her mother to lock up. I shake hands and leave.

Outside, buds are beginning to form on horse chestnuts. Grey smog lies over the darkening city, and lights blink on the hills surrounding Ankara — hills that have received libations to Cybele, Teshub, and Zeus. I try to imagine the world in the hands of an ultimate authority, try to envision being free of apprehensions about the future of the planet, try to visualize a world where there is no poverty, no environmental disasters, no dirty wars fought with increasingly brutal weapons.

Women in Islamic garb stroll through an upscale shopping centre called Karum in Ankara. (Semih Bilgen)

A car honks. Şerife is driving a Renault Twingo. Her daughter lowers the window to ask if I need a ride. "Thanks," I say. "I'll walk."

"Watch your step on the uneven pavements," Şerife says as she pulls away.

Islam, the religion born during the seventh century AD in a slave-trading nomadic tribe of Arabia, has determined the texture of Anatolian life for close to a thousand years. In the Dark Ages, the nomadic Turks galloping on horseback with their bows and arrows across the steppes of Central Asia were pagan and shamanist. Shamans were masters of ecstasy in women's robes, with long hair and high-pitched voices. They could enter the spirit world in a trance and mediate between people and spirits.

Ancient Chinese texts describe the Turks as people who drank *kımız*, fermented mare's milk, and who worshipped spirits. Their prehistoric religion bore traces of the matriarchal organization of their tribes — all of their protective spirits were feminine. Their men and women shared tasks and decisions equally; the women were highly skilled as equestrians and archers. In religious ceremonies, men and women consumed alcoholic drinks, danced together in circles, and offered sacrifices to the spirits.

Early Turkish men and women bathed in the nude together in lakes and rivers. An Islamic missionary named Ahmad ibn Fadlan, who visited the Oghuz Turks in southern Turkestan during the tenth century, related an anecdote that reveals how accepting the Turks were of women's bodies. Erdogan Aydın, in *Nasil Musluman Olduk (How We Were Converted to Islam)*, cites Ibn Fadlan: "During a visit in the tent of an Oghuz Turk, his wife lifted her skirt and scratched her private parts. We closed our eyes and whispered *"estagfurullah!"* but her husband laughed and told the interpreter that our presence did no harm to his wife and that her ease was better than if she had been secretive." The Arab explorer also noted that adultery was unknown among the Oghuz Turks.

During the eighth, ninth, and tenth centuries, the Turks resisted the Muslim Arabs who invaded North Africa, Persia, Spain, and southern Turkestan, spreading their faith by the sword. It took 300 years for some of the Turkic tribes to begin converting.

In the ninth century, the Arabs forced some Turkish slaves to become mercenary soldiers in Islamic armies. The Mamelukes of the tenth century were an army of Turkish slaves in Egypt who formed the first Islamic Turkish state in history. The Seljuk Turks, who built the first Islamic Turkish empire, were also slaves bought for the army of the caliph of Baghdad. They became the protectors of the caliph and began to spread through his realm. Not long after, nomadic Turkic tribes called the Turkomans started to arrive in Anatolia in search of new pastures for their herds.

Anatolian Islam took two different forms. The first was orthodox or Sunni Islam, based firmly on the Koran. It became the state religion and was embraced by those who held political authority. It thrived in urban, upper-class settings and produced a refined art and culture.

The second form of the religion was popular Islam, a heterodox version practised in rural Anatolia and among the nomadic Turkomans who blended pre-Islamic shamanist and Buddhist traditions of Central Asia with Islamic doctrines, elements of mysticism, and even Anatolian Christianity. Those who practised this heterodox popular version never segregated their women and never covered or veiled them. In prayer ceremonies called *cem*, men and women danced together in a circle. This humanistic blend eventually produced the Alawite sect, which is still alive in Anatolia.

☾

A village troubadour strums his *bağlama*, a stringed folk instrument, and sings verses in the Anatolian folk tradition. Ali, whose name recurs in the song, is the son-in-law of the Prophet Mohammad:

> *"Yemen ellerinde beri gelirken,*
> *Turnalar Ali'mi görmediniz mi?*
> *Havanın yüzünde Semah dönerken,*
> *Turnalar Ali'mi görmediniz mi?"*

> "While returning from the lands of Yemen,
> Cranes, did you not see my Ali?
> While turning round and round in the *semah*, facing the sky,
> Cranes, did you not see my Ali?"

Four young women in several layers of long skirts, their hair covered by flowing chiffon, stand up, perform a ritual salute by placing their right hands on their chests, and invite four young men to the dance by touching their shoulders. The men rise and return the salute, then the group begins a solemn dance in a circle, lifting and lowering their arms, imitating the flight of a crane. The dancers don't touch one another; they never turn their backs to the troubadour or to the white-haired man, the *dede* (elder), who sits behind a sheepskin spread on the floor. The sheepskin is sacred; it represents the lofty seat of the *dede*.

I am kneeling on the ground like everyone else, watching the ritual at a shrine on top of the sacred Hüseyin Gazi Mountain near Ankara on a September afternoon. Witnessing the *semah*, the Alawite dance of worship, for the first time in my life, I am spellbound. It has taken me all these years to glimpse the soul of the land of my birth.

The *semah* is the traditional worship of nomadic Turkoman tribes in Islamic guise. It takes place during the *cem*, a prayer ceremony/community session under the *dede*'s leadership. The *cem* is where men and women considered brothers and sisters confess their sins, reflect on moral decisions, receive guidance, learn self-discipline, and resolve disputes.

Alawism is not Turkey's official religion. It is a faith whose practice varies from region to region and which has survived more than 500 years through tradition and secrecy. Between 11 and 30 percent of the Turkish population is Alawite — the exact number is unknown.

I watch the dance and mull these things over. The dancers turn and turn, just as the world spins on its axis and orbits the sun. They take a step forward and a step back to the accompaniment of the *bağlama* and the song called *nefes* or "breath."

"Why *nefes*?" I ask the woman kneeling beside me.

"It's the breath of life and inspiration," she says. "The breath of hope."

When the troubadour ends his verse, the dancers prostrate themselves on the ground and kiss the earth.

I walk behind the shrine towards the mountain summit. The district took its name from a legendary Alawite hero/saint of the thirteenth century whose tomb, rumoured to be on top of the mountain, has become a place of pilgrimage. But the closer I get to the summit, the more I feel that this must have been a sanctuary long before the Alawites. A cluster of huge, strangely shaped boulders stand like surrealist sculptures above the hills, and I know in my bones that this is Cybele country.

On top of this wild, remote mountain, each and every thistle bush is decorated with colourful rags and ribbons. I have seen this practice in Anatolia at other "sacred" spots — the bits and pieces of fabric are there as pleas to a god, a goddess, spirits, or the universe. In the empty excavation site at Alacahöyük, beside the remains of Hatti houses from the Bronze Age, I once saw a large almond tree with rags tied around its branches. It was a startling sight — mysterious and strangely appropriate, as if the people of the region sensed that spirits were hovering over the ruins.

I have found no texts that explain this custom and can only speculate wildly about the vestiges of fertility rites, or about the pine trunks that represented Attis's body (or penis) and that were decorated with ribbons in late March to celebrate his resurrection. I can also guess that this is a remnant of the Turks' pre-Islamic practices in Central Asia. But there is one thing I know for sure: it is women who keep this tradition alive.

Do old women whisper instructions to their daughters? How do people know that a place is sacred? Why do people think that today, at the dawn of the third millennium AD, *here* on these boulders, their wishes will be heard by the sky, by a god, by a goddess?

For a long time, I sit on one of the lichen-coated rocks, enveloped in the mist, feeling close to the sky.

Three months later, on December 21, I hear on the radio that the winter equinox has coincided with the moment when the moon, on its elliptical orbit, is closest to the Earth. It will appear larger on that night than in more than sixty years. In a city full of concrete blocks, I ask myself, where can I watch this once-in-a-lifetime celestial show?

Hüseyin Gazi! I remember suddenly. I call my brother Semih's house. "We'll go with you," his wife, Melek, says. "Wait." Might others have celebrated the moon on that rocky mountaintop hundreds or even thousands of years ago?

The night is damp and chilly. A car is parked on a hill across from Hüseyin Gazi, arabesque music spilling from its windows.

"Someone has brought a girl for a romantic evening," Semih remarks.

Melek has brought a bottle of Russian vodka with three small crystal glasses. Beside the sacrificial altar near the shrine, we raise a toast to the sky and to the winter solstice, then climb on top of the boulders. The arabesque music stops when the car across the hill drives away. The wind picks up. We are alone on the sacred mountain as clouds glide over the largest, most glorious porcelain moon we have ever seen. It crosses my mind that I won't be alive the next time the universe puts on this magnificent show. The sky is so immense and the moment so exhilarating that the thought of my own mortality doesn't disturb me. Surprisingly, it's almost intriguing.

Zöhre *Ana*, Foreign Values, and the Rebirth of Islam

In the squatter neighbourhood of Keçi Kıran on the hills to the east of Ankara, a tall new building with a spiralling outdoor staircase and large windows stands out among the whitewashed houses with red-tiled roofs. Three giant portrait banners hang on its facade. Two of the portraits are familiar: Ali, the Prophet Mohammad's son-in-law, and Atatürk, the country's liberator. The third face is unfamiliar: a middle-aged woman with short hair and coarse features. A sign above the roof identifies the place as the Zöhre *Ana* Foundation.

The pictures of Ali and Atatürk side by side show that the foundation belongs to Alawites — fervent Kemalists who associate Atatürk's secularism with their own liberation from Sunni repression. But the image of a woman between Ali and Atatürk is odd.

My Alawite cleaning woman, Döndü *Hanım*, tells me about her. "She's a female *evliya*, a saint. A healer. People sacrifice rams to her. Her real name is Süheyla, but she's known as Zöhre *Ana*, Mother Zöhre."

At the gate of the Alawite building a swarthy young man with hazel eyes greets me. "I don't know if the Mother will see you," he says. "I'll give you some tea," he adds, "then I'll take word to her." The man's name is Erdal. He has been in the service of "Mother" ever since he graduated from university with a degree in French literature.

The Zöhre *Ana* Foundation is a cross between a shrine and a social-service centre. At the entrance, water gurgles into an indoor pool adorned with a brass statue of a boy and a girl in an embrace. Erdal escorts me to a coffee/gift shop on the ground floor where Zöhre *Ana*'s framed photos, *nazarlık* (evil-eye beads), and embroidered scarves are sold.

The woman who calls herself Zöhre *Ana*, Erdal tells me, was born Süheyla Toker in a village in the province of Yozgat in central Anatolia. At age fourteen she had a trance. Her family thought she was ill, but when she reported meeting the spirits of great Alawite saints, they understood that she was "chosen." The trances recurred, and soon the woman began to perform miracles. Her family had no choice but to bow before her.

"She's a source of light," Erdal whispers. "People seeking her healing touch come from far and wide. They come here with pain in their hearts and disease in their bodies, and they go away healed and transformed."

At the next table a young couple sits quietly. The woman's head is covered with an embroidered kerchief, while the mustachioed man wears a peasant cap and holds a baby whose face is raw with a rash.

"Malicious people have sued the Holy One many times," Erdal confides to me. "The *hodja*s and mullahs hate her because she's a woman and because she's Alawite. They've accused her of being a false prophet. But she wants nothing from those who flock to her." The devotees of Zöhre *Ana* set up the foundation as a defence against libellous attacks, he says.

Erdal takes me on a tour. In a dimly lit grotto downstairs, three women prostrate themselves in front of a sheepskin spread before a throne. "They're paying homage to the Mother's chair," Erdal says. "She isn't there, but her chair and the skin are sacred."

In the bright dining room where the poor get a free meal, a villager working as a volunteer cleaner tells me her life belongs to Zöhre *Ana*. "I was in a coma with lung cancer. My family was on a deathwatch. My husband brought blessed water from the Mother and dropped some in my mouth. I got up and walked. Not a trace of the illness left."

Behind the kitchen a ram is being skinned in a clean, modern sacrificial hall. A modestly dressed woman standing beside the butcher tells me that she asked the Mother to help her son and daughter-in-law conceive a child. "They were childless for eight years. They conceived a few weeks after I brought them here." The ram, I am told, is the *adak* or "votive sacrifice."

At that moment the girl behind the gift-shop counter comes running into the sacrificial hall to whisper in my ear, "The Mother will see you now. I'll take you to her." She removes her shoes before mounting the green-carpeted spiral stairs outside the building, then kisses the doorframe before entering the room.

While I linger in the doorway of the room, which is covered with machine-spun carpets, my guide falls to all fours and starts to crawl on the floor. An aquarium full of goldfish bubbles away in one corner of the room, and crystal vases hold red and yellow artificial roses. Mother, an ordinary-looking, thickset Anatolian woman with short hair and no makeup, is seated on a divan along one wall. She is dressed in pants, a flowered blouse, and high-heeled pumps. Two men in suits perch on chairs, while several people recline on the floor. A baby, taking unsteady steps, falls down and gets up again and again.

When my guide reaches Zöhre *Ana*, she kisses her feet and whispers something in her ear. I smile, but Mother doesn't smile back. Awkwardly, I head towards the divan across from her, sit, and mumble thanks to her for receiving me. She says nothing.

The people on the floor grow silent. Some of them crawl towards Mother from time to time to kiss her feet or to murmur something. Zöhre *Ana* touches their heads with her fingertips without lowering her gaze.

The silence continues. Is this a battle of wills? I imagine that Mother, displeased with my upright position and unsure whether I regard her with awe or contempt, is bracing herself. Then one of the men beside her speaks. "You can ask her questions."

So I ask an obvious one. "How has all *this* affected your personal life as a woman?"

"I don't have a personal life," she replies. "My life belongs to the people who need me." But, Erdal has told me, she does have a husband and two children. It took her husband, a furniture seller, a while to overcome jealousy, but he eventually accepted the "gift" and adjusted to it.

Then Mother says unbidden. "I am neither a quack nor a sorceress. As you see, I don't cover my head. All I do is share the inner beauty that is offered to me with people who want it. My enemies are in the religious establishment — those who think sainthood belongs to men. And quacks who are threatened by my gifts."

One of the young women on the floor, her eye on the baby, whispers to me that her home is in Germany and that she has come to visit the Mother because the baby belongs to the spiritual leader.

"How do you mean he belongs to her?" I ask.

"I wanted to have a child, so my mother came to see Zöhre *Ana*, who phoned me and said I would have a boy. And there he is."

"And does he have a mark?" one of the men on the chairs asks.

"Yes," the young woman answers. "Above his hips, just under the waist."

"What mark?" I ask.

"Zöhre *Ana*'s children all have marks," the man on the chair says. "Either apples or moons."

"His is an apple," the young woman says. "A small round birthmark."

I don't ask to see the birthmark.

In my mind's eye, the plain woman on the divan is transformed into a painted and plumed medicine woman, turning round and round to the sound of drums and flutes. When Zöhre *Ana* speaks again, I am jolted back into the carpeted room. "I would like to meet with academicians at a conference and discuss these things," she says. "Perhaps you can arrange such a forum."

"I can't promise anything," I reply. "Perhaps some anthropologists would be interested."

With that said, I take my leave, the bubbling of the aquarium echoing in my ears.

☾

In the late fifteenth century, during the reign of Sultan Yavuz Selim, the rulers of the Ottoman Empire pressured nomadic Turkomans to settle down. This policy coincided with the establishment in Persia of a rival to the Ottomans — the Shiite Safevi state led by Shah Ismail. The followers of Shah Ismail arrived in Anatolia, preaching to the heterodox nomads and indoctrinating them with the Shiite themes of the holiness of Mohammad's son-in-law, Ali, and the twelve imams who descended from Ali's line. The Turkomans, longing for a saviour to deliver them from Ottoman oppression, saw Shah Ismail as just such a saviour, and they idolized Ali as a divine protector. Thus, the heterodox, popular version of Islam in Anatolia was transformed into the Alawite sect.

Ottoman rulers had no tolerance for rivals such as Shah Ismail. They unleashed their fury against his Anatolian supporters and massacred more than 40,000 Alawites. From then on the Alawites kept their religion concealed. They married only within their communities, and throughout the centuries they kept their identities secret.

Early in the twentieth century, during Turkey's War of Liberation, the millions of Alawites who had kept their heterodoxy hidden fervently supported Mustafa Kemal. They welcomed Kemal's secularism and republicanism, hoping it would provide a release from the oppression of Sunni Islam.

Fearing the "corrupt values" of Western culture, Sunni Muslims and their religious leaders, who glorified the imperial past, organized riots to overthrow Atatürk's new republic. They were crushed and their leaders were executed. During the second half of the twentieth century, the rift between urban and rural people in Anatolia, between Kemalists and Islamists, continued to grow.

The internal dynamics of the young Turkish republic were complex enough. But soon a powerful outsider, the United States, began to meddle in Turkish affairs. During the presidencies of Harry Truman and Dwight Eisenhower, the Americans sponsored Islamic movements and organizations in Turkey and in Central Asian countries south of the Soviet Union as a bulwark against communism. Such policies anticipated later strategies undertaken by Presidents Jimmy Carter and Ronald Reagan, which in Afghanistan in the 1980s led to the direct arming of the *mujahideen* guerrillas who were trying to expel the Soviet invaders. One of those *mujahideen* was Osama bin Laden.

In my childhood in the late 1950s and 1960s, while American doctrines moulded Turkish society, American movies and songs shaped the people's dreams. There was a U.S. army base in Ankara, and GIs began turning up in middle-class neighbourhoods. An American couple moved to the green house across from my parents' pink stucco bungalow in Bahçelievler, bringing glamour and mystery to the street lined with lilacs. On summer evenings the American couple lounged on their balcony, drinks in hands. In my world, no one took a drink before dinner. When we had afternoon guests, my mother served tea with cakes. But in films I saw men and women at parties with glasses of whiskey in their hands. And back then it seemed as if movie scenes were being enacted on the balcony across from us, stirring vague longings.

The Americans appeared superior to everyone else we knew. They bought nothing from Turkish stores. They had their mysterious PX to supply them with the goods they were accustomed to. They ate American food, wore American clothes, and used American soap. They had their own look, their own smell.

American films showed us a charmed world in which the houses were large and had modern, airy kitchens, bright bathrooms where women soaked in sudsy bathtubs, and spacious gardens where men cooked steaks on barbecues. Our own house in Bahçelievler was small and had concrete floors. My mother cooked vegetable dishes and *köftes* on a hot plate in our tiny kitchen, and our bathroom only had a shower.

As awkward pubescent girls and boys, we danced to 1950s American rock-and-roll at secret gatherings arranged at homes where the adults were absent. I remember once lying to my parents on a Saturday afternoon when I was twelve, saying, "I'll study with Esin, a girlfriend," but instead I carried my older sister's high-heeled shoes in a book bag to one of those long-ago parties and, aching from guilty exhilaration, danced with a boy whose face I can't recall now. As we shuffled around in a clumsy embrace in a dim corner of someone's living room, he rubbed against me sheepishly to the tune of The Platters' "Twilight Time."

The Turkish republic was forty-something years old. At school we studied the history of the Ottoman Empire, the War of Liberation, and the heroism of Kemal Atatürk. We glorified the independence of our nation, stood to attention when we heard our national anthem, and were stirred by the sight of our flag. Islam was no political threat. We were proud of the secularism of our country.

Turkey was beginning to industrialize on a larger scale, and rural people flocked to the cities to look for work. Unemployed immigrants from Anatolian villages started to live in squatters' houses or *gecekondus* (literally "perched in the night"), forming a new class of people who were neither peasant nor urbanite.

In the mid-1960s, I left for Canada. With each return visit to Turkey, I noticed more and more squatter shacks around the country's cities. After the 1980s, the number of villagers who left their land and migrated to the cities increased in leaps and bounds. Today millions of people with rural origins live in squatter neighbourhoods. Although usually poor and jobless, the inhabitants of even the rudest shanties still have cable television or satellite dishes. While children play barefoot outside on dirt roads, their parents watch an endless parade of American soap operas and sitcoms.

Many of these people turn to arabesque, wailing torch songs with a Middle Eastern beat and lyrics that express pain, jealousy, and loss. In the cultural and spiritual vacuum that permeates these squatter towns in the age of globalization and high technology, an Islamic revival recruits new disciples every day. Ironically, the Communist threat has disappeared and the Islamic "alternative" that the Americans nurtured during the Cold War has become a dynamic force to be reckoned with. People who are marginalized by globalization, disturbed by relentless change, and frightened by foreign values find comforting certainties and a clear sense of identity in Orthodox Islam.

Turbans and Honour

One October day Maviye, the wife of a caretaker at the Middle East Technical University, offers to introduce me to an Islamic "evangelist" that she knows. After classes on a weekday afternoon, I accompany Maviye on a minibus to her house in Gülveren Mahallesi, a squatter neighbourhood with crooked, unpaved roads on the outskirts of Ankara.

We get off the minibus near a corner grocery store where barefoot children eye KitKat chocolate bars and bags of Doritos on the shelves. Maviye, a plump young woman with curly brown hair that escapes from the *yemeni* tied behind her head, walks ahead of me purposefully, following the dark and narrow alley until we arrive in front of a small whitewashed house.

The overheated sitting room inside is furnished with machine-spun rugs, wooden sofas, and a television. On the TV screen, two lovers in an American soap opera are in the middle of a quarrel. Several women wearing colourful kerchiefs and gold earrings recline on the sofas to witness my meeting with the neighbourhood evangelist. While we wait for the latter, Maviye serves us tea and cakes that she has made.

In honour of the guests, Maviye's daughter lights the wood stove and continuously feeds it with logs. Not long after I have been introduced to all the women waiting with me, the evangelist Bahriye *Hanım*, a middle-aged, heavyset woman wearing a large white turban, arrives.

When Bahriye *Hanım* is finished greeting everyone, I pull out my tape recorder and get ready to ask my first question. The born-again Sunni evangelist shakes her head, though, and says, "A woman's voice is an instrument of sin. I cannot let you capture my voice." I put the tape recorder away.

"Allah willed me to open up to the faith," she continues, raising her hands as if praying. "Just as Allah is willing you to drink this glass of tea intended for you today. Nothing happens without his will." Her voice is soft and gentle.

Bahriye *Hanım*, her husband, and their two daughters came to Ankara from a nearby village twenty-five years earlier. In the village, they worked so hard in the fields that they had no time for God. During the first years in Ankara, while her husband was jobless, survival was all she could think about. But twelve years ago, her husband became a carpenter and Bahriye *Hanım* found God.

"When you find God, you also find Satan," she says. "He is as real as God. Whenever a man and a woman shake hands, whenever a man hears a woman's voice, it's Satan who puts lust in the man's heart. The body of a woman, except her face and her hands —" she indicates her face and hands with a caressing motion "— should not be seen. If she goes around showing any other part of her body, that part of her body will burn in hell like kindling for all eternity."

Bahriye *Hanım* passes her days praying and spreading the Word and practising full submission to God. "My daughter's husband took a second wife and sent my daughter back to us," she explains. "'Son,' I said to him, 'if this is God's will, so be it. So be it. Glory to God.'"

She turns to the women in the room. "Full submission to God brings peace. These days are just like the days of our Prophet. Believers and non-believers are becoming enemies. We are in the eve of terrible turmoil."

☾

The first four articles of the Constitution of Turkey assert the secular nature of the republic as its fundamental and immutable quality. This means that religion and state are permanently separate, even though people are free to worship as they please. Religious attire is forbidden in state institutions.

And that has become an issue in the fight between Islamists and the state. The hijab and the jilbab, the head scarf and the loose floor-length gown that fundamentalist Islamic women wear, is banned in offices and schools. At the University of İstanbul the Islamists have organized rallies, polarized the students, and created turmoil. In some high schools, teachers who enforce the laws have been attacked with knives and guns.

At the beginning of the term at Middle East Technical University, I enter a classroom in the Faculty of Management and my heart sinks. In the second row, a girl sits in a hijab. METU is a state university, and students have to be easily identified on their ID photos. University rules forbid the hijab in the classroom, and instructors are required to ask students to remove their head scarves. If the student refuses, it is the teacher's duty to report the student to administration for disciplinary measures.

This girl, who has a pale, delicate face and whose name is Zehra, smiles easily and is a responsive student. I find myself liking her and dreading my task. After class I gently remind her of university regulations.

"I dress according to my faith," she replies.

"If you want a religious life, why didn't you choose a religious school?"

"I want to study management. I should have a democratic right to wear what I want."

I tell her I am required to report her, but I am uneasy. *Am I victimizing a woman?* I wonder. A part of me agrees that she has a right to believe whatever she wants, but her holy war disturbs me. I hand the department head a note about the incident.

Zehra, a hard-working student with average intelligence, continues to attend my classes in her religious costume. One day, about four weeks after our first exchange, she is waiting for me in the corridor after class.

"Have you reported me?" she asks.

"Yes, I have."

"You can withdraw your report. I'm going to drop your course."

I suggest that we talk. We walk outside under the horse chestnuts.

"I stay at an Islamic student residence," she says. "I feel safe there. They give me free food and shelter so I can study at university." She came to Ankara from Afyon, a smaller city in western Anatolia. The religious community offered her shelter on condition that she obeys the rules, which include the hijab.

"The classroom isn't a place of worship," I tell her. "Your marks are good. Take off your head scarf in class and complete the course."

"I can't. The Koran —"

"The Koran was written 1,500 years ago for an Arabic society."

"The Koran was written for all eternity. It's the Word of God." She pauses, then fires her last salvo. "I heard you defending women's rights. You're a hypocrite. You're preventing me from getting a university education."

"Look," I say, "it's your life. It's your choice. The rules say a religious uniform is inappropriate in a university classroom. I hope you stay in my class, but it's up to you."

"Yes," she says. "Good afternoon."

Zehra never returns.

☾

During a break in Dr. Fatmagül Berktay's presentation of a paper at a conference in the METU Convention Centre, I ask her to autograph my tattered copy of her book *Women and Monotheistic Religions*, which is so full of my scribbles and underlining that she chuckles. The professor agrees to let me interview her over coffee in the convention centre's lobby. As she perches on a windowsill beside me, she says, "It is neither Islam nor any of the other monotheistic religions that first made the veil a symbol of purity for women."

She then repeats what I have already read. "It was in Mesopotamia that women were forced to cover their heads for the first time 4,000 years ago. When men became dominant in Assyrian society, the veil became a mark of respectability, identifying women who belonged to a respectable man. Contrary to popular assumptions, the roots of the veil, which symbolizes the control exercised by men over women's bodies, lie deep in patriarchal eastern Mediterranean cultures — ancient Greeks, biblical Jews, and even the Byzantines. This shift in power and in values happened in Mesopotamia and in ancient Greece long before the appearance of monotheistic religions. All that Judaism, Christianity, and Islam did was confirm and entrench that shift."

"Yet today," I interject, "the veil has become a hot issue in Turkey, while other eastern Mediterranean cultures have abandoned it. What do you make of that?"

"Yes," she says, "the wearing of the veil as a particular symbol has become a political issue here. But remember, Islamic fundamentalism has a great many similarities with Christian and Jewish fundamentalism, including the similarity of attitudes towards women. The veil, or hijab, has become a cultural symbol in Islamic societies, perhaps partly in reaction to ever-increasing liberalization of sex and women in the globalized world."

The coffee break is over, and most of the conference participants have returned to the auditorium. I can see that Dr. Berktay is torn. She casts glances towards the auditorium, yet generously continues to answer my questions.

"One last thought," I say. "After researching goddess worship, I was struck by the fact that the snake used to be the goddess's companion. Yet in the Old Testament the snake becomes an accursed animal."

"Oh, yes. The snake is one of the most important symbols of the goddess. In Genesis the snake betrays Eve. The snake and the story of the Fall represent the end of shame-free female sexuality. After the Fall, female sexuality becomes shameful. It's allowed to express itself only in motherhood, in pain, and under the husband's hegemony. Patriarchy snatched away the sacred force of fertility from women."

I nod. "With monotheistic religions, even motherhood appears less of a generative accomplishment than it was under the goddess. In Judaism, Christianity, and Islam, it's the male seed that's the sacred life-giver, not the female body."

"Absolutely," Dr. Berktay says. "But that view is much older than monotheistic religions. It was very strong in ancient Greece, for example. Do you remember Aeschylus's trilogy *Oresteia*? In *Eumenides*, lines 658 to 661, Aeschylus says it isn't the mother who generates her baby. She is only a receptacle, but it's the father who places the generative seed inside her womb.

"During the reign of the goddess," she continues, "fertility gave women sacred power. That also meant guilt-free sex and pleasure. Patriarchy brought along the need to control women's bodies so that paternity could be established. It also separated sexual pleasure and maternity from each other."

Dr. Berktay crushes her empty coffee cup, wishes me good luck with my work, and returns to the conference auditorium.

Whirling in Ecstasy

In the beginning, God was alone in the void, and God was perfectly beautiful. But beauty wants to be admired. Perfection wants to be loved. So God created the universe to

mirror his own perfection. He created human beings so they
would love him.

— Nevin *Hanım*, High-School Teacher

In my mind's eye, I can still see my high-school literature teacher Nevin
Hanım leaning against her desk and lecturing us on Sufi mysticism — a
medieval religious movement based on the longing for a direct, ecstatic
experience of God, and also a fountain of great literature. I remember trying to imagine the lonely God she described, so perfect, so beautiful, and
failing because my mind couldn't conjure up any image corresponding to
the idea.

The philosophy she explained to us, the seeking of unity with God in
ecstatic love, is nowhere to be found in the Koran. The Koran sets out the laws,
sheri'a, by which Muslims have to live. It regulates people's relationships with
one another and describes their duties towards God. It inspires fear of God, but
the word *love* doesn't exist in the Koran.

Nevin *Hanım* told us that the notion of consuming love as a path towards
God entered Islam around the tenth century when religious and philosophical
works were translated from Sanskrit and Greek into Arabic and Persian. That
was how Hindu, Buddhist, Neo-Platonist, and Christian teachings began to
influence Muslim writers and thinkers.

In literature Sufi mysticism found its richest expression in the life and work
of Mevlana Celaleddin'I Rumi, born in 1207 in the city of Balkh in
Afghanistan. His family fled from the Mongol invasion and finally settled in the
south-central Anatolian city of Konya, then the capital of the Seljuk Empire.

Back in high school, Nevin *Hanım* read out sections from Rumi's collection
Mathnavi, and we listened in awe:

"Come, whoever you are, still come …
Even if you have broken your vows a hundred times,
Even if you are pagan, fire worshipper, or non-believer
Still, come.
Ours is not the door of despair."

Our literature teacher half closed her eyes and explained in a near-whisper
how, for Rumi, love was the creative force of the universe and the only path to

union with God, the Loved One. The writings and teachings of the mystic poet, she told us, were deeply humanistic and tolerant.

Rumi established the Mevlevi order of mystic dervishes in Konya and set out a path for them: a mystic first becomes a novice "quester," then a "traveller," learning to overcome his earthly self in order to be filled with the presence of God, and finally, when his being dissolves into the being of God, he becomes a Sufi sheikh, a "holder of the secret." A sheikh receives tremendous adulation from his followers. Many attain that exalted level after their deaths.

During his lifetime, Rumi became a sheikh and had thousands of Orthodox Christian Byzantines among his followers. He died in Konya on December 17, 1273. That date is still called Şeb-I Aruz, the Day of Final Union. On that date each year in Konya, whirling dervishes perform ceremonies that are open to the public.

☾

On the first Şeb-I Aruz of the twenty-first century, Jean and I take a bus to Konya to see a ceremony of the still-active Mevlevi order. The bus is half-empty. Jean reads a murder mystery beside me. An elderly woman across the aisle, her head covered with a scarf, sits still as a statue. During the three-hour ride, I watch the austere winter landscape of central Anatolia from the window — grey mountains under a steely sky — and think about Christmas in Canada.

Snow would be piled up in Winnipeg's streets, blowing across frosty avenues decorated with Christmas lights. People bundled up in parkas would rush in through the revolving doors of stores, puffing as they stomped their boots to shake off the snow. I used to wait for the Academy bus in front of the Hudson's Bay department store on weekday evenings. Day after day in December, I would pass by the huge red velvet bow hanging over the perfume counter. Day after day, Bing Crosby would drone "I Saw Mommy Kissing Santa Claus." Irritable shoppers would jostle one another in a frenzy that seemed contagious and inescapable.

Back in the bus on our way to Konya, the radio is on. The driver is listening to Anatolian folksongs. I recognize some of the refrains and hum along. Outside the window, grey, mauve, and rust hills rise and fall like sand dunes.

The lampposts on Konya's avenues are decorated with illuminated forms of whirling dervishes. Our hotel is in a narrow street close to the sanctuary, which houses a former dervish seminary (now a museum), a mosque, and a green-tiled mausoleum, a place of pilgrimage not only for Muslims, but also for Rumi's followers from around the world. Jean and I walk down a street lined with carpet stores, souvenir and antique shops, and grilled meat restaurants called *kebapcis*.

The sold-out ceremony of the dervishes takes place in the evening at a modern basketball stadium. More than 3,000 people, mostly Anatolians and some tourists, fidget on red benches. Women wearing head scarves hold children on their laps. The echo in the concrete hall elevates the din of the crowd to a roar as people shout to be heard. The occasion has the atmosphere of a carnival.

The event marks the 727th anniversary of the great poet's death, referred to as his *vuslat*, or "union with God." The ceremony, called a *sema*, represents the mystical journey of the dervishes' spiritual ascent to God, the turning towards the truth, the desertion of the ego, the maturing of the soul, the ecstasy and the return to life in order to love and serve all creation.

The performance, aided by a male chorus of a dozen singers, starts with a concert of Sufi music, played by an orchestra consisting of *kudums* (kettle drums), thirteenth-century string instruments, and the *ney*, a reed flute. First comes the sound of the drum, representing the Divine Command "Be." Then the *ney*, symbolizing the soul of the universe, introduces a cadenza whose melody rises in the quarter tones of the Anatolian scale while a male voice recites a verse from Rumi's *Mathnavi*.

> "The air flowing through the reed is fire
> Extinct, if with passion won't inspire
> Fire of love is set upon the reed
> We are as the flute, and the music in us is from thee,
> We are as the mountain, and the echo in us is from thee."

The male chorus sings some of Rumi's poems set to music that is monophonic but with a hypnotic beat. In the opening lines of the *Mathnavi*, Rumi says that the reed flute laments the brokenness of the human soul longing for the Loved One. Longing for wholeness. Longing for consuming Love, for Beauty.

I try to imagine the Anatolia of the thirteenth century, a world without steel, plastic, or electricity, dimly lit by torches and explained by religious wisdom. I imagine the sound of horses' hooves in the streets. I imagine the cruelty, the rigidity of that world.

And I think about the cruelty of our own world in this new century. More than a hundred political prisoners have died from hunger strikes in Turkey, protesting a move from dormitories to cells. Iraq is in chaos. North Korea tests nuclear weapons. Land mines maim farmers in Lebanon.

In the basketball stadium, sixteen dervishes in white robes and conical hats bow to one another in a ritual salute to begin the most sacred part of the ceremony — the whirling of the *sema*. To dissolve in all-consuming love for God and to attain wholeness in ecstasy, they spin, arms open, right palms turned towards the sky to receive God's mercy, left palms pointed at the ground to pass it on. One by one they start to unfold, to raise their arms, to bend their heads slightly to the right, and to whirl, as Rumi writes, "as atoms whirl around each other, and as the heavenly bodies whirl around the sun" in a trance around their own axis and around their sheikh. One foot remains on the ground while the other crosses it and propels the dancer in an even, harmonious movement to the beat of the *kudum*s and the otherworldly tune of the *ney*.

> "As waves upon my head the circling curl
> So in the sacred dance weave ye and whirl,
> Dance then, o heart, a whirling circle be.
> Burn in this flame — is not the candle He?"

I am surprised at my own response to the hypnotic movement and the ancient music. This is a glimpse into the soul of Anatolia. In a crowded basketball stadium, Mevlana's message of universal love and tolerance resonates with meaning. And when the *sema* ends with a recitation of the Fatiha, the opening chapter of the Koran, and the dervishes chant *"Hou,"* a call to God, I, an agnostic, am moved to tears.

Some months later I journey to another *sema* of the dervishes at an ancient Mevlevi temple at Üsküdar on the Anatolian side of İstanbul. Before the ceremony I meet Didem Edman, a thirty-three-year-old woman with large brown eyes and long curly hair. We have our talk at the MADO ice-cream parlour. Didem wears jeans and a T-shirt. She is a draftswoman and a whirling dervish, a seemingly unlikely novice of Sufi mysticism.

"I suggested meeting at MADO," she says, "because I love ice cream. I'm already plump and I shouldn't eat any, but the sundae dipped in pistachios here is so good."

We both order sundaes dipped in pistachios. I smile at her appetite, her spontaneity, and her ordinariness.

Ten years earlier, when Didem was a student in the Department of Fine Arts at the University of Mimar Sinan in İstanbul, she went to a *sema* to take photographs. "I can't find words to describe the longing that I felt," she says, "and the peace that I found."

A man gave her a booklet about Rumi and Sufi mysticism. She began to attend the discussion and prayer meetings of the group whose members were the disciples of a dervish called Hasan *Dede*.

"You could ask Hasan *Dede* any question you wanted," she tells me. "I wasn't aware of being in search of something. But as I heard the answers Hasan *Dede* gave, always urging patience, tolerance, and love, all his responses made deep sense to me. I gradually found that whenever I had personal troubles, I could rely on his insights to find solutions. I was free to ask him for advice whenever I needed it. I began to learn the path of Mevlana and discovered myself at the same time."

Didem Edman chats with me minutes before the sema in İstanbul.

Didem says the task of a *murshid*, a "leader," is to reduce the load of the novice by showing her the way. "That's what Hasan *Dede* was doing, and that's why I became more and more attached to him and to Mevlana's way." She had been a nominal Muslim until then. "Our *dede* explains Mevlana's views to us. Our *dede* nourishes us."

As Didem explains, "When someone wants to join the order, Hasan *Dede* asks that person if she has ever been in love. If the answer is no, he tells her to go away and to come back after having experienced love. If a person doesn't know human love, she can't know divine love."

Didem was the first woman ever invited to whirl in a ceremony. Now she trains other female novices.

"Something happens during practice," she says. "You learn to overcome the limits of your body. You may get nauseated, you may feel dizzy, but the trick is to transcend those sensations. You do that by concentrating on love." She speaks about these mystical challenges in the same way that she talks about pistachio ice cream — with a matter-of-fact enthusiasm.

That evening Didem takes me to the prayer meeting of the order. The ancient temple, a two-storey building whose first floor housed the tomb of an eighteenth-century mystic, is in an uphill, cobbled street in Üsküdar in a well-tended garden. Didem stands before the iron bars of the outside window and prays before leading me upstairs to the second floor. I find myself in a large hall covered with carpets and lit with hanging lamps. On the walls there are pictures of the Prophet Mohammad, his son-in law, Ali, Mevlana, and Kemal Atatürk. About a hundred people are gathered inside — half of them women, who look middle class, including two Americans. They welcome one another with embraces.

Carol, one of the two Americans, is middle-aged, while her countrywoman, Tuesday, is in her twenties. Carol says she is married to a Turkish man and has lived in İstanbul since the 1970s. She tells me she whirls, but not at public ceremonies. "In public I would feel like a false dervish," she says. Tuesday, who in her long skirt and dangling earrings, reminds me of a hippie, doesn't want to talk.

During the Mevlevi ceremony, Didem Edman (foreground) becomes a mystical and mysterious creature — a dervish.

145

At eight o'clock Hasan *Dede*, an attractive man in his sixties with white hair, a round belly, and a flashing smile, appears and greets his followers by placing his left hand on his heart and bowing his head. He was born in Skopje, Macedonia, and immigrated to Turkey during the late 1950s. He speaks with a Roumeli (Balkan Turkish) accent. His own guru was a sheikh named Hakkı *Dede*, who belonged to the Skopje Mevlevihane.

For the discussion session, the followers sit cross-legged on the carpeted floor. Carole whispers to me that I am about to get to know a wonderful person and that I should ask him a question so that the entire group can be enlightened by his reply.

Hasan *Dede* is a retired shopkeeper. He is married and has six children and many grandchildren. The *dede* opens the evening discussion by condemning the 2001 terrorist attacks in the United States. Those who did that, he says, weren't Muslims despite what they called themselves. Then he greets me and invites me to ask him a question about his order.

"How is it that this 'brotherhood' includes women?" I ask.

"Mevlana discriminated against no one," he answers. "Men and women, Muslims and non-Muslims, Turks and foreigners, were equal in his eyes. Our doors are open to everyone as his were. We don't ask our followers to convert to Islam. Mevlana included women in his own order. The human soul is the human soul. It longs for the beauty of God and has a right to attain that beauty."

A middle-aged woman wearing expensive clothes asks him how she can discern her ego from her soul. Hasan *Dede* replies in parables. The ego, it seems, strives for earthly satisfaction while the soul longs for lasting beauty.

Others ask the *dede* questions about the history of the Mevlevi order and about reconciling daily lives on a mystic quest. At 8:30 Hasan *Dede* ends the discussion. Carol and two other women serve tea in slim-waisted glasses accompanied by store-bought cookies. Then it is time for prayers.

A woman nudges me and gives me a chiffon head scarf. All the other women have covered their heads. People settle on the floor once again, and the prayers start with a rhythmic repetition of the word *Allah*. Then a man with a rich and tuneful voice reads some sections from the Koran. At the end of each section the congregation chants a refrain.

As people unfold their crossed legs and get to their feet, a group of eight musicians, called *mutrip*, take their places and prepare their instruments. A choir of twenty people sit behind the musicians in a semicircle, and the music begins. Hasan *Dede* stands. Five dervishes, including Didem, circle the floor in slow steps before him, saluting him and one another by bowing their heads. Then, gradually, they raise their arms and begin to whirl.

The hymns, sung by a mixed chorus of men and women, are melodious, soothing, and arousing. I am mesmerized as the three women and two men whirl so close to me that I could touch them. They are clearly in another world. The rhythm speeds up towards the end of a hymn, and the whirling does, too. Then a new hymn starts, and the dervishes seem to go deeper into the trance. Watching them, I feel as if I am also in the grip of a trance. The young woman who ate a sundae dipped in pistachios with me that afternoon now appears unreachable, intimidating.

> "Draw near, draw near!
> I'll whisper in thy ear
> His name, whose radiance
> Maketh the spheres dance."

Dazed by the music, the rhythm, and the movement, I try to understand mystical love. Love for the sun, the wind, the world, and life — yes! But when I strain to imagine the great force before and beyond worldly beauties, my mind draws a blank.

To catch the night train back to Ankara, I have to leave before the end of the ceremony, before the dervishes' call to God. Outside the temple the istanbul night is balmy and noisy. Two guards in the cubicle at the gate watch television. There will be a war in Iran, too, one of them tells me. I ask him if he can call a cab. In a couple of minutes, I am in the back seat of a taxi lurching through the congested streets of the city, already far away from the world of the whirling dervishes.

Chapter Six
RISING WATERS

Dilmun, a pure, clean, bright land where there is neither sickness nor death lacks water. The great water god Enki orders Utu, the sun god, to fill it with fresh water brought up from the earth. Dilmun then becomes a divine garden, green with fruit-laden fields and meadows.
— Sumerian legend, cited in Samuel Noah Kramer, *History Begins in Sumer*

Sumerians were the first to imagine a paradise, a "garden of the gods." They called it Dilmun. In the 5,000-year-old Sumerian legend, fresh water was the only resource that Dilmun needed to be transformed into a green garden. Today the world is beginning to run out of water, and the Sumerian lands — Mesopotamia, Iraq — are burning, scorched not only by drought, but also by cluster bombs and depleted uranium.

Mesopotamia and Anatolia are sister cradles of civilizations. Their destinies are tied to each other. Upper Mesopotamia (southeastern Anatolia) is a place of turmoil and sorrow and will remain so because of water and oil. The water that flows in two unruly rivers, the Tigris and the Euphrates, gives life to the entire region; and the oil that oozes out of the ground in Mosul and Kirkük fuels wealth around the world.

All industrialized countries covet Upper Mesopotamia and meddle in its affairs, but it is the U.S. empire that is consolidating its hegemony there. The people who live in the region, mostly Kurds, are among the poorest in the world. Feudal social structures still determine their relationships. Landowners control landless peasants. Men own girls and women. In a treacherous arena of shifting alliances, powerful nations play local tribes against one another.

In the 1970s, Turkey began an ambitious development project called Güneydogu Anadolu Projesi (GAP), the Southeastern Anatolian Project, with plans to build twenty-two dams and nineteen power stations to harness more than fifty billion cubic metres of water that flow annually through the Tigris and Euphrates rivers, representing 28 percent of the country's waters. Big hopes rest on the giant project that will eventually cost about $32 billion, irrigate more than 1.7 million hectares of land, and annually produce 27 billion kilowatt hours of electricity. GAP is expected to be completed by 2020.

The waters of the Tigris and the Euphrates are of tremendous interest to all of Turkey's neighbours: Israel, Syria, Iraq (i.e., the United States), and Iran. At a time of hitherto unseen economic, political, and military U.S. hegemony, when nation states have all but lost the right to determine the use of their own resources and the protection of their own environments, it is safe to assume that the ancient geography of southeastern Anatolia is being transformed with imperial consent.

During the last two decades of the twentieth century, an undeclared civil war raged in the GAP region between the Turkish armed forces and the Partiya Karkerên Kurdistan (PKK), the Kurdistan Workers' Party, Marxist separatist Kurdish guerrillas. The war petered out without fanfare early in the twenty-first century when the Israeli secret police delivered PKK guerrilla leader Abdullah Öcalan to the Turkish government, but flared again not long after with the establishment of an autonomous "Kurdish State" in northern Iraq.

Encouraged by the foundation of a "Kurdish State," the PKK guerrillas use the mountains of northern Iraq as a safe haven. The Turkish armed forces' desire to wipe out PKK training camps in those mountains meet with firm opposition from the United States; after all, the Kurds are the only American allies in Iraq. The invaders can't afford to disturb the only "stable" region in that country.

Meanwhile the European Union pressures Turkey to give more autonomy to southeastern Anatolia, thus stirring deep misgivings among nationalists in Turkey that the West might have ulterior motives to divide Turkey. The 10 percent barrage or threshold (to be assigned seats in parliament a political party needs at least 10 percent of the national vote) in the election laws of Turkey prevents Kurdish politicians from entering the Turkish parliament, while the "Kurdish issue" continues to simmer on low heat. And the *Global Trends 2015 Report* prepared by the U.S. State Department, the CIA, and the National Intelligence Council states that in the next decade Turkey will face issues of control and ownership of the waters of the Tigris and the Euphrates.

Terrorists and Heroes

"They shot a shepherd," says twenty-eight-year-old Feride. "They said he was a terrorist. They shot a farmer and said he was a terrorist. Then they shot my husband and said he was a terrorist."

Feride wears a flowered cotton skirt and a purple embroidered kerchief tied behind her ears as she sits on the bed, the only piece of furniture in her one-room squatter's shack in the Batı Kent Mahallesi district of Diyarbakır in south-eastern Anatolia. She was married at age thirteen and became a widow with five children at twenty-two. Four of her children are lined up beside her on the bed. Her eldest son, twelve-year-old Abdullah, watches us from the doorway.

People in western Anatolia consider Diyarbakır a dangerous place. An ancient city on the northern banks of the Tigris surrounded by medieval

Feride, a Kurdish woman, lines up her four children for a photograph on the only sofa in their shack.

Byzantine fortifications of black basalt, Diyarbakır has the highest concentration of Kurdish people in Turkey. During the last fifteen years of the twentieth century, millions of Kurds whose villages were burnt or demolished by the Turkish armed forces flocked to squatter neighbourhoods in this city.

Feride is one of those refugees. Her neighbourhood is filled with Kurds whose villages were destroyed, whose husbands, brothers, and sons were killed, and whose children work on the streets shining shoes or selling sweets. Feride's husband died in 1994 in the village of Kelekçi. "The soldiers gave the villagers twenty-four hours' notice," she says. "I grabbed the children and left. They burnt down the village."

The mud-brick houses with flat roofs and small courtyards in Batıkent resemble village houses. A discarded couch with rusting springs stands outside Feride's fence. Children play on the dirt roads.

Feride speaks only Kurdish. Necla Hattapoğlu, president of a charitable organization called Women's Platform, translates for me. Feride's son, Abdullah, wears a t-shirt advertising *Deliyürek* (*Wild Heart*), an action-filled television series.

"Abdullah is our breadwinner," Feride tells me. "He sells sweets on the streets and earns our rent for this shack. Abdullah is in grade four at school, but he says he wants to quit. He says he doesn't want to be in a classroom with kids who are younger than him." Feride says there are no men left in her family. "My brothers, cousins, in-laws, and uncles are all either dead or fugitives."

While we walk between the shacks, Necla Hattapoğlu explains to me that the war has destroyed an entire generation and the survivors are scarred. "Some people profit from the war — even civil servants receive double pay for working here. But the local people are devastated. Most were caught between the guerrillas and the armed forces and have been terrorized by both."

In an empty lot between the houses, we see an eight-year-old girl carrying her three-year-old brother. Both are barefoot. The girl tells us her mother is sick at home, which is a wooden shack leaning against an apartment building. We knock on the door.

The mother, who is curled up on a floor mattress, looks up. "*Buyurun, hoşgeldiniz,*" she says. "Welcome." She tells us the doctors said there were spots on her lungs, but she has no money for treatment.

Her name is Hamsa. She, too, was married at thirteen and gave birth to six children, two of whom died. Her husband is also sick with bleeding ulcers. She explains that there used to be an underground shelter at her village, Üçkoran, near the city of Mardin. The soldiers burnt the village, and all the villagers moved to Diyarbakır. Hamsa's two oldest sons, eleven and thirteen, shine shoes ...

☾

The Kurds are an ethnic group that has lived in southeastern Turkey, northern Iraq, and northern Iran for more than 1,000 years. They were nomadic tribes, depending on herds of sheep and cattle for a livelihood, and like the Turks, they converted to Islam during the twelfth century. Under Ottoman rule they were one of several ethnic communities in Anatolia.

After the collapse of the Ottoman Empire in 1918, during the Turkish War of Liberation, the Kurds fought beside the Turks against the Ottoman aristocracy and the British, French, and Italian invaders of Anatolia. Britain, the United States, and France manoeuvred to establish a Kurdish state under their control to gain access to the oil fields in Mosul and Kerkük, but they failed when Kemal Atatürk abolished the Islamic caliphate and established the secular Turkish republic.

The Lausanne Treaty of 1923 delineated Turkey's borders and defined the Christian and Jewish communities within those borders as minorities who could teach their own languages in private schools. But the Muslim Kurds weren't identified as a minority, so they weren't granted the right to use or teach Kurdish.

Many Kurdish tribes wanted an Islamic state and reacted angrily to the abolishment of the caliphate. Their rebellions to overthrow the new regime — encouraged by Britain — were crushed. The feudal tribal structure of the region remained unchanged during the twentieth century. Various Kurdish tribes waged war with one another while Britain, France, and the United States coveted the rich oil fields of Mosul and Kerkük. Meanwhile southeastern Anatolia, mostly Kurdish, remained the most underdeveloped, impoverished part of Turkey.

The vast GAP scheme, the largest development project ever undertaken in Turkey, has brought no benefits to most Kurds. Moreover, the venture worries neighbouring countries such as Syria and Iraq, which depend on the waters of the Tigris and Euphrates and fear losing a vital resource.

In 1987, when the PKK started a guerrilla war against the Turkish state to establish an independent Marxist nation, neighbouring countries hostile to Turkey and to the GAP project supported the Kurdish rebels. Some Europeans and Americans were also suspected of covertly assisting the guerrillas. Turkey fought back. During the 1990s, tens of thousands of Kurds were imprisoned and tortured. More than 30,000 people died, and five million Kurds took refuge in squatter neighbourhoods around cities such as Adana, Mersin, and Antalya.

Doğu Beyazıt

In the summer of 1998, while Jean was still in Quebec City, I drove a rented car from Erzurum and headed for the town of Doğu Beyazıt in the easternmost corner of Turkey, near the border with Iran and Armenia. Village houses made of mud bricks with flat roofs rose out of the arid, dust-coloured land like geological formations. On the hillsides, I saw flocks of sheep that were also dust-coloured and that blended into the landscape. As I drove by, I waved at mustachioed shepherds who raised hands to greet me.

It was late afternoon when I arrived at Doğu Beyazıt in the foothills of Mount Ararat, whose snowcapped summit towered above the clouds to the east. As I checked into a little hotel on the main street, a military helicopter circled above the roofs. The people in the hotel spoke Kurdish among themselves.

The mountainous land was magnificent. The remains of a medieval Islamic château, İshak Paşa Sarayı, glowing rose and gold in the evening sun, dominated the landscape. Across from the château, the masonry of 3,000-year-old Urartian walls almost merged with the hill. I walked up that hill until I was above the château. A treeless valley of mauve craters spread before me. I lingered there, waiting for the sunset.

A young man came out of the little coffee shop on top of the hill, carrying a chair. He brought it down to the clearing on the hillside. "You'll be more comfortable if you sit down," he said in accented Turkish as he went back to the coffee shop. I sat there alone until the sun turned crimson and slid behind the valley. Then I forced myself to get up and walk down the hill to the town before dark.

The next morning I returned to the hill and climbed all the way to the coffee shop. Music, unlike traditional Turkish music, unlike anything I had heard before, spilled from the terrace. A flute sustained a long note, and a woman's voice rose in a plaintive wail. Inside, four swarthy men with thick black moustaches played cards. The youth who offered me a chair the evening before recognized me and smiled. I asked him for tea.

"Military helicopters were circling above the town yesterday," I said when he brought it. "Is there a lot of fighting around here?"

154

Perched on rugged cliffs five kilometres from the town of Doğu Beyazıt, ishak Paşa Sarayı is a superb example of seventeenth/eighteenth-century Ottoman architecture.

He nodded, then changed the subject. "Where are you from?" he asked. "I figured you weren't Turkish. A Turkish woman wouldn't be walking around the hills alone in the evening."

I saw him talk to an older man behind the counter. They both glanced at me, and then the youth came back. "Most tourists visit the château and the Urartian walls and go away. Why do you ask about the fighting?"

I told him I was a writer.

That got him talking. "There isn't a single family here who hasn't lost a brother or a father or a husband. We all know someone in the mountains. In our hearts, we support the guerrillas."

His name was Hasan and he was seventeen. He said that until two years earlier he had been determined to stay out of trouble, that he had been working as a tourist guide and had hoped to manage a hotel one day. Then his cousin, who was in the PKK, was killed crossing the border to Iran.

"The killers didn't return the body to the family," Hasan said. "They got rid of it in the night. About a hundred of us, the relatives, went into a house for a wake. On the way back, the police appeared and ordered us to disperse. We locked arms. They opened fire on us. I was wounded in my leg."

Hasan said that night he was arrested with thirty-three others. At the police station they tied his eyes, made him lie on the ground, and beat him.

"They kept us in there for fifteen days. They beat us every day, asking us for names of others in the PKK, asking for the relationships between people. Whether you had anything to do with the PKK or not made no difference. They thought anyone who went to the funeral of a terrorist had to be a terrorist."

The irony was that jail was like a political academy for him. At first he thought he had no business there, that he wasn't interested in such things, and that the authorities had made a mistake. But by the time he was released, he had become an enemy of the Turkish state.

"Wouldn't you be?" he asked me. "But it's no life, hiding in the mountains, hungry, thirsty, cold, in constant fear. I realized the PKK can't win without the support of the people. The people here are scared and divided. They inform on each other, so I left the PKK."

He had met some French tourists who said they could get him a fake passport. He was waiting to hear from them, hoping to immigrate to France.

While Hasan talked, the men playing cards left their game and gathered around us. One of them, a tall, thin man with very white teeth, introduced himself as Ahmet. He said he had been a schoolteacher in a village but was fired for teaching the children Kurdish. Ahmet said that many young men joined the PKK because they had no jobs. "But," he added, "the local people are so ignorant, so poor, that they inform on their own people for a little money."

Ahmet volunteered to take me for a drive on an old moped to show me the land and some of the villages nearby. I hesitated.

"It's just a twenty-minute ride," he said.

Raising dust clouds, we drove uphill to a plateau awash with an ocean of tall, blue-green grass that rippled in waves. We came to a clearing where earth-coloured mounds with flat roofs sprang out of the ground. They were the remains of houses made of mud and straw, and they were empty.

"There was a bloodbath in this village a couple of months ago," Ahmet explained. "A group of guerrillas came down to eat a meal with their families. A village woman said, 'I'll go get some snow so you can drink cold water.' She walked a little distance from the houses. She didn't know that one of the villagers had informed on the men and that the police had surrounded the village. A policeman saw the woman. He lifted his gun and shot her in front of all the villagers. If that hadn't happened, the guerillas would have escaped. But seeing the woman shot, they opened fire. Thirty policemen died. Villagers must have died, too, I don't know how many. After that the people deserted the village. Some went to cities and to other villages. Some live in tents."

At the centre of the village a fountain dripped. Heaps of rubble lay here and there.

We took a winding road up another hill and came to second cluster of houses made of earth. Here a couple of women washed sheep wool at the fountain.

In the pasture beyond the houses, we discovered a man guarding a small herd of sheep. Ahmet told him something in Kurdish. The man nodded and began to talk, squinting and pointing towards the hills. Ahmet translated.

"Some women from this village were picking grass in the fields. They met a few guerrillas. Normally, when guerillas run into people, they take hostages. This time they let the women go. One of the women was the wife of the village mayor. She ran straight to her husband and told him, and her husband went to the police. Police surrounded the area. They killed several guerrillas, but one of them escaped. Now, if you were the one who escaped, wouldn't you avenge your dead comrades? Sure enough, he returned to the village with other guerrillas and killed the woman and her husband in front of all the villagers."

After telling this gruesome story, the old man complained that the army was killing herds of sheep. "They want to discourage the villagers from feeding the guerrillas. But the people are poor, anyway. Without the sheep they're left with no milk, no cheese."

On our way back to the coffee shop, we drove past an army truck full of soldiers in camouflage uniforms. I was scared. Ahmet laughed. "They'll think I'm on the make with a tourist."

I strolled back to town under the midday sun and set out in the rented car to return to Erzurum.

"Were you visiting İshak Paşa Sarayı?" the young guard at the barricade asked. "Would you believe that I've been here for two years and I haven't seen it yet?" He returned my passport and waved at me with a smile.

I drove out of Doğu Beyazıt. At the Erzurum airport I boarded a plane to return to Ankara where neither the Kurds nor the war officially existed.

Weeks later, near my parents' summer house on the Aegean coast, my mother and I took an evening walk. Two men sauntered towards us across the road. I felt my mother's hand tighten on my arm. She stopped talking and began to move faster. "What's the matter?" I asked her.

"Nothing." She remained silent and continued to make an effort to walk faster — at a surprising pace for her age and health.

"Wait a minute!" I stopped on the road. "What's going on?"

"Those two men who passed us," she whispered." They're not from here. Both were dark with black moustaches. They could be Kurds."

"So?"

"Terrorists are everywhere these days. You never know ..."

We reached the house where bougainvillea cascades over the garden gate, and where inside, my father was listening to the evening news on television.

The announcer's voice gave the daily, official tally: "Sixty-four terrorists 'captured dead' in a village near Batman. The armed forces have confiscated their cache of weapons ..."

Outside, crickets chirped, and dance music poured out of an open window.

Hero

A little later in the summer of 1998, on my way by bus from İzmir to Ankara, I met a hero and his mother. As we left the lush Aegean region and entered the dry central Anatolian plateau, the landscape outside the window changed. I glimpsed craters formed by dry earth, brittle yellow grass swaying along rocky ridges, and stretches of grey-brown land rising and falling under a white sky. The heat seemed to hiss and rustle as lizards darted between dry thorns.

The bus driver was listening to arabesque music. A *nazarlık*, a blue glass charm against the evil eye, dangled from his rearview mirror. All the seats in the bus were occupied. A couple of middle-class folk, probably returning from vacation, turned the pages of magazines. Little girls with long braids and little boys in shorts sat on the knees of village women in flowered shirts and long, loose pants gathered at the ankles. Some passengers dozed.

In the back row, across the aisle from me, a teenage village boy slept, his shaved head lolling against the shoulder of a middle-aged woman beside him. His face was thin with delicate features and thick eyebrows. The woman stared out the window. I noticed her hands — rough red fingers fidgeting on her lap, thumb rubbing the other thumb, turning around and around, squirming like hungry animals.

She turned towards me and caught me staring at her. Out of embarrassment I smiled. She hesitated and smiled back. I averted my eyes and waited for her to glance out the window again so I could continue to observe her and the dozing boy.

The boy moved in his sleep as if he were trying to get comfortable in the narrow seat. He pulled up his knees, licked his lips, and pushed his head more towards the woman's chest. The woman accommodated him and squeezed closer to the window. She lifted one of her hands to the sleeping boy's shoulder and let it rest there, the bony knuckles now still.

The afternoon heat settled in the bus. Some people made fanning motions with their hands. A fat man expelled a loud sigh. The woman beside the sleeping boy held a newspaper over the boy's head to shade his face from the sun. He squirmed, opened his eyes, slid away from the woman's chest, and stroked his head. Yawning, he peered out the window, then surveyed the bus with dark eyes. He, too, caught me staring.

The boy said something to the woman, who picked up a plastic bag from the floor and extracted a little box of cookies. Fishing out a cookie, the boy bit into it, then made a sudden move towards me, offering the box. "Take one, please."

I did, embarrassed that he had caught me watching him. We both chewed on cookies quietly until he asked me where I was from.

"No wonder you speak such good Turkish," he said. He was terribly interested in Canada, the land of affluence and peace for most Turks. He knew someone who tried to immigrate but who couldn't get a visa. I asked him if he was a student.

"Student? No. I'm a soldier." He seemed half outraged, half amused.

"How old are you?"

"I'll be twenty in September."

The woman beside him smiled at me timidly. "I'm his mother. He was at home on leave for two weeks. Now he's returning to the front. I'm going to see him off from Afyon."

The front! "Do you mean you're on duty in the southeast?" I asked.

He nodded, his eyes dark, serious.

"Have you been there already?"

"Yes. Three months now."

"It must be rough."

This comment unleashed a torrent of words. "You can't imagine how rough. We're tense all the time. Sometimes they attack our barracks in the middle of the night. It's happened several times. Each night when I go to sleep I tell myself I might never wake up. Some nights I'm so scared I want to run away. You learn never to relax. Never. If you relax for one moment, that might be when they get you. You can't trust anyone. No one. None of the peasants in the mountains, not even the children. It's so hard to live while suspecting everyone around you. We're all scared. We try not to show each other."

I wanted to ask him what was going on in Şırnak and Hakkari, towns reportedly demolished by the army, but I was ashamed to make light conversation about horrors. With new fascination, I studied the mother, thinking how her heart must ache to send her young son to kill or be killed.

Then the boy suddenly started talking again, even though I hadn't dared ask any more questions. "One night, just before I took my leave, after we went to sleep, they invaded our post. If the guard hadn't seen one of them crawling behind the building, they would have blown all of us to bits. As it was, we captured all of them."

"What did you do?"

"The usual. You try to get as much information as possible about who's in their organization, about who supports them, and about their strategies for attack."

"How do you try to get information?"

"You beat them. Scare them. They're like animals. You do anything you have to do." His big, dark child's eyes gazed warmly into my eyes. He was almost boasting.

"And you," I heard myself asking, "have you seen people killed? Have you killed?"

He continued to look at me, then nodded. "Of course. It's our duty."

I let my eyes drift back to the lunar landscape flowing outside the bus window. The driver announced Afyon in ten minutes, and the soldier's mother began to gather her plastic bags. As the mother and son got off the bus, the boy said, "Iyi yolculuklar. Bon voyage."

I watched them walk towards the little restaurant beside the bus depot — he, carrying the bags; she, holding his left arm tightly, as if afraid she might trip on a stone.

Peace

The war zone became fertile ground for a brisk arms and drugs trade. The PKK relied on the contraband to finance its war. The state recruited counter-guerrillas and armed local village guards, thus creating gangs of out-of-control vigilantes.

In February 1999, Turkish forces (with the help of the American and Israeli secret services) captured PKK leader Abdullah Öcalan, who was tried and condemned to death for treason. From death row, Öcalan called for peace "in a democratic Turkish republic" and asked his guerrillas to abandon the armed struggle. The PKK announced in late September 1999 that it was ending its armed campaign for Kurdish self-rule and transforming itself into a political organization called KADEK, which would seek cultural rights. In January 2000, the Turkish parliament decided to stay Öcalan's execution. More than 10,000 Kurds remained in prison for supporting the PKK.

((

"Is the war over?" I ask Kurdish lawyer Feride Laçin in Diyarbakır while drinking tea in her cozy office, which has a plush couch and chairs.

"War was never declared," she replies. "Peace won't be declared, either. But we no longer fear for our lives when we go out on the street."

Feride was on the board of the Human Rights Association of Diyarbakır, an organization that was harassed constantly by the Turkish armed forces and counter-guerrilla groups. Now she is chairing the women's commission of the Diyarbakır Bar Association.

"Women face a lot of violence," she says. "The war and the mass migration have worsened unemployment and poverty. Now, in squatter shacks in big cities, parents become alienated from their children. Most parents speak only Kurdish, yet their children speak Turkish. The children have witnessed terrible violence. They seethe with anger. Child crime is rising. In the village, children helped their parents. In the city, they roam the streets."

The war is over, but it has caused social degeneration. Tens of thousands of Kurds have been displaced and estranged from their values. Feride explains that there has been a great rise in prostitution and in teenage suicides. "Families sell their own daughters to soldiers and to policemen," she says. "Several

These Kurdish children in a squatters' neighbourhood in Diyarbakır in southeastern Anatolia likely face a grim life.

teenage girls have killed themselves during the past year. And it's people from this region who sell drugs in the European markets."

When Jean and I walk inside the medieval basalt fortifications of Diyarbakır towards the Tigris River, hordes of small children run after us. Some of them are barefoot. As their numbers swell, many of them fight among themselves. Suddenly, I am terrified of the army of street children, fearing the kids might get out of control at any moment. I ask the children to stop following us, but they ignore me.

A storekeeper who hears me yells at the children, "Don't behave like a pack of dogs! Leave the tourists alone." He makes a hand motion as if to hit someone. The children disperse, and a great sadness descends upon me.

Dead Terrorist

On a March morning, just before the Islamic sacrificial holiday of Kurban Bayramı, I visit Mehmet and Naime Yılmaz in the Teoman Paşa district of Antalya. When I arrive, Naime is sitting on a stone floor in a whitewashed room

162

redolent with the sweet smell of flour. She is making baklava for the holidays with her daughter-in-law and two other women. A large bowl of dough stands between them. The women break off pieces of dough, roll them on wooden boards, spread thin sheets of dough on trays, sprinkle walnuts over them, and cover them with more layers of dough. When the trays are finished, Naime cuts diagonal and perpendicular lines in the dough to make diamond-shaped pieces. I sit on the floor with the women, Mehmet settles on the windowsill, and the daughter-in law gets up to make tea.

I take a photograph of Mehmet and Naime in front of a portrait of their dead son, Servet, who was killed in a village near Diyarbakır by police in 1992 when he was nineteen. Plastic flowers in red, green, and yellow — the outlawed colours of the PKK — are stuck under the frame. The middle-aged couple stand solemnly side by side in their living room in a squatter's shack, which has a flat roof like the houses made of mud bricks in the villages of southeastern Anatolia. Naime wears a white turban, the headdress of Kurdish village women.

"I went there a week later," Mehmet says. "To see my son, I made someone dig open the grave, and then we knew it was true. Servet had joined the guerrillas. He was dead."

Mehmet and Naime came to Antalya in 1968 from their village in southeastern Anatolia.

"We fled from a blood feud," Naime says. "Someone from my husband's clan had a fight with a man from another clan and killed him. My husband was the youngest in his family. The enemy clan would go after him. We came to Antalya to cover our tracks. But we never found happiness."

Mehmet and Naime Yılmaz stand solemnly before the simple "shrine" they prepared in memory of their dead son, Servet.

163

Antalya is a beautiful Mediterranean city on the ridges of the Taurus Mountains. In ancient times, the city was called Attaleia, named after the Pergamon King Attalus who founded it during the second century BC. Today it is a tourist haven with Roman walls, an ancient port now restored as a yacht harbour, and bistros and tea gardens perched on cliffs.

In March, when the sky over Ankara is grey and the ground muddy, there is sunshine in Antalya, and plum trees are in flower. A blue light rises from the sea and covers the craggy silhouettes of the Taurus peaks across the bay. Ripe bitter oranges hang on branches like forgotten Christmas ornaments.

Neither the tourists nor the middle-class Turks in the city seem to notice the tens of thousands of Kurds from southeast Anatolia, many of them jobless, some driving taxis, some doing occasional labour, most living on the outskirts of the beautiful city. Kurdish children shine tourists' shoes in the city's palm-lined avenues. Many of them have brothers, fathers, and uncles in prison. In humble living rooms every evening, the Kurds tune in to an outlawed Kurdish-language television station, "Med TV," whose signal comes from Britain. They consider *terrörist başı* (head terrorist) Abdullah Öcalan a hero.

For many years Mehmet Yılmaz found casual work in Antalya as a private security guard. He and Naime had four sons and a daughter and barely enough to eat. Now Mehmet has no work. One of the sons is dead, one is unemployed, one sells tomatoes to provide for the entire family, including his own wife and child, and another son is doing his military service in the Turkish army.

When Mehmet tells me this, I look up at him in surprise.

"Yes," he says. "I know the irony. That's our situation. Servet had also received his papers for military service. That's when he disappeared. He decided to join the 'other' army."

"Servet was the first from Antalya to join the guerrillas," Naime says with pride. "He grew up here, not in the southeast. After him his cousin also went, and he also died."

After Servet's death, the police came for Mehmet. They kept him for three days, wanting information. "That's how it is," Mehmet says. "When they know someone in the family has joined the guerrillas, they go after the others in that family."

Most people in the neighbourhood are Kurds, but not all. "We have Turkish neighbours, too," Naime says. "When Servet died, they came to offer us their condolences. That was before they found out how he died." But word got around, and the Turkish neighbours now stay away.

"We pity the Turkish children who die in this war." Naime says. "But they don't pity ours. Terrorist, they call him. My son died for his people. I want to believe that Servet's death wasn't for nothing." Naime looks at me, her blue eyes pleading. I glance away.

☾

Thirty-two-year-old Remziye, mother of three small boys, lives on the second floor of a two-storey building above a grocery store. Her brother-in-law opens the door for me. I take off my shoes in the hallway and enter the living room furnished only with a sofa. On the wall, there is beadwork in red, green, and yellow, with two doves in the palms of handcuffed hands.

"I made that in Diyarbakır Prison," Remziye says. "I did time on three different occasions. The last was in 1994. I stayed for three months." Her crime was always the same: *yardım ve yataklık*, "aiding and abetting" the PKK.

"My husband died in prison five years ago," Remziye says. "They arrested him on a Monday. On Thursday he was dead. He was thirty-five."

As she speaks, I suddenly recognize her. "Don't I know you? I think I interviewed you eight years ago. I still have those cassettes. You were pregnant at the time. Do you have an eight-year-old child?"

"Yes," Remziye says. "Bişar. There he is." She points to a thin boy at the door.

In the autumn of 1994, when the war was at its height, I came to this shantytown in Antalya to interview people at a wake for two men killed in the southeast. One of those people, a young pregnant woman from Batman, pointed to her swollen belly. "I'm willing to spill the last drop of the blood of this one to fight against the Turkish state," she said. That was Remziye!

In the eight years since then, two of Remziye's brothers have also died, Remziye has been in prison twice, and her third brother is still in prison.

"One of my brothers died last November," she says. "I received the news on New Year's Eve." She and her father went to Diyarbakır to identify the dead man from a photograph of the corpse. "They didn't give us his body."

Remziye tells me that *all* the children in her native Batman are father-less. *All.* Not *many*, not *most*, but *all.* Families are without sons, brothers, and husbands. "Our men are dead and dying," she says. "On holidays everyone goes to the cemetery."

I remind Remziye of what she said seven years ago about the child she was then carrying.

"I remember you now," she tells me slowly, "but I don't remember saying those things. I want peace now. I want it for the sake of my kids."

☾

On our way from Diyarbakır to Tatvan on the western shores of Lake Van, Jean and I stop at Baykan, a town of 9,000 people in the mountains. The café on the main street has a view of a pine forest to the north. We buy water and *leblebi* (roasted chickpeas) and drink exceptionally flavourful tea. From then on we are in the mountains. The land appears much less arid than the plains near Batman. Close to Tatvan, irrigation hoses in tobacco and cotton fields form rainbows. Villagers bent from the waist hoe cotton fields.

The *öğretmenevi* (teachers' guesthouse) at Tatvan is a happy surprise. It is a clean new building with spacious rooms and a balcony from where we watch a crescent moon slip behind the mountains.

At 9:30 p.m. the city is closing up shop. We see lights at a restaurant on the fourth floor of an apartment block and walk up dark stairs. Inside, only one table is occupied; the sole waiter in sight is tidying up the tables.

"Just soup and salad," we say.

The two young men at the occupied table look to be in their twenties. One of them asks if my husband is French.

"We like Tatvan very much," I say.

He stares at me.

"Don't you?" I ask.

"Well," he says, "we're public servants." He pauses. "Terrorism ..."

"Were you affected much?"

"We're in a special commando team. We're trained to fight in the mountains. We think about *them* as traitors. We want to get rid of them."

"But the fighting seems to be coming to an end," I say. "Will it be hard for you to return to civilian life?"

The second man, who has remained silent until now, nods. "When you carry out 'operations' in the mountains, you suspend all emotions," he says.

"You know that sooner or later you'll have to fight, so you want to get it over with."

"Why did you choose this job?" I ask.

"It's well-paid," he answers.

The men get up, wish us a good evening, and head to the door. Just as they are leaving, the one who started the conversation returns to our table with a smile. "There's a beautiful crater lake at Mount Nemrut," he says. "No, not the famous Mount Nemrut with the Commagene kings' statues. This one is different. It's less than ten kilometres north of Tatvan. You can see the mountains, the tall grass, and the sky in its mirror-like surface. Make sure you stop there."

"We'll do that," I say. "Thank you."

A Dirge for Zeugma

> A flood will sweep over the cult centres;
> To destroy the seed of mankind …
> Is the decision, the word of the assembly of the gods.
> — Sumerian tablet inscription cited in Samuel Noah
> Kramer, *History Begins in Sumer*

I wake up in the night grieving over Zeugma. I imagine the turquoise waters of the Euphrates dissolving the eggshell-coloured earth over the mosaics of gods and goddesses celebrating celestial victories — the world's finest mosaics, unseen for a thousand years, lost forever to human eyes. I imagine columns collapsing in slow motion underwater, bronze statues sinking into the depths of a vast man-made lake. And I ache with sadness.

I have seen the huge dam lake over Zeugma glistening between whitish hills rising like sand dunes.

The Tigris and the Euphrates and the fertile crescent between them have nurtured more layers of civilizations than any other piece of land in the world. Prehistoric societies, Sumerians, Babylonians, Assyrians, Romans, various Islamic states, and the Ottoman Turks have lived and died there.

The soil in this region receives little rain. For thousands of years the Tigris and Euphrates rose wildly in winter but shrank to brooks in the summer. They

Broken columns of ancient Zeugma rise on the banks of the Euphrates River.

either caused disastrous floods or they shrivelled under the scorching sun. In prolonged droughts, crops withered and the land cracked and turned into dust. The searing heat and the parched earth seemed like pronouncements of God's wrath, as cited in the Bible's Revelation 16:

> And the fourth angel poured his vial upon the sun; and power was given unto him to scorch men with fire.... And the sixth angel poured out his vial upon the great river Euphrates; and the water thereof was dried up, that the way of the kings of the east might be prepared.

In the first summer of the twenty-first century, however, the age of globalization and technology brought an end to the droughts. The GAP project began to dam the waters of the Tigris and Euphrates, transforming the ancient geography. Their waters rose, as in the Sumerian creation legend, to flood towns, orchards, and the ruins of ancient cities in Upper Mesopotamia. Hundreds of settlements and dozens of archaeological sites were submerged and many others were doomed.

The development had economic and strategic importance beyond irrigation and electricity. Water would be the prized resource of the twenty-first century, scarcer and more precious than oil. With GAP, Turkey hoped to dramatically increase its bargaining power over its neighbours.

The modern world didn't hear of Zeugma, a Roman city on the west bank of the Euphrates, thirty kilometres north of the Turkish city of Gaziantep, until the late 1980s. Its sumptuous remains lay buried under ten metres of soil. Only a couple of rock tombs and the remains of the temple of Tyche, the goddess of fortune, were visible above the ground on a slope rising 300 metres. Pistachio trees grew in the blanched soil.

Southeastern Anatolia — Upper Mesopotamia — is a place that knows poverty and sorrow. Struggling to live under the scorching sun, the Kurds and the Turks didn't explore the many ruins. Ruins don't feed children.

Treasure hunters knew better, though. Secretly, in the late 1980s, they dug up the ground near the graves, carted away sections of mosaics, and left behind gaping holes. Archaeologists took up where the smugglers left off. They unearthed wall frescoes, statues of Roman nobles, and a bounty of bronze objects, including oil lamps, medallions, miniature statues of Hermes and Eros, and weapons. And they discovered magnificent mosaics, parts of which were stolen by the smugglers.

Rumoured to have been built in the late second century AD during the reign of the Roman emperor Septimius Severus, this stone bridge over the Cendere, one of the tributaries of the Euphrates, is still used. (Jean Burelle)

In 1992 the guard on the site found a tunnel, also dug by smugglers, on the northeastern side of the mound. More excavations revealed a villa whose floors were covered with mosaics, one of which portrays a celestial wedding scene where Eros, the god of love, offers a love potion to Dionysos and Ariadne. In 1994 three large burial chambers and five more villas adorned with mosaics were discovered.

The word *zeugma* means "passage" in Greek — appropriate for a city at one of the two narrowest points of the Euphrates, and on the Silk Road to China. The city was founded by one of Alexander the Great's generals in the fourth century BC, and Alexander himself crossed the river there on his way to Persia.

The city prospered from trade and became a legion centre under the Romans. It was pillaged and burnt by Sasanid invaders during the third century BC and gradually lost its splendour. In the seventeenth century, a Turkish village named Belkis was built near Zeugma's remains. When human eyes once again beheld Zeugma and some of its treasures in the late twentieth century, the site was already doomed. A dam was planned at Birecik, 800 kilometres from the ruins.

Work started on Birecik Dam in 1996. During construction, workers discovered pieces of mosaics and notified archaeologists. Emergency excavations uncovered a large Roman bath and gymnasium right on the dam's axis. Researchers barely had time to take photographs of the baths and to remove thirty-nine pieces of mosaics from the site.

The ancient city lay on a slope, which meant that it would be flooded in two stages. The first level would be submerged in July 2000, and the second level would go under three months later in October. Only a small section on top of the mound would remain.

In 1997, as the dam neared completion, excavations took a desperate, frenzied pace and revealed a grave site from the Bronze Age. More mosaics, an archive, and a collection of stamps also appeared one after the other. Zeugma had more than 5,000 square metres of mosaics, and archaeologists wanted to find and salvage whatever they could.

The governor of the city of Gaziantep decided in 1999 to postpone the building of a school and a hospital so he could spend money on the digs. "We can build a school and hospital next year," he said. "But Zeugma will be lost by then."

Archaeologists from Gaziantep Museum and from Nantes University in France found new mosaics. In one of them, Dionysos stands with Nike on a chariot pulled by two leopards while Bacchae twirl in an eternal dance before them. One dancer's shawl catches the light and flies. Another mosaic depicts

Queen Pasiphaë (the wife of King Minos and the mother of the Minotaur) commissioning a wooden bull from a father-and-son team of carpenters. Pasiphaë's gaze is sad, and baby Eros awaits with his bow and arrow behind her stool. The older carpenter rushing away to obey the order holds a saw. Tiny stones are laid in such a way that they convey movement and emotion.

During the last two nights before the flood, as the water was beginning to seep through the ground, some archaeologists toiled through the night in a cave that could have collapsed at any moment. They worked feverishly in the light of a generator to remove the mosaics portraying the birth of Venus. The face of the goddess of love had been stolen earlier, but her long, slender waist and her perfectly shaped legs were unmistakable.

And then it was over. The water rose through the caves and through the floors of half-excavated villas, and the Euphrates claimed the treasures that still remained underground. "A catastrophe," French archaeologist Catherine Abadie-Reynal said. "An archaeological catastrophe."

I first saw Zeugma after the first layer of ruins was flooded, while the second layer was awaiting the waters. The arches of the dam were visible from behind the columns of the ruined Roman city. Ripe pistachios hung in crimson clusters on tree branches above — a silent, magnificent landscape. It was the dam against the ruins, and the ruins had lost.

I also saw some of Zeugma's mosaics in the museum, images fashioned from small pieces of local stones in thirteen different colours, each piece of stone no larger than 1.5 centimetres. One showed Oceanus and Thetis amid sea creatures. I saw light in Oceanus's eyes. Light and shade made of stones! Human minds and human hands create such strange beauty.

Riverside villas belonging to Roman officers and nobles had been carpeted with tapestries made of these tiny stones, but no human eyes will ever see them on the slopes overlooking the Euphrates again. And that, too, is the work of human minds and human hands. It isn't God's wrath but human choice that now forces the ancient river to swell like a sea, swallowing thousands of years of human heritage.

☾

On the slopes overlooking the blue-green dam lake, I meet a peasant woman with stern eyes who holds a small child. I ask if she lives in the village of Belkis, which is also submerged. She nods.

"We're in a mess now," she says. "Hundreds of us in tents behind that hill there like earthquake survivors. Without electricity, without sewage. Our village lies in the water. Our pistachio trees, too. They say they'll give us houses. But when?"

"Did you know your village was near the ruins of an ancient city? I ask.

"Yes, we did."

But this woman hasn't seen the mosaics and isn't sure what they are. She turns away from me.

Twenty-five kilometres upstream from Zeugma, half of Halfeti, a town nestled on the south shore of the river at the bottom of a steep incline, is also submerged. The roofs of some buildings stick out of the lake, and empty half-ruined houses sit on the shore waiting to be flooded.

"A school was here," says Mehmet Erdogan, a fisherman on the Euphrates, pointing at the depths of the water as we float in his small boat beside the tops of palm trees poking out of the water. "And here was a park."

When Mehmet stops the motor, an immense silence falls on the lake. Shadows alternate with the glow of late-afternoon sunlight on the steep, rocky banks that soar beyond the town, forming a canyon. It is a magnificent but eerie sight.

"The water rose suddenly in May," Mehmet says. "We knew part of the town would be flooded, but everyone thought his own house would be safe. We took refuge in tents and in prefab houses behind that hill," he adds, indicating the slope with an outstretched arm, "but most of us don't have electricity, water, or sewage. We weren't prepared for this."

Ten minutes by boat from Halfeti is Cerkem, a village of 105 houses and 600 people that was flooded in May 2000. I talk to a villager from Cerkem standing on an island of abandoned pistachio orchards in the middle of the dam lake.

"We had pistachios, plums, apricots, walnuts, olives, grapevines, and figs here," the villager tells me. "They moved us to a place called Karaotlak. At Karaotlak there are only black stones and red earth. No roads, no telephone, no sewage. Hopelessness hangs over all of us. My pistachios are ready for harvest. There are no roads to transport them. These little boats are dangerous. They sink as soon as the wind rises. I've lost 400 pistachio trees to the water. Now I'm losing 300 tons of ripe nuts."

As if to prove the greatness of his loss, he gives me a cluster of fresh pistachios. I eat the tender nuts and throw the crimson coating and shells into the water.

((

Street vendors sell fresh pistachios in the streets of Gaziantep. In the narrow alleys of marginal neighbourhoods, Kurdish women string red peppers and eggplants to dry for winter, while their children polish shoes in parks and avenues. Destroyed mosaics and statues are one thing, but on this land of ancient injustices, people also grieve over lost lives. Tens of thousands of people died in an undeclared war in this region while the dams were being built. Can silent stones and shards of ancient pottery be of any use against poverty or sorrow? Can memory or beauty?

One of the mosaic fragments I saw in the Gaziantep Museum was the portrait of a young woman whom the archaeologists called *The Gypsy Girl*. Smugglers had stolen the lower part of her face, but her dark eyes were so expressive that they seemed to follow you wherever you walked. Now they looked sad. Next they seemed gay. Then they appeared scared. Mysterious eyes on a mysterious face, dug up at the very end before Zeugma sank like Atlantis.

And how much more remains underground? How much more is unseen, forgotten? The eggshell-coloured land has no memory, and neither does the turquoise Euphrates. Memory is for people. Beauty, too.

In the small hours of the night when fears and longings emerge like phantoms, I lie awake to mourn discarded history, hidden beauty. Words become monsters in my mind. Technology. Progress. Prosperity. Strategic-bargaining tool. Control of resources. My grief seems absurd viewed against poverty and human lives, and grows even sharper when I tell myself that I will never fully know what I have lost with Zeugma.

Hasankeyf

Soldiers stop Jean and I twice to check our passports on the way from Diyarbakır to a medieval town named Hasankeyf. We pass bald mountains where sheep graze beside mud-brick houses, then descend into a valley and suddenly come upon the Tigris flowing southwards between the mountains in a steep canyon sliced like a piece of cheese and perforated with caves.

I have never known a place that feels more remote, more like the setting of a science-fiction movie. The houses of Hasankeyf huddle against buff caves, and the

Hasankeyf awaits the floodwaters that will submerge thousands of years of human heritage.

remains of a medieval bridge rest in the water near a modern bridge. An ancient minaret rises at the foot of the bridge beside the ruins of a medieval mosque.

There are no hotels in town, so we check in at the teachers' residence. A dozen policemen sipping tea on the sidewalk greet us, then watch as we take our bags out of the trunk of our rented car.

Later we take a stroll. As we gaze at the massive river cliffs, a thin boy with blue eyes appears before us. "Welcome to Hasankeyf," he says in English.

When I answer him in Turkish, he pauses. Then he switches to Turkish and sounds as if he is quoting from a book. "These steps will take you to a Byzantine fortress that was built from a single block of stone, perhaps the only one of its kind in the world. Inside its walls there are the remains of palaces and mosques. I can show them to you."

Rıdvan is an eleven-year-old Kurdish boy in a doomed town. His mother died when he was two, and his father abandoned six children to elope with a woman. Rıdvan's eyes are serious — the eyes of a man with responsibilities. He works as a self-appointed tourist guide and earns the equivalent of a Canadian dollar a day.

"I take the money to my grandmother," he says. "She gives me bread and cheese and some pocket money out of it."

174

From a dollar? I think.

Hasankeyf will be flooded when a dam is constructed at Ilısu, upstream on the Tigris, but no one knows when.

"They want us to go away," says the grocer who sells us bottled water. "New construction is forbidden in Hasankeyf. The town is dying. They want it to become a ghost town even before they flood it."

Ali, a man in his thirties, holds a ten-month-old baby as he tells us that the people of Hasankeyf feel betrayed. "To earn a living I have to leave this town. I work as a cab driver in Batman, thirty kilometres north of here. I have to leave my wife and children alone during the week. What kind of a life is that? People used to fish on the Tigris. Some used to sell sand from the banks. Those jobs are banned now. Even tourism is being discouraged. That white building in the corner was built as a hotel, but they won't give it a licence."

The origins of Hasankeyf are unknown and its early history is obscure, but the caves pitting the cliffs have been inhabited from time immemorial. During the third and fourth centuries AD, the Romans and the Sasanians (from Iran) fought over the town. The Byzantines built the fortress and kept Hasankeyf until the arrival of the Muslims in the seventh century.

In the early twelfth century, under the Islamic Artuqid Dynasty, Hasankeyf became an important medieval city, but the Mongolians invaded it in the thirteenth century. A century later the Islamic Ayyubid Dynasty rebuilt it and 200 years later passed it on to the Ottomans.

"This fortress was impenetrable during the Middle Ages," Rıdvan says as we walk up the steps. "It has secret tunnels that go down to the river. That's how people got their water during sieges."

Other children working as guides gather around us, speaking Kurdish to one another.

"There are no jobs for the adults," thirteen-year-old Şehmuz says. "My father used to go to Diyarbakır to work at construction sites. He'd come to see us from time to time. He ended up staying there. I have a mother and three sisters. Now I look after them."

"Our cultural heritage will be destroyed," Rıdvan says, still sounding as if he's reading from a book. "The water will rise nine metres and will cover everything up to the top of the ancient minaret that you see there."

"Where will people go?" I ask him.

"Maybe they'll give us houses somewhere else."

"Tell you what," Jean says to the children. "Our rented car needs to be washed. How about we drive it down to the Tigris and you guys wash it with bucketfuls of water?"

There are cheers, and a solemn agreement to share the pay.

On the river, right on the water, there are shelters made of dried poplar branches. People with their shoes and socks off sit at tables, eating and drinking with their feet dangling in the Tigris. Some even swim — more like wade — in the gurgling river.

The boys strip to their underwear and throw bucketfuls of water at the car, laughing and screaming. Afterwards they share the pay, as dignified as a group of businessmen, and disappear into the half-light.

Jean and I soak our feet in the river and drink tea. Tiny fish nibble at our ankles. The setting sun gilds the ruins and broken minarets, while the Tigris mirrors the burning sky. Hasankeyf puts on an eerie and spectacular show to break our hearts with beauty.

A group of men sitting around a table across from us get up to dance the *halay* to music blaring from their car radio. They lock arms and step sideways together, shimmying their shoulders as the sun settles behind wine-coloured mountains.

On a summer evening in Hasankeyf, men dine out while the Tigris River cools their feet.

Rıdvan appears beside the rented car the next morning while Jean and I are stowing our bags in the trunk. "I got up early to say goodbye. Can I get into the car with you? I'll get off when you cross the bridge."

In the back seat, he raises Jean's binoculars to his eyes to stare at the hills on the west bank. "I dreamt of you last night," he tells me, the binoculars covering half his face. "I dreamt of a wedding. You two were getting married." He pauses, then adds, "I also dreamt I was your son."

Jean stops the car on the west bank of the Tigris. Rıdvan puts down the binoculars and gets out. As we drive away, I turn to look at the slim figure on the bridge, slowly walking towards Hasankeyf. My final image of the dying town is that of a little boy in a blue shirt against a medieval castle on a steep cliff pitted with ancient caves.

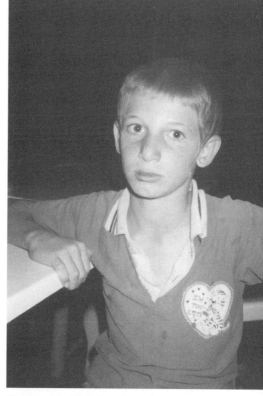

Eleven-year-old Rıdvan is serious about his job as a freelance tourist guide in Hasankeyf.

Chapter Seven
DEADLY HONOUR

Çiğdem means "crocus" in Turkish — a wildflower that pushes through the debris of winter. Çiğdem is also a girl's name.

On April 5, 2001, the Turkish daily *Cumhuriyet* carried a short item about a seventeen-year-old girl named Çiğdem in the city of Ağrı in the easternmost corner of Anatolia. Her family had given her in marriage to the son of the *mukhtar* (headman) of a village. The groom had complained that he had found "the goods defective," that Çiğdem wasn't a virgin, and had sent her back to her family. (He had already returned two other girls to their families on similar grounds.)

Çiğdem's family left the village in shame. They went to a squatter neighbourhood in Ağrı. There, to cleanse the family's honour, an elder of the tribe strangled Çiğdem to death.

An autopsy revealed she was a virgin.

In the same newspaper, a couple of months earlier, I read another news report. In a town in southeastern Anatolia, six men strangled a young woman and cast her body into the Euphrates River. One of the men was her husband. He and his relatives meant to kill her to clear the family's honour because she had run away with another man. Somehow the woman survived and assumed a new identity at an undisclosed location.

On a summer night, a car screeches to a stop at a secluded bend of the Euphrates. Three men pull a whimpering, pleading woman out of the back seat. Dry grass rustles as they drag her to the edge of the fast-moving river. The men stand there for a moment, then as if another second's pause might weaken their resolve, they nod to one another. One of them squeezes the woman's throat until her body grows limp, then pushes her into the water. Three men, shadows in the night, remain still, watching the woman's body rise to the surface a couple of times before floating away.

I imagine the above. The newspaper report was brief. It did say the men threw her into the Euphrates. It also said her name was Gönül, which means "soul." She was nineteen.

Hairy hands squeeze your throat and you choke. Dread paralyzes you. Then you wake up in cold, dark water, rise to the surface, gasp for air, and stroke against the flow. You see the black silhouettes of the willows whose low branches arch over the water on the shore. A savage hope rises in you, but the flow drags and pulls you under. Cold to your bones, you choke. Black water fills your nostrils and lungs. You push your head above the water, coughing and spitting. You grasp a branch that slips from your hands. You stroke harder, grasp again. Finally, you pull yourself out and collapse onto the shore.

Gönül survived somehow. The men neglected to tie her hands and feet, and she managed to pull herself up to the shore. Perhaps she lay on the riverbank staring at the stars, listening to the sound of the water and to the crickets. She might have crawled to a dry spot between pistachio trees and waited for the first light of day. She might have hobbled to the road, stopped a car, and asked the driver to take her to the police.

The rest of the story is even more astonishing. Gönül went to the police, and on this occasion, instead of returning her to her family, the police helped her to escape. She fled to another town in another region of Anatolia, assumed a new name, and is still alive.

The newspaper report said the husband and his accomplices stood trial and were acquitted. The judge concluded that "severe provocation" incited the men to the crime and judged unreasonable Gönül's refusal to testify in court on the grounds that her life was in danger.

I dream about finding Gönül, whose name, of course, is no longer Gönül, and hearing the story of her survival.

Honour and Shame

To explain the inexplicable, to understand how it can be possible for a father or a brother to murder in cold blood a daughter or a sister, I explore the ancient code of honour and shame that predates all monotheistic religions. In the 1960s in *Honour and Shame: The Values of Mediterranean Societies*, anthropologists John

Peristiany and Julian Pitt-Rivers referred for the first time in an academic work to the notions of honour and shame that have been entrenched in traditional agrarian and especially Mediterranean societies for thousands of years. Their book focused on the customs that sanctioned the killing of women for even suspected sexual improprieties.

Agrarian communities of the Mediterranean were, and are, fiercely patriarchal. Girls and women belong to men — to fathers, husbands and brothers — and their sexuality is strictly controlled by men. Eking out a living from the land in regions where water is scarce, people in such traditional communities depend for survival on members of extended families and clans to such a point that the individual feels useless without the group. Group sanction has tremendous weight in people's lives. Decisions such as choice of partner, child-bearing, and punishment of offences are never indi-

vidual matters but always communal. In order to produce and to reproduce, people need three crucial resources: arable land, water rights, and women. They fight over all three.

Honour, the public recognition of a man's worth and standing, was, and is, a key concept in communities where the group (the family, clan, or tribe) directs all actions. Honour is a combination of the man's own sense of self-worth, his assessment of his worth in the eyes of others in his group, and the actual opinion of others about him. Although admirable qualities such as honesty, competence, and hospitality may confer honour on a man, his honour depends primarily on the sexual behaviour of his women: his daughters' and sisters' virginity before marriage, and their (and his wife's) absolute fidelity after marriage. Even a rumoured or suspected breach

In a park in southeastern Anatolia, a Kurdish woman weaves brightly coloured kilims to catch the eyes of tourists.

of sexual purity is cause for tremendous shame. To erase the shame, the woman is killed. Such a murder is decided upon by an assembly of the males in the group not only to restore the honour of the group, but also to increase the status of the killer.

In traditional Mediterranean societies, shame, that terrible stain on men's reputations, has a completely different meaning for women. For daughters, wives, and sisters, shame is the natural and desirable state of modesty, reticence, innocence, and self-effacement, an appropriate state of constant vigilance to guard chastity.

Some sociologists make a distinction between patriarchal Western communities, where an individual man holds power over women, and traditional, neo-patriarchal societies, where a group such as family, clan, or tribe holds power and sanctions the violence of an individual man against "his" women. But whether a society is patriarchal or neo-patriarchal, there is no doubt that most of the violence against women in the world is based either directly on the code of honour and shame, or on unacknowledged remnants of that primitive code.

Another newspaper clipping from the Turkish daily *Cumhuriyet* dated October 1995 sat for years on my desk in our apartment in Quebec City. It described two murders — executions in broad daylight at a square in the city of Şanlıurfa in southeastern Anatolia. Both victims were young girls. Both had their throats slit by a man from their own families. One of the killers was the seventeen-year-old husband of the twelve-year-old victim, a child bride. The other killer was the fourteen-year-old cousin of the seventeen-year-old victim, an unmarried girl later found in an autopsy to be a virgin. Both events were called *töre cinayeti*, "murder according to custom." The girls had defied taboos and had stained their clans' honour.

In Ankara, when I began to research those murders, I discovered there were five more known "honour" murders in or near the same city between 1994 and 2000. Fathers, husbands, brothers, and cousins had killed young women because of an obligation to clan custom. Family councils made up of men had passed death sentences and chosen execution methods least likely to draw the wrath of law. Choosing the youngest male in the family as executioner was a regional tradition.

In March 1994 in a house in Beykapisi, one of Şanlıurfa's squatter neighbourhoods, thirteen-year-old Mohammad Felhan killed his seventeen-year-old sister, Hacer, from close range with a shotgun. Hacer and Mohammad were two of eleven children of an Arabic sheep breeder named Mustafa Felhan. The day before the murder Hacer left her clothes and a suicide note beside the well in their courtyard and disappeared. Her family searched the well and found no body. The next day Mustafa Felhan was called to the police station. The men of his clan went with him and waited with stony faces outside the station while Mustafa entered. His daughter was there with a girlfriend. Police records say that Hacer wanted to free herself from the pressures of her family and had run away to her girlfriend's house but that she had gotten scared and gone to the police. The police returned her to her family.

The men of the clan felt dishonoured by Hacer's attempt to escape from home. That night, while Hacer sat in a locked room, they held a meeting. Mustafa wanted to spare her daughter. He told his relatives that she was still a virgin. But the other men wanted blood. As executioner, they chose Hacer's thirteen-year-old brother, Mohammad, a minor. In his statement to the police, as quoted by Mehmet Faraç in *Töre Kıskacında Kadın* (*Women in the Trap of Custom Killings*), Mustafa Felhan described the execution:

> My brother, Adnan, brought a gun to my son who, as a shepherd, knew how to use a gun. He loaded it, and when we gave him the order to shoot, he shot at his sister, who was kneeling in her room three to five metres away from him. She fell, but was still alive. My father, Omer Felhan, told Mohammad to aim at her head. My son reloaded the gun and fired again. At that moment I left the room not to see my daughter's death. I went to the police station. When I returned home accompanied by the police, Hacer was dead. I am deeply saddened by the event, but we had to cleanse our honour according to the traditions of our region.

In the village of Kısas, twenty kilometres from Şanlıurfa, a man named Ismail Sevinç dragged his cousin, twenty-year-old Rabia Oğuz, by her hair out of a grocery store, where Rabia had run for refuge, and threw her under the wheels of a tractor in the early afternoon of August 29, 1995. The dusty village square was full of villagers who witnessed the murder. Rabia's uncle, Halil Konak, ran the tractor back and forth over the girl's body. When he stopped, another cousin lifted the girl's head to see if she was dead. Then he and Ismail

Sevinç pulled pistols out of their belts and fired shots into the air to announce to the village that their clan's honour was cleansed.

An autopsy showed that Rabia was a virgin.

In court the killers claimed Rabia had died in an accident, and they were acquitted. But anonymous villagers wrote letters to the prosecutor, insisting that a murder had gone unpunished, which triggered a second trial. This time the victim's uncle, Halil, and her cousins, Ismail Sevinç and Ismail Konak, each received prison sentences of twelve and a half years.

((

The name of the city gives me the shivers, yet I decide to go to Şanlıurfa. So, during a session break at METU, Jean and I fly there.

Şanlıurfa, one of the oldest cities in the world, is in Upper Mesopotamia, close to Turkey's border with Syria and on the ancient Silk Road. Assyrian documents from 2000 BC refer to it as Ruhua or Ru'ua. During the fourth century BC, the Seleucids named it Edessa because of its resemblance to the Macedonian city of the same name. Between 132 BC and 214 AD, Edessa became the centre of an Arabic dynasty named Abgar. In 1098 a crusader army led by Baudouin of Boulogne captured it, built a castle on its dust-coloured cliffs, and kept the city until the twelfth century when the Seljuk Turks conquered it.

The people of the region call Şanlıurfa the City of Prophets. Biblical patriarchs Abraham, Job, and Jacob, as well as Saint George, are all said to have lived there. The cave near Harran where Abraham was born is a place of pilgrimage.

Şanlıurfa is about fifty kilometres southeast of Atatürk Dam, the sixth largest in the world and a cornerstone of GAP, Turkey's Southeastern Development Project. More than 300 settlements and several archaeological sites are now submerged in water, and the irrigation has transformed the parched lands around Şanlıurfa into cotton fields. GAP has also led to a sudden surge in Şanlıurfa's population. Thousands of villagers steeped in feudal and tribal traditions now fill squatters' houses on the hills surrounding the city.

As the plane descends, I look out the window at the treeless hills and valleys of Upper Mesopotamia and think about Inanna, Ishtar, Astarte, Ashtoreth, Anath, Asherah, the Queen of Heaven, the Goddess of Life and Love and Death, the Great Whore, the Mother of Harlots — the same great goddess who was worshipped all over Anatolia as Cybele. Before the Bible and before the patriarchs, this was her realm. For thousands of years, as in this Akkadian prayer, Mesopotamians invoked Ishtar fervently:

> Praise Ishtar, the most awesome of the Goddesses, revere the queen of women, the greatest of the deities. She is clothed with pleasure and love. She is laden with vitality, charm, and voluptuousness. In lips she is sweet; life is in her mouth. At her appearance rejoicing becomes full. She is glorious.

Priestesses representing Ishtar annually mated in a sacred marriage with a priest or a king who stood in for the god Dumuzi (Tammuz, Attis). The fertility of the land and of people depended on the sexual power of the goddess. During the celebration of the symbolic enactment of her sacred marriage, her male worshippers in and around the temple grounds made love to temple girls to glorify the goddess and to bring health and abundance to the world. But in time, the Jewish Yahweh took his revenge on Ishtar.

At midmorning in Şanlıurfa, sunlight falls on the medieval fortress that dominates the city. It also bathes the flat-roofed houses made of beige limestone clustered on the hillsides. The man at the reception of the Harran Hotel on Atatürk Caddesi, the city's main street, brags to Jean and me that in summer Şanlıurfa sizzles. "Last summer," he says, "it went up to 58 degrees Celsius." But on this late January morning the temperature is 12 degrees Celsius and the sun is gentle.

Jean and I stroll down Atatürk Caddesi towards the old market, past pistachio sellers with their cartfuls of nuts, past pastry shops whose windows display several varieties of baklava sprinkled with pistachios. We walk through thick, greasy smoke wafting from stalls where swarthy men roast pieces of lamb on skewers. Many of the men have thick, dark moustaches, clench cigarettes in their mouths, and wear *şalvars*. Their heads are covered with *poshus*, white or checkered turbans that give them an exotic, macho look.

The city feels medieval. The streets of the old town are no wider than two metres. High walls surround the houses and their courtyards. On the ground floor of one home, we see a stable.

The labyrinthine old market is organized by craft guilds. In one alley, blacksmiths bend red-hot irons; in another, coppersmiths shape trays and pans. There is a carpenters' alley and a lane where men cure bloodstained sheepskins.

In the tailors' street, men sit in cubicles behind antique Singer sewing machines with foot pedals. In the alley of textiles, women covered with draping mantles bargain for gaudily coloured silk scarves and fabric. Many of the women have grey tattoos on their faces and gold teeth in their mouths. The air smells of burning fat and horse manure.

Beyond the old market is an attractive park with mulberry trees and a large pond surrounded by a picturesque wall of arches and columns and three mosques. A plaque on the wall beside the pond states that the idolater King Nimrod threw the Prophet Abraham into a fire, but the flames turned into water and formed this pond while the logs were transformed into fish. Now the pond swarms with sacred fish: large carp that open and close their yellow mouths near the water's surface. At noon a chorus of prayer calls resounds throughout the city.

Later, in the living room of a squatter's house on the outskirts of Şanlıurfa, I meet middle-aged Sabahat Gilan, who clutches the arm of Nursel, her twenty-two-year-old daughter. Both women wear kerchiefs and cotton dresses with long sleeves and skirts.

"I don't allow her to get out of my sight," Sabahat says. "She can't even go out to see her girlfriend. It's a question of honour. If *something* were to happen, I'd be held responsible."

Something. The glance or the touch of a man. Love is forbidden to Nursel. Her mother seems to accept the ancient customs related to honour, and she calmly explains why male children often become executioners. "Everyone accepts a family that cleanses its honour. Everyone knows that a child will receive a light sentence. Imagine a family with many children. If the father were to kill a tainted girl to cleanse his honour, he would go to prison and the family would be left without a provider. A disaster."

The Gilan family migrated to Şanlıurfa from a village. Sabahat and her husband, Mustafa, have six children. Mustafa does casual work as a porter in the marketplace. Their twelve-year-old son, Orhan, earns the equivalent of $2 Canadian a day shining shoes in Şanlıurfa's parks and streets.

"Many honour murders are made to look like suicides," Sabahat says. Then she tells me about an event that took place in a village a couple of months earlier. A young man returned from military service and heard rumours that his wife was seen with another man. He spoke to her parents, and together they decided she should be forced to drink poison.

"The woman had a small child and a baby," Sabahat says. "She pleaded with her husband to allow her to hold the children one last time before taking the poison." Then the woman drank the poison and died.

Sabahat goes on to tell me that the family of the dead woman put pressure on the family of the man who was seen with her, saying, "We have cleansed our honour. Now you have to cleanse yours." The young man refused to commit suicide, so his father killed him with a rifle.

"The court couldn't find sufficient evidence to convict the father," Sabahat says, "and the whole village supported him. The father who shot his son to cleanse his honour now walks around proudly."

The next day, in a sunny office on the second floor of a dingy apartment building, I meet with Özcan Güneş, the *Cumhuriyet* reporter in Şanlıurfa. Özcan is the journalist who wrote the story that obsessed me in Quebec City. He tells me now that the texture of social life in Şanlıurfa is still medieval. "With GAP, people who have cotton fields are making money. And you know what they do with the money? Buy themselves more wives. The money buys cars, apartments, and wives."

The region still lives within feudal economic and social structures, Özcan says. Most peasants are landless. They work on the land, which belongs to an *aga*, or landlord, who has connections with political parties and big business and who controls the lives of his "serfs." *Aşiretler* — clans organized through the male bloodline — are the fundamental units of society. To survive, individuals rely on the clan's support and behave according to clan rules. Men pass their possessions on to their sons. Most women own nothing. Daughters are sold in marriage to the highest bidder, or they are given in religious marriage to a close male relative, very often to the father's nephew. Sometimes young people are given in marriage within a system called *berdel*, in which a family gives their daughter to another family and takes the daughter of that family for their son in exchange, thus avoiding payment. Polygamy is common. Girls have very little say in their own marriages. A girl's virginity represents her clan's honour.

"The status of a woman," Özcan says, "is somewhere between that of a farm animal and a slave. As small children, girls fetch water and work in the fields. At fifteen they're sold in marriage. They give birth. They work in the fields and at home. Sometimes they're beaten. Sometimes their husbands take other wives."

187

For these two young women in the village of Kısas, love can still mean a death sentence.

But television is causing trouble. "Women see on TV that other women in the world live by different rules," Özcan says. "Some try to push the boundaries in their lives and pay for it with their lives."

Urban migration is weakening clan relations and challenging feudal values. The medieval fabric of society is beginning to unravel slowly in Şanlıurfa — a gruelling process.

Feride Lacin, a Kurdish woman lawyer from Diyarbakır, tells me that honour murders are increasing with urban migration. "Violence and flux, and the intrusion of urban values, make traditional men ferocious," she says.

Thousands of Kurdish villages in northern Iraq and southeastern Anatolia were destroyed during the last quarter of the twentieth century. Lacin says the violence that devastated the social, economic, and cultural fabric of Kurdish communities produced more incidents of honour killings and an epidemic of female suicides (many of which were actually murders).

"Contradictory forces in a community," she says, "such as modernization on the one hand and traditionalism on the other produce great anxiety. Poor, unemployed men lose all control over the circumstances of their lives, so they grasp the only power that remains to them — control over women. At a time of flux, and in a consumer society where self-worth is becoming associated with purchasing power, the poor are even more obsessed with their honour because they have little else."

Lacin's words echo the analysis of feminists who argue that in times of social change and upheaval (economic crises, ethnic wars, globalization), patriarchal forces will tighten their control on women. But how and why did patriarchal forces gain such murderous command over women? Gerda Lerner says in her book *The Creation of Patriarchy* that a social and economic transformation in Mesopotamia established patriarchy and slavery at the dawn of history. Accumulation of property and the emergence of hierarchies accompanied the establishment of early states. When slavery became institutionalized, men began to make laws to dominate women's bodies.

The fact that women were vulnerable to rape and could give birth to the children of unknown men came to be seen as a fundamental threat to society. A man who couldn't protect his wife, sister, or daughter was scorned. The rape of conquered women dishonoured the women and served as a symbolic castration of conquered men. As Orlando Patterson points out in his book *Slavery and Social Death*, men in patriarchal societies who couldn't protect the sexual purity of their wives, sisters, and children were truly impotent and dishonoured.

On a Saturday morning, Jean and I take a minibus from Şanlıurfa to Kısas. In cotton fields on both sides of the road, women pull out stubble. At the entrance to the village a sign says: "Population 2,000."

We get off at the square where Rabia Oğuz was killed and walk up the dirt road that encircles the village of mud-brick houses devoid of running water or sewage. People stop us on the road and invite us into their homes. Mustachioed men shake our hands and offer us tea.

Jean and I eventually come across a group of men sitting in a circle in a warehouse whose door is open. We greet them and they beckon us in. The primary school teacher Muzaffer Özbay tells us that the men have gathered to offer condolences after a funeral. According to local custom, men and women are separated.

The men are so welcoming that I feel uneasy asking about the murder of Rabia. "Individuals get caught in the clutches of tribal custom," says an elderly man named Imam Ozbay. "If Rabia's father had decided to spare his daughter, he would have had to take her away from here. But even then, as long as the men of his tribe had felt dishonoured, someone would very likely have followed them and killed her." He shakes his head in sorrow. "What a shame," he murmurs.

The villagers are now shunning the killers. Rabia's mother, Rahime, is devastated. Her father is a recluse.

After we leave the group of men, twenty-six-year-old Fatma and seventeen-year-old Hatice wave to us from the courtyard of a mud-brick house. We enter Fatma's one-room house and sit on the kilim covering the dirt floor.

"Rabia fell in love with a man in the city," Fatma says. "They spent a night in the cemetery and made love there. But then Rabia got scared and went to the police. The police should have protected her, but instead they returned her to her family. They should have known that the family would kill her."

Fatma herself was married to a cousin when she was fifteen. "Here there's no permission to fall in love," she says. "What Rabia's family did was horrible. The entire village cut them off after that murder. But most girls wouldn't have dared do what Rabia did."

Most Kurdish and Arabic women in southeastern Anatolia aren't even allowed to eat in their husband's presence, Fatma tells us. A woman can't speak or even pick up her child in her father-in-law's presence. She has to care for her husband, give birth (preferably to sons) in rapid succession, and work all the time at home and in the fields. "When a man brings a second or a third wife, a *kuma*," Fatma says, "some women are relieved because it means less work. But it can also mean less food. Women have no money of their own."

When Jean and I leave Fatma and Hatice, we notice satellite dishes protruding from many of the flat roofs made of mud. Soon we approach a group of women sitting on the steps in front of a mud-brick house. Two of them are old and have tattoos around their mouths. A young girl runs inside to bring Jean a chair, but I sit on the steps. The young girl, Didem, is a student who is preparing for university entrance exams. "I want to go far away from the restrictions of this village," she says. She boasts that her parents are progressive and that they are encouraging her to leave.

The older women speak no Turkish. Elderly Emine talks to Didem, who translates. "They say television is corrupting the young girls of the village and that American soap operas cause tragedies like the death of Rabia."

"She isn't saying that Rabia's family were right," Didem interjects. "But what else could they have done? Who could face being shunned for dishonour? Girls see these foreign programs where people fall in love and they get ideas. How else would Rabia have gotten the notion to run away with a storekeeper?"

Didem says she loves television but that she isn't interested in love. "My parents wouldn't give me away in marriage without asking my opinion," she insists. "That's good enough for me. My parents are educated."

☾

In the Archaeology Museum of İstanbul, I saw cracked clay tablets with Sumerian cuneiform writing. The script was deciphered by British Sumerologist Samuel Noah Kramer and Muazzez Ilmiye Çığ, his Turkish student. It contained invocations to Ishtar, the epic legend of Gilgamesh, and Sumerian legal codes.

Those codes reveal that around 2000 BC the women of Mesopotamia were still enjoying a relatively high status, especially if they worked in temples as housekeepers or as sacred women. The laws allowed women to manage and bequest the dowries their fathers gave them when they married. Husbands and wives had equal rights over their children. An upper-class wife could conduct her own business affairs.

Yet the laws of Sumer recognized the importance of paternity and required women to bear only the children of their husbands. Adultery was forgivable for a man but punishable by death for a woman. A woman was valued for the number of children she had.

In 1750 BC the Sumerians were overcome by the Babylonians, whose greatest king, Hammurabi, gave his famous code to history, fully institutionalizing the patriarchal family. Under Hammurabi's laws a woman could be divorced on virtually any grounds: childlessness, adultery, even poor household management. All that a husband had to say to divorce his wife was "Thou art not my wife," then return her dowry. Yet a woman who said those words to her husband would be killed. A woman couldn't divorce her husband but she could leave him and return to her parents' home if she could prove that she had been faithful but that her husband had been cruel. A wronged husband had the right to kill his wife and her lover.

Hammurabi's code clearly acknowledged women as property. Fathers could determine who their daughters married, and they could sell their daughters to a prospective husband for an agreed-upon price. Marriage was monogamous for women, but men were free to visit prostitutes or to take concubines.

The Assyrian civilization followed the Babylonians in Mesopotamia, and during the first millennium BC, women lost many more rights and freedoms.

Assyria was more militaristic and needed more soldiers than Babylonia, so it honoured women who gave birth to sons.

During the time of the Assyrian Empire, Middle Assyrian Laws fiercely restricted women's rights. These decrees firmly entrenched the sexual regulation of women. The virginity of respectable daughters was now a financial asset for a family. Sadly, those laws still determine the lives of many women in Upper Mesopotamia.

Another major transformation took place with Abraham, the first biblical patriarch. Not just law but religion established and sanctioned the harsh patriarchal codes of society. Now an all-powerful god, Yahweh, ordered the repression of women. Sexual control of women was Yahweh's will, expressed in his covenant with the men of Israel. The revolution was complete.

Who created life? Yahweh and the godlike male he created, we are told in Genesis.

Who brought sin and death into the world? Woman in her alliance with the snake, Genesis tell us.

The snake, which from time immemorial represented the goddess, and which symbolized free female sexuality, was now the instrument of original sin. And shame was heaped on women. Shame on their hairless skins, on their fertile wombs, on their passions, and on their affections.

In Western civilization, the work of Aristotle formed a solid patriarchal foundation for Western science and philosophy. In Arabia and Upper Mesopotamia, the Koran and Islamic philosophy buttressed the patriarchal tradition. But those who now present the ancient codes of shame and honour in an Islamic guise, who say the Koran ordains the oppression of women, are simply repackaging the 3,000-year-old patriarchal codes of Upper Mesopotamia.

☾

In Harran, the supposed birthplace of Abraham, children come out of beehive houses made of mud bricks. Self-appointed guides, they follow Jean and me to the ruins of the ancient fortress and ask us for pens. We stop near the ruins of the world's first Islamic university to eat the oranges we brought along, but a goat steals Jean's orange.

Abraham was the first of the Jewish patriarchs. His barren wife, Sarah, offered him a concubine, Hagar, who gave birth to a son. Hagar was proud. She forgot her social place in relation to Sarah and took on airs. Abraham, the just man of God that he was, sent Hagar into the desert with his son, Ishmael. The men of this region still continue Abraham's tradition and bed new women if their wives fail to give them sons.

It isn't Islam that oppresses women in this region. The Islamic edicts about women come directly from the Old Testament, which is marked by Mesopotamian myths and laws. Religion didn't cause the subordination of women. It simply reflected and sanctioned the social and economic transformations that had already entrenched patriarchy in Upper Mesopotamia.

Back in Şanlıurfa, in Yakubiyye, another shanty district, I meet with a group of young women gathered in the small room of a ÇATOM (Multi-Purpose Community Centre). Some of the women cut fabric around a table, while others embroider. Their teachers, Adalet *Hanım* and Emine *Hanım*, both middle-aged women in head scarves, listen affectionately to their younger charges' chatter.

ÇATOMs were established during the past decade by the community development administration of Turkey's GAP project. At each one of the twenty-one ÇATOMs in southeastern Anatolia, local women are asked to choose and organize educational and recreational programs. At the one in Yakubiyye they are learning sewing, embroidery, cooking, and healthcare.

Near Şanlıurfa, Harran's ancient beehive houses now stand empty.

The women's heads are covered with scarves. They chat with one another and with me eagerly, candidly.

"Our daughters won't suffer like us," seventeen-year-old Ayşe tells me. "We'll try to make them freer. Look, our mothers can't read or write, but we can. Our mothers could never do embroidery like this or sew like this. We're learning to do these things." As if to support her optimism, Ayşe shows me the white cotton tablecloth with gold garlands of roses that she is embroidering.

Sixteen-year-old Gündüz is sewing a baby bunting for her hope chest. She, too, is proud of her work, but she disagrees with Ayşe. "You say this now, but you're not even married. Once you get married it'll be your husband who decides how your daughter will be raised."

If only the deadly code of honour and shame could be defeated by the time this little girl in Kısas grows up.

"I could try to reason with him," Ayşe replies. "I wouldn't be as passive as my mother. I'm sure of that. Before this ÇATOM was opened I never went out. I did housework and looked after my younger sisters and brothers. Some neighbours told my mother about the ÇATOM. They said there were no men here and that girls could learn sewing and cooking. She talked to my dad to let me come. I love it here. I will keep coming as long as I can."

"Since I've been coming to the ÇATOM, I've started to hate men," sixteen-year-old Naime declares.

"Why since coming to the ÇATOM?" I ask.

"Because before, I never went out. I didn't even finish primary school. But on my way here, boys harass me. They whisper, 'Pst, pst, girl. Will you keep it all for yourself, girl?' Things like that. If my parents knew this, they would never send me again. I hate boys. I hate men. I don't ever want to get married. I feel such rage that I understand how a person could lose her temper and physically attack a man one day."

Eighteen-year-old Ülkiye says she envies Naime's freedom. "She's so lucky that she isn't married," Ülkiye tells us. At fifteen Ülkiye's parents married her to her cousin. Now her husband refuses to let her out. She sneaked out of the house one time to come to the ÇATOM while he was away for his military service. But her husband phoned one morning while Ülkiye was out and threatened to come and beat her. She's taking a chance being here again.

"Does he beat you often?" I ask.

"If I disobey him," she says matter-of-factly. Ülkiye has a six-month-old daughter. "When she was born, my husband said it was too bad the baby wasn't a boy."

"How will you raise your daughter?" I ask.

"My daughter's future isn't up to me," she answers. "Her father and the elders of the family will decide."

Outside, dirty water races down the irregular stones of the alley, and children play in the mud. A couple of men in *poshu*s and *şalvar*s crouch like sentinels beside the grocery store on the corner, smoking and talking in the sunlight.

Chapter Eight
THE CURSE OF DIONYSOS

Once upon a time, when gods and kings reigned in Anatolia, the god Dionysos offered to grant a wish to the great Phrygian King Midas.

"Let everything I touch turn into gold," Midas said.

To test his magical powers, Midas went around his palace touching things and turning objects into gold. His eyes glittered like the shiny metal. He laughed out loud. His doors became gold! His bedding changed into gold! Gold! More gold!

But then Midas got hungry. He lifted bread to his mouth, and it, too, turned into gold. He raised a goblet of wine to his lips, and the dark liquid became gold. Midas picked up a peach, and it changed into gold. Then his young daughter entered the glittering hall, and he rushed to embrace her. She also became gold.

Horrified, Midas begged Dionysos to take back the gift. The god took pity on the king and said, "Go bathe in the spring of the Pactolus River near the city of Sardes in Lydia."

Midas bathed in the spring and returned to his court a wiser and less greedy king.

Sardes (Sart in Turkish) is an hour's drive from the city of İzmir in the Aegean region of Turkey. The magical Pactolus River, Sart Deresi in Turkish, still runs there, and some say the specks of gold left behind from Midas's bath still sparkle in it.

In the legend, Midas freed himself from the curse of gold. But a similar curse hovers over Anatolia today. A gold mine started in 2000, 500 kilometres from the temple of Artemis at Sardes, threatens the vineyards, olive groves, and villagers in the region. In the once-great Hellenic/Roman city of Pergamon, now Bergama, a mining company is turning the Garden of Eden into a wasteland. And Dionysos no longer responds to pleas.

((

On a spring morning near Bergama, the ground is covered with daisies and blood-red anemones. The air is scented with thyme and the cows suckle their calves. More than 2,000 villagers from surrounding mountain villages take an ancient cobblestoned caravan route through the olive groves and descend towards the village of Çamköy. I am among them. As we march, we jump over boulders and pass through bushes.

"This is what we're defending!" Rahime Özyaylalı, a young woman in şalvars and a flowered kerchief, shouts at a riot policeman, showing him the olives in the bowl in her outstretched hand. "Look at these olives. This is what we're fighting for!"

The cops push and shove the crowd of villagers sitting in the middle of the İzmir-Çanakkale highway, blocking traffic. The villagers yell, shove back, resist. A water truck arrives and turns its hose on the crowd. There are screams, and some villagers stumble and fall, while others lie on the highway. In the mayhem, Rahime's bowl is tipped over and her olives are scattered onto the road. She pounds with her fists on the shoulders of the policeman trying to push her away.

After the melee, when we begin to march again, Rahime walks beside me. She picks some wild grass resembling dandelions with red tips and offers it to me. "*Kuzu kulağı*, lamb's ear," she says. "It's tangy and rich in vitamins." Changing the subject, she tells me, "I was only fourteen when the resistance started. Now I'm twenty-seven. My parents didn't send me to school because they thought I'd get married. But I'm not getting married. I'm fighting for my land."

The villagers assemble in Çamköy's village square. A sharp whistle rings through the community, and Oktay Konyar, a small man with a drooping moustache, stands on a fence to address the crowd. Oktay is an olive producer and the villagers' leader in civil disobedience.

"Remember," he calls out, "no provocation! No violence! We walk in single file, women in the front, men in back. We'll pass in front of the mine and towards the highway. No exchanges with the police. No throwing of stones. Let's go!"

The villagers form a single file on the dirt road beside the huge pines at the edge of the village. Colourful scarves fly in the breeze, *şalvar*s flap against legs. Armed policemen start a parallel line on the other side of the road, and everyone begins to march.

Across the road from the village, riot police in helmets and shields stand at the gates of the gold mine once named Eurogold, later owned by the American mining giant Newmont, and now taken over by a Turkish company called Koza. The villagers proceed quietly past the gates, casting bitter glances at the mills, cyanide tanks, and belts of the mine.

They continue their procession along the highway until a sharp whistle from their leader signals them to sit down to rest. Hunched on the roadside, the women make garlands from the daisies. Then another sharp whistle sounds, and they get up, circle the village of Ovacık, below the infected wound on the land, and settle on the highway once more. "We are the people!" they shout. "Our cause is just. We shall win!"

At Anatolian weddings people attach gold coins on the bride's dress as a symbol of a bright and prosperous future. But that shiny metal brings me visions of craters carved into the land and a murky jade-green tailings dam filled with poisoned mud — a festering gash on a hillside once covered with olive trees and nut-bearing pines. Şahsine Dikmenoğlu, an elderly peasant woman hobbling on knees swollen with rheumatism, says, "They are killing my land! My grandchildren's land!"

Ayşe Kurhan, another elderly villager, adds in her accented regional Turkish, "We were the keepers of the

Village women lead the march against the gold mine in Çamköy near Bergama.

199

land. We were living off the land with the light of our eyes. We were the guardians of the earth. Away from the land we'll die."

I had no idea until I got to know the story of the gold mine in Bergama that gold is extracted from ore with sodium cyanide. Now I know. I know that even for the one gram of gold in a wedding band a minimum of one ton of earth is poisoned forever.

In Canada's northern wilderness, gold mines have destroyed large sections of aboriginal lands and have provoked outcries from people who depend on the forests and lakes for food and water. Now gold miners are in Anatolia where there is no wilderness.

The alluvial soil of the Bakırçay Valley on the northern Aegean coast of Turkey is among the richest and most fertile in the world, even after thousands of years of tilling. Today's town of Bergama was a thriving Hellenic/Roman health centre 2,000 years ago. With its thermal springs and its fragrant air, it was the city of Asclepius, the Greek god of healing. There, for centuries, people's lives were tied to the land and seasons. Aegean farmers produced the finest long-fibred cotton in the world, the sweetest figs, the best olive oil, and the juiciest grapes.

But at the beginning of the twenty-first century a company named Eurogold came to the valley to extract ore from the soil. Earlier, in 1989, Eurogold received a licence from the Turkish government to dig a gold mine in a 100-hectare area above the village of Ovacık.

"Gold was a magical thing," fifty-two-year-old Tahsin Sezer from Çamköy says to me over tea at the village café. "We thought we would be rich." He tells me how the villagers at first welcomed the foreigners drilling in their fields. "These foreigners said they would build new roads, new wells, and even a new mosque. Some people sold their fields to them. But then Sefa Taşkın, the mayor of Bergama, brought university professors here to tell us what gold meant — a curse!"

The villagers learned that the ore would be leached with cyanide, that the process would activate toxic elements and heavy metals in the soil, and that eventually the underground water would be contaminated. Gold mines have caused environmental disasters in the United States, China, Guyana, Bolivia, Romania, the Philippines, and Zimbabwe. The villagers visited the city of Lefke in Cyprus and saw the reddish wasteland that a gold and copper mine closed in the 1970s had left behind.

Soon the mayor of Bergama joined the villagers. He and 652 villagers launched a lawsuit against Eurogold.

In November 1996, while the case was before the State Council, Eurogold cut 2,500 nut-bearing pines and 850 olive trees on the slopes overlooking Ovacık. The day when electric chainsaws went to work Sebahat Gökçeoğlu, an "activist" and grandmother, was picking olives.

"It was an autumn day," she says on our march. "Our olive groves were just behind the mine site. I heard a dull roar. I stopped picking and listened. My heart pounding, I ran back home and phoned the mayor. 'Help!' I cried. 'They're murdering the pines!'"

When middle-aged Mustafa Umaç describes that day, tears well up in his eyes. "Those pines — we froze in winter but never cut a single branch. We were penniless, but we didn't cut them. We didn't let anyone else cut them, either. Pines mean life. They mean air. We watched over those pines. They cut them by the thousands. The roar of the saws echoed through the hills. That roar jolted us into action. Thousands of us went down to the highway and closed it to traffic that day."

Three months after the protest march, on a hot, dusty afternoon in June, I take a bus from the coastal town of Dikili to Bergama, get off at the junction of Çamköy, and walk one kilometre to the village of Süleymanlı. I find Mustafa Umaç's wife, fifty-two-year-old Gülizar, making tomato sauce in the yard. She has blue eyes, a sunburned face, and the whitest teeth I have ever seen. A tray of ripe tomatoes rests on a table as she sweats beside a boiling cauldron. "We used to grow such sweet tomatoes," she tells me. "We've stopped. No one buys produce from us anymore. Look at that field covered with dust! The water in our wells has turned cloudy. We're scared."

To eject the gold miners from their land, the villagers organized under a man who loves Mahatma Gandhi and olive trees. Oktay Konyar grew up in Bergama and served as the regional leader of the social democratic Cumhuriyet Halk Partisi (Republican People's Party). He told me he and the villagers had vowed to resist the mine with Gandhi's civil disobedience methods.

In 1997, 3,000 people from the villages surrounding the mine held a referendum in accordance with the Bergen Convention (to which Turkey is a signatory). The result was a resounding no, but the construction of the mine continued.

I leave Süleymanlı and pay a visit to Rahime Özyaylalı in Çamköy. In the living room of her parents' house, she serves me stuffed vine leaves. While I eat she stands as if to enact scenes from the evening of April 30, 1997.

"I'll never forget the spring night we occupied the mine. Thousands of us! At 1:00 a.m. there was a knock on our door. I knew this was the night. We would invade the mine. The committees were meeting, the village was buzzing. It was as if everyone knew but no one knew. When the news arrived, I sat outside and cried. Then I grabbed a stick and got on our tractor with my father. Everyone prayed as if we were going to war. All the villagers were on tractors. No lights on anywhere. The night was pitch-black. My heart pounded. Our tractors ran over the barbed wire, and we entered the site. The guards fired some shots in the air, then fled. It was around 4:00 a.m."

Once inside the mine site, the villagers wanted to stay. The governor of İzmir arrived to negotiate with Oktay Konyar. After hours of hard bargaining, the governor agreed to halt construction for a month and the villagers reluctantly left the site.

"We wanted to destroy the sheds and the buildings on the site," Rahime says. "We didn't want to leave that place. But Oktay Konyar said we should touch nothing. He said the governor would close the mine, so we should leave."

The Environmental Impact Report of the mine claimed there were no settlements within a thirty-five-kilometre radius of the site. The nearest settlement shown in the report was Bergama, which was a blatant lie. Tens of thousands of people live in the seventeen villages around the mine site. According to data from the Bergama Chamber of Commerce, the value of the olive oil, cotton, and tobacco registered in 1995 exceeded $42 million U.S.

An active fault line that passes from Kaynarca, only 1.5 kilometres away from the mine, represents an earthquake risk that could be catastrophic. The Environmental Impact Report says nothing about that and nothing about the soil erosion that will result from the destruction of the tree cover in the region.

On May 13, 1997, the Turkish State Council, the highest court in the land, announced its decision. The villagers had won! When I drop by Tahsin Sezer's place down the road from Rahime Özyaylalı's house, he recalls the exact wording. "The court decision said there was no public interest in the operation and that it would violate the Turkish Constitution that guaranteed the citizens' right to life and to a clean environment." Sezer laughs as he relives that day. "The ants have friends, we said to each other. We celebrated. Our women made sweets. We held a huge picnic under the pines, and many people celebrated with us that day. Environmentalists, people in trade unions, students. Thousands of them came to feast with us."

But fifty kilometres from Çamköy, construction of the mine continued at an increased speed. Even at night heavy machinery laboured feverishly under floodlights.

The villagers escalated their civil disobedience.

"I walk through Çamköy at night and tap gently on the windows," Oktay Konyar tells me when I sit with him on the balcony of his house in Dikili overlooking the Aegean Sea. "One tap means the man has to come outside. Two taps — the woman. A basket containing olives, cheese, bread, and water stands by the door. She silently picks it up and walks in the dark towards another village house and taps on the window. No one puts on any lights. They can be seen from the mine. People walk through hidden paths and gather near a van waiting in a clearing. No one asks any questions. We travel at night to reach the location of our demonstration in the morning.

"Faced with ordinary peasants, uncles, and aunts," Oktay continues, "sunburned men whose hands are gnarled from work and women whose bodies sag and stoop from toil and from childbirth, the police are at a loss. Trained for violence, they can't beat these people with truncheons as they beat the students who demonstrate for free education or for better prison conditions. They can't manhandle the peasants who resemble their own parents. They take them in for questioning, and the peasants give simple answers that ring true. 'We're here because foreigners are poisoning our lands,' they say. 'We violate no laws. We are afraid of cyanide. Without lands we would die.'"

Early one morning in August 1997, three buses arrived at the European side of the Bosphorus Bridge in İstanbul. Villagers got off the

Tahsin and Fatma Sezer stand in the yard of their house in Çamköy.

buses and calmly tied themselves to the parapets of the suspension bridge. Before long, riot police arrived. Traffic stopped, and the cameras and microphones of all the television and radio stations in Turkey were pointed at the villagers of Bergama.

"I'm scared of heights, but I was prepared to jump that morning," twenty-nine-year-old Ayşe Yüksel from the village of Yenikent tells me when I visit her. "We were surrounded by police. The place was swarming with reporters. Drivers stuck in the blocked traffic honked in support of our action. The TV cameramen put down their cameras and applauded us."

The resistance was changing the villagers, especially the women.

"Before the struggle you never saw a woman's face in these villages," Gülizar Umaç says to me as I wait for a bus on the road to Bergama. "We wore draping covers all the time. We used to ask our husbands for permission even to visit our sisters. But during the resistance, a time came when a knock on the window meant the woman had to go. When that time came, no husband asked his wife where she was going. Women gained confidence and freedom. We stopped using our head scarves because they got in the way. Now women walk in the front. We lead the way in demonstrations and protest actions."

☾

"How can we dismiss a foreign investor?" asked İmren Aykut, Turkey's minister of the environment at the time. "What if they demand compensation? How can I take such an economic risk?" These words were reported in several newspapers in late 1997. Back then it looked as if the Turkish government considered the State Council ruling a mere embarrassment.

In August 1999, the Prime Minister's Office commissioned a new environmental study from scientists associated with an institution called TUBİTAK and obtained a report stating that Eurogold had installed new safety equipment after the high court ruling. Now, the report said, the cyanide would no longer pose a threat to the environment. One of the scientists on the committee gave a dissenting view. Dr. Enver Küçükgül, of the Department of Environmental Engineering at a university in İzmir, objected that all the environmental impact reports prepared for Eurogold were based on information supplied by the company. He said no one had independent data on the amount of gold to be extracted from the ore or the amount of cyanide to be used.

Dr. Küçükgül said the mine's information was insufficient and approximate at best. It seemed likely that the gold to be extracted at Ovacık would increase threefold, he said. That would mean a lot more cyanide would be used.

Still, the TUBİTAK document, which had no legal validity, was employed to endorse the mine.

The mining company, now named Normandy, bought full-page advertisements in major newspapers announcing Turkey's golden age and promising jobs. Normandy began to distribute job application forms. Rumours circulated that ordinary miners would be paid upwards of $1,000 U.S. a month.

One evening, when the villagers got word that cyanide tanks were on their way to the mine, they surrounded the site with homemade torches and began to keep watch around the clock. The company was forced to transport the cyanide to an unknown place.

In November 2000, hundreds of villagers, some women wearing only slippers on their feet, marched 350 kilometres from Bergama to Çanakkale. "Our feet had blisters," Sebahat Gökçeoğlu tells me while we sit side by side under a walnut tree in Çamköy. "We soaked them in cold water every night. People greeted us along the way. They offered us food and beds every evening. It took us eight days to walk the 350 kilometres."

The villagers of Bergama became folk heroes. All over the country, people cheered their independence, courage, and creative energies. But soon the mine began to blast their land with dynamite. The company called it "trial production." In April 2001, dynamite explosions shook village houses four times a day. A thin, sticky dust coated tobacco leaves and olive branches.

☾

Jean and I drive to Çamköy on a hot day in July. We go past the mine's barbed-wire fence and park. I get out of the car to take a picture of the belts, pipes, and mills. The guard inside the fence stares at me but says nothing.

In the yard of the village café, elderly men play backgammon. The owner of the café comes outside with a pitcher of cool water. Jean and I sit in the shade of the walnut tree in the yard. Soon villagers arrive and shake our hands. The café's owner has sent word that we're here, and before long, more than fifty people gather around us.

"It's like an earthquake," seventy-two-year-old Ayşe Girgin from Ovacık says. "The rumbling wakes us up at 4:00 a.m. I curse the miners after each explosion. 'May your lungs explode,' I say."

Sebahat Gökçeoğlu raises a delicate issue. "Some young men in our village have applied for jobs at the mine. We shun the families of those men. We don't even greet them anymore. But it hurts. This is such a small village. Is it right to treat people as if they're the enemy just because they want work?"

"They're cowards," my old friend Tahsin Sezer says. "They've sold out! We shun them!"

A murmur ripples through the crowd at the café. "We shun them!"

In April 2002, the Turkish Ministerial Council gave the mine secret and special permission to begin full production. The villagers assembled before the riot police at the gates of the mine and cried, "No to cyanide! Get out of our lands!"

The riot police stared at the men with their peaked caps and the women with their *şalvar*s and head scarves. Inside the mine's barbed-wire fence, special agents spoke into walkie-talkies and filmed the demonstrators.

Dynamite explosions continued to tear the earth, heavy earth-moving machines roared all day long, and a dam lake contaminated with dull green cyanide tailings grew behind Ovacık, only fifty metres from Çamköy.

When Jean and I attend a rally in Çamköy's café, we hear Oktay Konyar shout, "We'll resist! We'll resist until the mine leaves our valley! We'll plant trees on that site. We'll turn it into a national park!"

"Our olives have shrivelled," a young man wearing a peaked cap says. "A fine dust has settled on our tobacco plants. When they explode dynamite, our houses shake. Dust covers all the plants and chokes us."

"Birds are dropping dead," a young woman adds. "Our forest used to be full of birdsong."

An old man with a white moustache shakes his head. "We're abandoned, left alone with the angel of death."

"Dursun *Amca*," Oktay calls out to the old man, "don't spread despair! Haven't we trusted each other all these years? Haven't we stood shoulder to shoulder to face the police? Haven't we marched bare-chested under the rain? We shall march again, all the way to Ankara, to make our voices heard. I promise you." He then raises his fist and shouts, "We are the people! Our cause is just! We shall win!"

The peasants repeat his words with a resounding roar: "We are the people! Our cause is just! We shall win!"

I leave the café and walk over to the grocery store where three youths smoke under the awning. One of them, a blond fellow with a thin moustache, glances at the café and shakes his head in disapproval.

"Why aren't you at the meeting?" I ask him.

"It's no use," he replies. "The people of this village have given enough energy to this cause. We've struggled for ten years. We won in the courts, yet the mine is operating. What's the point of wasting more time and energy?"

"We need jobs," another youth says. "There are jobs at the mine."

"In summer we take tourists around in boats," the blond one says. "The officials refuse us visas for the Greek islands. If you're from this village, you're considered a radical. We grew up during the resistance to the mine, so we're all marked."

A light rain begins to fall on the village houses, the olive groves, and the craters filled with cyanide-contaminated mud as I head back to the café.

Later, Oktay Konyar accompanies Jean and me to his olive groves. The thin rain has given way to snow. As we walk up to the summit of the hill, he tells us about the magical self-generation of olive trees. "After hundreds of years, you trim them and new branches grow with the strength of young trees."

In the village of Sağancı, we visit an olive oil press built at the turn of the nineteenth century by Anatolian Greeks. "After the ethnic exchange, the Turks took over," Oktay says. "This olive oil has less than .05 percent acidity, the best in the world. But it's expensive to maintain the factory. The owner wants to sell it." He pours greenish-yellow sparkling oil into large tins for us. "Take back the soul of this coast with you," he says. "This golden liquid contains the Aegean sun."

The next time I take the winding road to Çamköy the dull hum of the mine envelops the village. I visit slender Günseli, the wife of Çamköy's *mukhtar*, or head administrator. She brings me a tray of food from her garden: spinach cooked in olive oil, hard white cheese from their cows' milk, and a salad of tomatoes, onions, and green peppers. Reminders of paradise.

"People who can leave the village are leaving," Günseli says. "But we have nowhere to go. There are so many empty houses that we're afraid of vandals. People know the village is dying. Strangers come in and break into empty houses."

Tobacco leaves now curl up and die. Animals are born with birth defects. Dynamite explosions have damaged olive flowers. Olive oil merchants in Ayvalık have notified the villagers around Bergama that they won't buy olive oil from their region anymore because they fear cyanide contamination.

Some young villagers have gone to work at the mine, even though they are afraid of the cyanide and ashamed of betraying the resistance. "We're hungry," they protest. "We're poor. Our backs are against the wall."

The *mukhtar* of Narlıca, a man who was in the front lines of the resistance for an entire decade, suddenly acquired a brand-new minibus and began to work for the mine. "The government has decided to give permission to the mine," he said to his villagers. "Who are we to argue?"

The villagers are confused, bitter, divided. They whisper that the mine has bought the *mukhtar* of Narlıca.

Sixty-eight-year-old Münir Aldaş and his forty-two-year-old son have become enemies. "He wanted to work at the mine," toothless Münir says. "'Over my dead body,' I said. So he took off, left for İstanbul. Never writes or calls. My only son. It hurts."

On August 22, 2002, a family of miners who were shunned in the village of Pınarköy got in a skirmish with a family resisting the mine, and the miners shot to death a thirty-five-year-old man. After more than ten years of nonviolence, the villagers were stunned by the sudden outburst of violence.

It is early fall when I visit the region one last time. I set out on foot from Çamköy to Narlıca, about two kilometres uphill. When I hear the sound of an engine behind me, I turn. A tractor stops beside me. "Narlıca?" the driver asks.

I nod.

"Jump on the right fender," he says.

I tell him I am on my way to the village to talk to people about the mine. He says nothing. "Are you a farmer?" I ask.

"I used to be," he replies.

"What do you do now?"

"I manage," he says, then grows silent. "Okay, okay," he adds suddenly. "I work at the mine."

I say nothing.

"I joined the demonstrations against the mine for many years," he volunteers. "But when the government decided to permit the mine to operate even after the high court decision, I decided to work at the mine. Let's face it, the mine is working whether I work there or not. If it's causing damage, it's doing that whether I work there or not. So I work there."

"What do you do?"

"Something beyond my wildest dreams. I work underground with heavy equipment to dig a passageway in the pit."

"How did you feel when you went to the mine to apply for a job?"

"I prefer not to talk about that."

I jump off the tractor's fender at the village square in Narlıca. The driver, who remains nameless, waves at me and drives away.

In Ovacık cracks appear in the walls of village houses from the dynamite explosions. The villagers who first refused the prefab houses built by the mine begin to move into them. Old women like Şahsine Dikmenoğlu and Ayşe Girgin stay in their own houses.

"To the death," Ayşe says. "This is my land. I have nowhere to go."

Ovacık shakes with dynamite explosions several times a day, and a thin dust settles on the crumbling, empty houses. Şahsine has high blood pressure. She still hobbles to rallies and shouts through a megaphone, "No! No! No, to the gold mine, no to cyanide!"

When her blood pressure gets too high, we take her to an emergency clinic where the paramedic puts a pill under her tongue. "No more stress," he says.

"I'll dance with Oktay Konyar when the mine is closed," Şahsine tells the doctor and the rest of us.

☾

A strange image from my last visit to Çamköy haunts me. It is after dark but before nightfall. Chickens sit on the branches of a walnut tree inside a wooden fence around the yard of a village house. They are large chickens, maybe a dozen, black silhouettes against a dusky sky. Beside the tree a young woman stands at the gate and holds out her hand to me. I see her only in silhouette, but I know her. It's Rahime. "Please take this," she says. "It's this year's crop. Who knows what may happen next year."

I take the offering — a large jar of olives.

She remains at the gate as I go down the earth road towards the village square. I turn back and wave at the silhouette beside the walnut tree full of chickens.

After more than thirty years in the New World, I am in Anatolia rediscovering its immense heritage, dreaming of growing old in an olive grove. But the dream turns into a nightmare in which I am forced to witness the destruction of that heritage.

I have seen the silvery tips of olive branches swaying in the wind. I have walked on ground covered with daisies between olive trees and sat in their shade in the spring. I have tapped on their fruit-laden boughs and picked the ripe olives that fell on a sheet spread on the ground in December. I have stroked the rough bark of a 200-year-old olive tree whose new shoots heralded renewal. I have even seen a blizzard in olive groves, a solemn ritual between the land, the trees, and a white sky, branches bending with the wind, enduring, and receiving the benediction of snow.

With their 4,000 years of presence in Anatolia, olive trees connect this land's past to its future.

Its future?

Early in this new millennium, in a world that is hostage to globalization, the Republic of Turkey has found itself in the grip of an economic crisis. Spiralling debts and dwindling reserves have led it to crawl on its knees to a global pawnbroker called the International Monetary Fund. The IMF (51 percent of which belongs to the U.S. Treasury) has hemmed and hawed and said it can offer Turkey a loan if the country passes new legislation allowing transnational companies to mine anywhere in Anatolia without being hindered by laws protecting the environment, agriculture, or cultural heritage.

As I write, a new mining law has indeed been passed in the Turkish parliament. It will open up olive groves, historic sites, coasts, fields, and orchards to miners, including gold miners who will leave the land forever poisoned with cyanide and heavy metals.

While resting during a demonstration against the Çamköy gold mine, Hatice *Hanım* fashions a garland of daisies.

I watch Anatolia, the sacred land, at a time when glittering shopping centres on the outskirts of cities and summer houses in the countryside crowd out the fields and forests as sparrows begin to drop dead among the poppies. I see Şahsine Dikmenoğlu standing in the valley below the village of Ovacık, staring at the mills and tanks of a gold mine on the hill in her village, her ballooning *şalvar*s and blue head scarf flapping in the wind. Her wells are drying. Her land is turning into a bald, barren wound. Her house shakes from dynamite explosions four times a day. Hard, shiny gold extracted with cyanide is defeating the ancient, healing, magical green gold of olive oil.

Once upon a time, a great king begged a god to be relieved of the power to turn objects into gold. When all the nut-bearing pines and olive trees are cut down, will the valleys in Bergama remember Şahsine *Hanım*? Will they remember the spring morning when thousands of villagers marched through fields covered with poppies and daisies while the police stood with their riot gear and watched the women walk in single file as a small man with a drooping moustache ran from one end of the procession to the other, calling for order? The land has no memory. Memory is for people. I was there. I bear witness.

Will the wind blow toxic dust in the Garden of Eden?

Chapter Nine
MEMORY IS FOR PEOPLE

"In this country," Jean says, "I rediscover the playful child I once was."

Jean has taken early retirement to join me in Ankara and glows with devotion to Turkey. He spends twelve hours a week at a language school learning Turkish. Hours of homework — filling the blanks in sentences — keep him humble. In public he calls me *yumuşak eşim*, "my soft partner," to make waiters and salespeople laugh. He examines the map of Turkey to find untravelled roads for his motorcycle excursions and gets furious with any Turk or foreigner who criticizes anything about this country. He says he has no wish to return to Canada.

I feel a jolt of anxiety when he says that. My Canadian public health insurance has expired. My furniture is in storage in Quebec City. My books, CDs, and photo albums are packed away lovingly in cardboard boxes. The Turkish carpets I took to Canada over the years, the marble-topped washstand I bought on Winnipeg's Logan Avenue and used as a buffet, the old pressed-back chairs I refinished with my own hands in the backyard of the house on Winnipeg's Montrose Street — objects that hold so many memories — are all in storage. My dearest friends ... My two sons ...

I dismiss Jean's comment with a cliché. "We never know what life will bring."

While he was in Quebec City, I "camped" in Ankara with borrowed furniture and secondhand appliances. Now the two of us are beginning to accumulate possessions: bookshelves, an antique lamp with a frosted blue shade, and chairs handmade from hornbeam with olive-green upholstery that we ordered at an imitation antique store on the fortress hill. They cost less than what we paid for simple chairs at IKEA in Quebec City.

"I, too, used to make furniture in Quebec," Jean says to Cengiz *Bey*, the owner of the store, in careful Turkish. "It was my hobby."

"Why did you stop?" Cengiz asks.

"My tools, my workshop, they're in Quebec City."

"That's not a problem," Cengiz says.

A month later, on a Saturday morning, the phone rings. "I've found a furniture workshop for your husband," Cengiz tells me.

Jean will pay the equivalent of $100 Canadian a month to share a fully equipped furniture workshop with two *marangoz*, or carpenter brothers.

Küçük cennet, Jean whispers to me when he returns from his first visit to the workshop with Cengiz. A little paradise. Within days he and the two carpenters form an unlikely trio.

Turks have a quirk that is endearing and irritating (to a Turk) at the same time. They are extremely fond of foreigners, and if the foreigner makes the feeblest effort to speak their language, they will fall over backwards from an excess of hospitality. Turks must be the only people on the planet who take their own kind for granted and honour the Other.

So the two Turkish carpenters wrap Jean in a cocoon of affection and generosity. Jean makes furniture with *marqueterie*, the French art of wood inlay, impressing his partners. They show Jean how planks are pressed and cut in Turkey. Whenever Jean has to buy wood or a tool, his *ustam*, or master, takes him to a place he trusts and bargains for him. Jean respects the competence of the carpenters and cherishes their friendship. "How skilled these people are with their hands," he says. "How hard and how well they work for such a pittance!"

I bake a cake, and Jean wraps pieces in foil to take to his *ustam* and the man's brother. "This will go well with tea," he says, grinning. "At ten every morning it's *çay zamanı*, tea time, at the workshop. My *ustam*'s brother brews tea, we stop work, sit around the little wood stove, and chat. Yes, in Turkish. Other carpenters from nearby workshops visit and drink tea with us. At noon we all go to a nearby *dönerci* to eat chicken *döner* sandwiches and salad. At 4:00 p.m. it's *çay zamanı* again."

It's true. Jean is at play.

((

"So you've returned to Turkey for good?" my students ask me.

"I don't know what 'for good' means," I say. "We're here for now."

After the dark stories I've explored in this book, it seems odd to say that our lives in Anatolia are richly fulfilling. Why then have I focused on such dark themes?

First, because I feel that breaking taboos and shedding light on forgotten memories is an act of hope. Second, after spending my adult life exploring the stories of a prosperous "new" country such as Canada, I find the dark secrets of this "old" land extremely compelling. And finally, because here I feel more at the centre of the ailing world, closer to the tensions of the Balkans and the Middle East, than I ever felt in Canada. Suddenly, the perilous condition of the world is much more real than it ever was.

And paradoxically that is why Jean and I love being here.

☾

Spring arrives in Ankara with apricot and cherry blossoms, and with the heavy perfume of oleasters. I plant pansies and geraniums in clay pots to make the most of our balcony, then splash bucketfuls of water on the stones. I splash, sweep, and think about the fragility of the simple patterns of daily life.

Years ago I parked my car on the corner of Winnipeg's Portage and Spence every morning. I bought a coffee from the Salisbury House Coffee Shop at the Mall Centre beside the city bus depot and stepped into the elevator to go up to the seventh floor. Familiar faces in the elevator. Good morning. Good morning. Small talk. The "ding" of the elevator at the seventh floor. The illusion of seamlessness, continuity, routine. That morning scene has disappeared from my life so completely that its ordinariness is the most astonishing element of the memory.

On my balcony in Ankara on this April afternoon, the sparrows chirp, the magpies cackle, the heat rises, and the Mall Centre across from the Army and Navy Surplus Store on Portage Avenue becomes a remote, exotic place.

Through all those years while my home was in Canada I played tourist during family visits to Turkey. Now I'm the host when my friends or sons visit us, and in my eagerness to please my Canadians, I discover new pleasures. The *hamam* or Turkish bath is one of them.

One autumn my eldest son, Errol, brings his new partner, Leisa, from Toronto to Ankara for the first time. Leisa announces that she would like to go to a *hamam*. "Why bother?" I object. "We have a perfectly functional bathroom at home."

She has heard about Turkish baths and wants to see one. "If not now, when?" she asks.

So, on a damp, chilly evening, we take the subway to Cebeci and walk several blocks to the oldest *hamam* in the city, a squat building from whose chimney thick smoke pours out.

A plaque over the front door says "Karacabey *Hamamı*, Built in 1440." We open the door and gasp at the scene. A brothel parlour? An Ottoman harem?

Half-naked women, breasts dangling, bellies and thighs blooming, lounge on chairs and benches, eating, drinking tea, and smoking around a crackling wood stove whose pipes are attached to a renovated wooden ceiling.

"It's hot," Leisa says.

"If you don't want to stay, we can leave right away," I tell her.

A plump woman in a white bikini bottom is reclining on a bench beside the stove. She takes a bite from the *börek* on the table and looks up at us.

"Do you want to change your mind?" I ask Leisa again.

But it's too late. A woman in black underpants hurries towards us, her small breasts quivering as she runs. "I'll get you settled right away," she says. "My name is Elmas."

"She means she'll get you into a room," says another woman in *şalvars* behind the tea counter, smiling at our bewilderment. "So do you want a room? Have you made up your minds? Are you coming in or not?"

"At least you understand the language," Leisa whispers to me. "Let's stay and find out what this is all about."

We hang around the overheated lounge in our coats and boots, not daring to sit with the naked women. Elmas returns with a key and leads us to the second floor to a gallery surrounded with doors overlooking the parlour.

"You undress," Elmas tells us. "Leave your things here and lock the door. I'll come and get you. Did you bring bath slippers and towels?"

I shake my head.

The room has two brown leather-covered cots, wooden hooks, and a mirror on one wall. Leisa and I begin to undress. Elmas knocks on the door and hands us cotton plaid wraps, large blue towels, and plastic slippers. We wrap the sheets of cotton around our torsos, tucking the ends over our breasts, and follow Elmas downstairs, across the parlour, and through a marble hallway into a world where time and place dissolve in hot steam.

Naked women move slowly like apparitions in the steam. Marble chambers with arched entrances lead into more marble chambers filled with the scent of soap, where women sprawl on marble platforms under points of light spilling from the domed ceiling. Speechless, Leisa and I collapse on the heated marble platform where Elmas tells us we should lie down. "Just relax," she says. "Don't use any soap, because I'm going to scrub you first." She disappears.

How much time passes in the steam on the warm marble platform, I can't say. Across from us a woman and a young girl — mother and daughter — soap each other's back, then pour water on each other's head from a marble basin as they play and laugh.

A couple of weeks earlier I took Errol and Leisa to Topkapı, the palace of the Ottoman sultans in İstanbul. "And this is the *hamam*," the guide said while we were going through the harem, leading a herd of tourists into a vaulted marble hall. In the dry, chilly space, I tried to imagine the steam and heat that once filled the *hamam* and the women who dreamed, gossiped, laughed, and intrigued during their ablutions between those walls.

The *hamam* provided a sensual escape for women sequestered in the hothouse atmosphere of the Ottoman harem. They wrapped their bodies in embroidered sheets, put on ivory-inlay slippers called *nalın*, and headed for their bath, accompanied by eunuchs bearing trays of food and drink. The *hamam* was the only place where they could bare their bodies, check one another out, and play, perhaps even take part in sexual games.

"Excuse me," one of two slender girls asks, interrupting my reverie. "Do you think we could also lie down on this platform?"

While I make space for them, I note the girls' complicated *hamam* kits: combs, razors, perfumed oils, special loofah sponges, all stacked tidily in a copper bowl. I nudge Leisa.

"I feel almost drugged," she says.

I have seen the remains of 2,000-year-old Roman baths in Ankara and wandered between the *frigidarium*, the cold chamber where bathers start from; the *tepidarium*, the warm chamber; and the *caldarium*, the hot chamber near the furnace. I have read that bathers used to wear special sandals with thick soles to protect their feet from the heated floors. Those magnificent structures with high vaulted ceilings, marble panels, and mosaics are now in ruins.

The Muslims adopted hot baths when they discovered Greek and Roman ones in Syria in the seventh century. At first only men were allowed to go to the *hamam.* Eventually, women were granted permission, but only after an illness or forty days after giving birth. Gradually, the privilege became a right.

While I dreamily ponder these things, Elmas materializes through the steam, takes Leisa by the hand, and leads her to another marble chamber. I get up to see what is happening. Elmas inserts her hand in a *kese,* a rough, sandpaper-textured cloth bag, and scrubs Leisa's back, shaking her like a rag doll. Leisa's back quickly turns a tender pink. I return to the no-soap chamber, close my eyes, and slowly, deliberately, inhale the fragrant steam, awaiting my own fate.

Eventually, Elmas takes me by the hand.

"That's rough!" I object when she lifts my arm and begins to rub my chest. "Don't touch my breasts with that thing, please."

"Just look at that dirt," Elmas says, showing me round clumps of something brown that I'm shedding as she scrubs.

"That's not dirt," I say. "That's my skin you're peeling."

She chuckles and continues her work, scrubbing with enormous strength. I, too, become a rag doll.

"Just you wait until I give you a massage," Elmas says. "You'll fall asleep on the marble."

When my entire body is covered with scrubbed-off dead skin, she orders, "Now go and rinse all this."

I hobble over to the next chamber, sit beside a *kurna* (a marble basin full of warm water), and pour water over myself.

I've read in the newspaper that the tradition of the *hamam* that has been in Anatolia for thousands of years with the Romans, Byzantines, Seljuk Turks, and Ottomans is dying out because heating the water and the marble chambers costs too much. How can it be dying out when this place is so vibrant with female bodies?

When I return to Elmas, she soaps up a washcloth with rose-oil soap for my massage. *Oh, the rose-oil scented steam that enters my lungs and pores while I lie limp on the warm marble platform!* I hear soft moans echoing somewhere in the dome. Am I the one moaning? Does Elmas think I'm crazy? She kneads my shoulder muscles, firmly tapping my back muscles, then works on my calves. The marble slab is slippery. If she gives my foot a push, I'm liable to slide off the other end of the platform and land on the floor.

Oh, that's good. Oh, that smells great. Oh, my back. Oh ... Where am I?

"Now stand up carefully," Elmas says. "Don't slip. You can wash off the soap, you can stay as long as you wish, but I'm done." I look at her in a daze. She laughs and moves on to wash another customer.

Leisa lies beside the marble basin pouring water over herself. "You're lucky," she says to me. "You'll come back for sure. In Toronto I'll dream of this."

"Hey," I ask, "do you feel as if you can hardly move your fingers, and as if you've lost all sense of time and place?"

"Absolutely," she says.

So we fall silent and loll around the marble basin.

"I suppose we should think about going home," I say after a while.

"Yeah," Leisa sighs.

Two rosy, scrubbed initiates to the *hamam*, we wobble slowly through the steamy passage and back into the parlour. The crackling fire in the wood stove now seems delicious. No longer bewildered outsiders, we lounge around for a while and smile at the woman behind the tea counter. "Would you like tea now, or would you like to get dressed first?" she asks.

"After we're dressed, please," Leisa and I reply.

In our room, we dry ourselves, cream our faces and limbs, put on dry clothes and, with languid steps, descend the stairs to join the community of half-naked women reclining and drinking fragrant reddish tea out of glasses with slender waists.

The woman at the tea counter calls a cab for us. Outside it is dark and still raining. "Two hours," Leisa says as our taxi begins to negotiate Ankara's congested traffic. "We arrived around 4:30 and now it's 6:40. It seemed so much longer and so much shorter. Strange."

"Snow is coming," our driver says. "I heard it on the radio. By morning snow will replace the rain."

"Next week at this time you'll be in Toronto," I say to Leisa.

She sighs.

((

"I'll take you to a tavern," my brother, Semih, announces on the phone one winter afternoon. "It'll do us all good."

After our daily late-afternoon tea at my parents' place, Semih and his wife, Melek, drive Jean and me to Meyhanemiz (Our Tavern), a dim, smoky room

219

where a variety of *meze*, cold appetizers, sit on small plates on tables: marinated octopus, pinto beans in olive oil and tomato sauce, feta cheese, eggplant salad, and *kavun* (honeydew melon). The *rakı* (anise-flavoured spirit) in our glasses turns creamy white when we dilute it with water. We take a forkful of cheese and a piece of *kavun* and clink our glasses.

The hours pass, the *rakı* starts to take effect, and a quartet of musicians appears at our table — a drummer, a *kanun* player, a *saz* player, and a singer. The *kanun* player asks for our requests from the classical Ottoman repertoire.

"Anything you wish," Semih says. The drummer begins, the *kanun* player follows with a plaintive introduction, and the aging man called Ismet *Hoca* starts his song. He sits motionless, eyes closed, and sings as solemnly as if he is praying.

> *"Ah . . .*
> *Dönülmez aksamin ufkundayız*
> *Vakit çok geç . . ."*

> "Ah . . .
> We are at the horizon of an evening of no return
> It is late . . ."

Village men while away the time at a tea garden in Şığacık.

Ismet pauses. The *kanun*, a horizontal string instrument on which the fingers of the player seem to fly as they pluck the strings, and the *saz*, a lute with five strings and a long neck, pick up the lament. The melody rises by quarter notes, and the melancholy of all journeys of no return fills the tavern. When the singer continues with the next stanza, people sing along: "We do not seek consolation in hopes of another life. This is the last phase, my soul. Live it as you will . . ."

A middle-aged woman at the next table calls out, "*Makber* please!"

Makber is a dirge for a dead lover, hardly a tavern song, but the *kanun* player begins a prelude and the singer listens with rapt attention like a shaman in a trance, then suddenly launches into an invocation. During the slow cadenza, someone turns out all the lights. A hush falls over the tavern as the singer's voice rises, holds a sound, and becomes a wail. There is a split-second pause during which we hold our breaths, then the lights come on as the drummer bursts forth with the refrain. Everyone joins in.

The mode of the music reminds me of the chant of a Greek Orthodox priest. Of course, when the Ottomans conquered Constantinople, they found musical scores, and Byzantine music entered the mix that already contained elements from Central Asia, Arabia, and Persia, making up Ottoman court music. Anatolian modes, Middle Eastern rhythms, and the poetry of the Ottoman court — all these things go to my head as much as the *rakı* and the *meze*. The modes and rhythms are hard for Jean to catch, but I pick them up right away.

Half-drunk with the *rakı* and the music, I join in the refrain of the sad song in that smoky tavern and keep singing until I grow hoarse, until the tables begin to empty.

☾

How do you make friends in the country of your birth after an absence of thirty-three years?

While researching the brothels of Turkey, I visit an anthropologist at the Bureau of the Status of Women in Ankara. Dr. Hanife Aliefendioğlu, a tiny woman with a huge personality and stores of energy, information, and critical thought, is a feminist in her early forties and active in an organization called The Flying Broom. At the end of our interview she invites me to a fund-raising social for a women's shelter.

I take the subway to the district of Yenimahalle and walk through dark streets clutching my bottle of wine. In the lobby of the neon-lit wedding hall in the basement of an office building, I buy a ticket and glance at the rows of tables where several hundred women are already eating *meze*. I know very few people there, yet the mood of defiant celebration is familiar from the socials of aboriginal women and women's health collectives in Canada.

"This is Nurhayat," Hanife says, pointing to a woman in a short black dress dancing with abandon, arms raised above her head, hips and belly rolling to the beat of the music played by an all-woman band. "Nurhayat was in an illegal left-wing group more than twenty years ago. Her husband was in the same movement. They had a son. In 1980, after the military coup, Nurhayat was arrested. While she was in prison, her husband fled to Germany with another woman from the same political group. Now Nurhayat lives with her son and runs a small pizza parlour. She serves edible violets with her pizzas."

The women — middle-aged, young, plump, thin, some made up and dressed up, some flaunting grey hair — dance in a circle now, belting out old tavern songs along with the band. I stare at Nurhayat's dangling earrings while she tosses her head and think about rat-infested prisons and about how life allows reincarnations.

The Turkish parliament is considering changes to the Turkish civil law that declares the man the head of the family and gives him ownership of all family assets, but the Islamist Party, reluctant in the name of protecting the texture of Turkish families, is dragging its heels.

"Let's meet at the parliament park at noon on Monday," a woman lawyer calls out from the podium. "Women, let's push for these changes!"

The musicians leave the stage, and a young woman arrives with a guitar slung across her chest. The dark timbre of her voice reminds me of Manitoba singer Heather Bishop. Heather would be right at home in this basement hall in Yenimahalle.

I win a telephone address book in the after-dinner draw. The music grows louder, the air turns opaque with cigarette smoke, and the hall heaves with the mass of women dancing between the tables. I leave around midnight.

Outside, the air is damp and windy. The sounds spilling from the wedding hall follow me as I walk gingerly on the irregular pavement, my head full of memories of Winnipeg juxtaposed against the images of the night. The subway train clunks across Yenimahalle Bridge. Cars pass beside me. The lights of squatter houses glitter on the hills surrounding Ankara. I stroll by a cherry tree in bloom in the yard of an apartment block. It is mid-March. The snow might be starting to melt in Winnipeg.

Thanks to Hanife I also participate in a sorcery session in Ankara.

She has accepted a teaching job at the University of the Eastern Mediterranean in Northern Cyprus and asks me to join her old friends at a farewell dinner for her. There are five of us — a doctor, a sociologist, a translator of books, a computer programmer, and myself, who all arrive with bottles of wine and pots of food. I am the eldest of the group; the others are in their late thirties. Only Nuran and I are married.

During dinner, we talk about patterns of neighbourly behaviour in different societies, difficulties of love relationships, tension between the need for change and the need for stability in women's careers, and about whether sex is overrated or underrated. After dinner, Nuran presents our parting gift to Hanife — a wall hanging on which a Turkish translation of a quotation from Faust's song ("Walpurgis Night") in Goethe's *Faust* is embroidered. The English version reads:

> A lovely dream I dreamt one day
> I saw a green-leaved apple tree,
> Two apples swayed upon a stem,
> So tempting! I climbed up for them.

"Here Faust is addressing biblical Adam's first wife, Lilith," Nuran explains in a speech. "Apples refer to sin, dear Hanife. They refer to ensnaring sexuality, and to pleasure. Let those be the secret ingredients of success in your new academic career. This wall hanging will remind you to keep climbing for sweet apples."

The speech is greeted with applause.

We settle on cushions on the floor in the living room, in candlelight, with second helpings of tiramisu.

Hanife turns to Nuran. "The candlelight reminds me of the sorcery we did for Nilgün last year," she says. "We're anthropologists, remember?" She explains to the rest of us, "We know all about sorcery."

"It wasn't so successful that time," Nuran says, "because two men were present — my husband and your brother."

"No men are present tonight," Işıl, the computer programmer, points out. "How about casting a love spell for me tonight?"

Hanife hesitates, then says, "It's getting late."

Işıl won't give up, though. "Come on. You're going away. This is my last chance."

"Look," Nuran says, "we can offer you a speeded-up, concentrated love spell."

Hanife and Nuran turn off all the lights and disappear into the bedroom corridor. A little later the two anthropologist/sorcerers re-enter carrying lit candles, wearing summer hats, and singing a love song in unison. Nuran has a book under her arm, and silk shawls are draped over Hanife's right shoulder. Hanife places her candle on the floor, walks over to Işıl, and slowly covers the programmer's head with three layers of shawls. She then whispers to us to kneel in a circle around the veiled figure.

Nuran opens a random page from the book under her arm, a collection of love poetry, and reads a verse about the fear of change.

When she falls silent, Hanife opens the same book at random and reads another poem, this one about sensuality. She then hands the book to me. "Make a wish for Işıl, then open the book at random and read," she tells me.

I obey her. "I wish you a new love full of vitality," I hear myself saying. Then I read a verse about waves of longing that crush resistance.

"I wish you a love full of surprises," Nilgün says.

When Zeliha wishes Işıl "a lasting love," Nuran objects. "That's not love. That's marriage."

"Love, by definition, is fleeting," Zeliha retorts, and a long discussion ensues.

Finally, from under the layers of veils, Işıl contributes her piece of wisdom. "I don't want love sickness," she says. "Not even waves of longing. I want companionship and sexual pleasure."

"Well, then, that's what we wish for you," Nuran says, clinching the argument.

When the six of us finish taking turns reading wistful, sensuous verses and blessing Işıl, Nuran leaves the room and re-emerges with a bowl full of grains and seeds from her kitchen. "Each one of you will take a seed or a grain," she tells us. She wraps the remainder in a transparent cloth and gives it to Işıl. Nuran then burns some of the anise, wheat, peppercorns, and coriander seeds in a little ashtray, producing an acrid smoke. "The spell is cast," she pronounces, then turns to Işıl. "You'll have to tell us what happens next."

"Eros has already slung his arrow," Hanife says. "The poor man must be looking around frenziedly."

"Sweet apples," Hanife whispers to Işıl when it is time to leave.

We all exchange the Turkish ritual kiss on two cheeks and repeat the new greeting inspired by Goethe. "Sweet apples."

☾

Jean and I take the train to İstanbul for the sumptuous final concert of the annual International Music Festival. La Scala Philharmonic Orchestra, choir, and soloists are performing Verdi under the direction of Riccardo Muti. A humid heat hangs over İstanbul. At Eminönü fishermen fry fish in their boats, docked beside the ferries crossing the Bosphorus, and sell it with bread. The sidewalk smells of grilled meat and onions. Jean looks longingly at the *kokoreç*, grilled lamb intestines. I drag him away.

The terrace in front of the concert hall overlooking the Bosphorus glistens with beautiful people — women in strapless evening dresses and high-heeled shoes, men in expensive designer linen suits. Concert tickets cost upwards of $60, yet the Atatürk Cultural Centre is packed. I recognize prominent businessmen in the crowd and point them out to Jean. "And those two beautiful women in leather pants are the Pekinel sisters, both famous pianists," I say.

After the concert, the crowd files into Borsa Restaurant, adjacent to the concert hall. Smells of grilled meat and *rakı* and the sounds of laughter, chatter, and clinking cutlery rise from the terrace overlooking the Bosphorus. Leander's Tower sparkles in the distance.

Later that week I take İstanbul's new subway from Taksim to Levent, the new business centre of the city, to see a French film at a luxury theatre in a bank complex. Huge blocks of glass and steel tower around the subway exit. The one I'm looking for, the İş Bank Centre, looms in front of me, yet I have no idea how to reach it. A busy highway runs between the sidewalk where I stand staring and the block before me, which shimmers like a mirage.

"Excuse me, how can I get to that building over there?" I ask a shopkeeper.

"You turn this way and go through the underpass," says the shopkeeper, pointing me in a direction away from the bank building. "Ask again if you get lost."

225

I do get lost and stop several people to ask for directions. When I finally reach the security gates of the bank complex, I find myself in a time warp (and a place warp) somewhere in the industrialized world.

The office tower is air-conditioned, all glass and mirrors and large television screens, with a shopping centre to one side. Constantinople, with its chaotic streets, its haze, its domes and minarets, has been replaced by the contemporary office tower complex. Here there are no smells of *kokoreç* or fried fish.

I hear Muzak and observe young men and women, ID tags dangling from their necks, who wear fashionable, conservative clothes that suggest uniforms. Shop windows resemble shop windows in Toronto or Munich, and a food court in the basement boasts Pizza Hut, Chinese Lily, Schneider's Deli, and Norma Jean's Coffee counters. Oh, yes, and there are Sultanahmet *köftecisi*, traditional meatballs. Even though the steel tables and chairs, the self-serve counters, the halogen lighting, and the steep escalators are identical to those in any other business tower/shopping centre in the industrialized world, there is the *köfteci* to anchor me in İstanbul. While I eat from a foam plate on my tray, I stare at gyrating half-naked girls on a giant video screen.

☾

One day my mother walks with difficulty to the porch outside her apartment to sit surrounded by flowering cacti and geraniums and chat with her neighbours. The next day she is bed-ridden. Just like that. Her face turns pale, her skin becomes almost transparent. "Her bones are like Kraft paper," the doctor tells my brother. Tiny cracks in her spine have finally immobilized her.

To look after her around the clock, we hire Nuriye, a woman who has six children and an unemployed husband. "We left our village near Yozgat in central Anatolia eight years ago," Nuriye tells me. "It's been poverty every since." She has a round, kind face and black velvet eyes. Nuriye covers her head with a lace-edged kerchief. Her youngest son is six.

"He was crying on the phone last night," she says. "He said he wanted to lay his head on my chest to sleep."

"I'm not bed-ridden, you understand," my mother tells Nuriye. "I'm just resting until my back gets better." My mother rages against the bedpan and against dependence. When my brother and I visit my parents after work, she asks my brother to help her walk to a chair, but she collapses, nauseated from the effort.

My father considers my mother's condition his personal tragedy. "Just a month ago she could sit in the living room and I could read to her," he says. "We were reading novels together. Today she won't get out of bed. Why can't she make a greater effort?"

My friend Heather writes from Winnipeg that her own mother has also become frail and that she is on a waiting list at the Riverview Nursing Home.

My parents own a modest summer house near the town of Seferihisar on the Aegean coast, built as part of a cooperative during the 1970s. The co-op, with white houses, fruit trees, nut-bearing pines, and an environmentally sound sewage treatment system, has become an attractive holiday village.

In late June, Jean and I travel from Ankara to İzmir and then to the town of Seferihisar, Europe's mandarin orchard. A farmer once told me, "We supply 80 percent of the mandarins the Europeans eat."

There, each summer, we enter what we call the Aegean coast routine.

I start the morning with a swim in the sea, one of my greatest pleasures. At Seferihisar, after an early-morning swim, my skin tingles throughout the morning. I hang my bathing suit on the line behind the house and wash the stone patio where we will spend the entire morning breakfasting, reading, and writing. Since the house faces east, the sun bakes the front terrace all morning,

In the sheltered cove of Şığacık, fishing boats await the next day's catch.

so we take refuge in the back, under the grapevine that has climbed over a frame to form a lush green roof. The large apricot tree beside the grapevine bears fruit as large as eggs.

I make at least a dozen jars of apricot jam. I pour sugar on the fruit, lay the dish out in the sun for a couple of hours, and then simmer it on low heat, filling the house with a tangy fragrance. But ripe apricots fall from the branches I can't reach. *Plop.* The fruits burst open on the ground, offering glistening nectar to ants. So I wash and sweep that terrace every day, getting high on the smell of wet stones.

In the afternoon, the heat rises and the cicadas whine. Like lizards on hot stones, we doze on lounge chairs, waiting for the late-afternoon breeze. When the bathing suits and towels hanging on the line beside the grapevine start to flutter, we know it is time to stir. By around six, the heat subsides and we stroll down the cobblestoned road lined with black pepper and oleaster trees to the sea. While I marvel at the ripening black peppers that hang in red clusters between feathery leaves on drooping branches, Jean dons his goggles and flippers to contemplate the underwater realm. I prefer to see the light over the water and to swim towards the line where the sea meets the sky.

"It's time for a cold glass of wine," Jean says as he walks out of the sea, panting and dripping. I want to stay in the water, to play with the rays of sunlight that dance on the sea. But the garden has to be watered and I don't want to miss out on those sweet early-evening hours. I swim to shore, and when my knees touch the pebbles, I get out of the water. Born of the sea like Aphrodite . . .

Watering the garden requires patience. You have to unwind the long garden hose attached to a tap on the back patio and begin with the hibiscus — the yellow one is extremely delicate, the red one hardier — in the lower yard. You form a pool around each plant. For lemon and mandarin trees, you lay the hose on the ground for about five minutes. Bougainvillea and oleanders need no watering, but the jasmine and the roses have to be drenched. I place my portable cd player on the front terrace and put on an opera. A frosty glass of white wine in one hand, the hose in the other, I go down the steps. As the light dies and the water gurgles, I sip my wine while the Marschallin in Richard Strauss's *Der Rosenkavalier* resigns herself to loneliness.

About fifteen kilometres from my parents' summer house on the Aegean coast there is a fishing village named Sığacık inside the walls of a half-ruined medieval fortress. Through the arched gates of the fortress, you enter narrow streets of whitewashed houses that have blue doors and high garden walls hiding courtyards with fig trees, bougainvillea, and lantana. On summer evenings, women sit on cushions thrown on doorsteps, chatting and crocheting lace right in the street.

Jean and I ride to Sığacık for dinner and stroll through the village streets. Through gates that are half open we stare at gardenias growing in olive oil tins and shoes lying on the stones. We nudge each other, stealing glances at scenes from people's lives: one woman stuffs vine leaves in a kitchen, another squats over a basin and hand-washes clothes.

"Good evening," we greet a group of women in one courtyard. Voyeurs that we are, we feel like intruders.

They invite us in.

"We're admiring the courtyards," I say. "They're sort of hidden but so lovely."

"If you admire them so much, why don't you buy one of these houses and become our neighbours?" an elderly woman asks. "Just a couple of weeks ago a French couple bought that one in the corner." She points with her chin at a well-maintained two-storey house with wooden shutters. "They didn't pay much for it. The owners needed the money. They sold the house and went to İzmir to look for work."

With a mixture of envy and resentment, I peer at the house where bougainvillea cascades down the garden wall. Will these houses be sold one by one to Europeans, exiling the villagers to squatters' shacks at the edge of heaps of concrete on the outskirts of big cities?

"Don't mope," Jean says. "Change is a condition of life. Nothing remains constant."

We walk out of the fortifications and along the wharf towards the coloured lights strung on the patio of a restaurant. After the sun sets, apricot streaks quiver on the surface of the sea. We settle at a table by the water with white wine and plates of eggplant in olive oil and garlic, marinated greens, and fried calamari. Jean and I watch the fishing boats return to the bay, their lanterns throwing flames of light on the water. Fishermen in rubber boots jump out, tie their boats to steel rings, pull out nets smelling of seaweed, and place them in heaps to dry.

A foreign-looking couple arrives. The young woman in a white backless dress has short, spiky red hair. The bearded blond man wears cutoff jeans. Waiters usher them to the table behind ours.

"*Langoustines, s'il vous plait,*" the woman orders.

I turn around to glare at her. Jean tells me I am acting like a jealous lover. "Don't forget," he says, "we, too, are outsiders here."

A three-quarter moon glides up from behind the hills to the west of the bay and coats the sky with a gauze of light. A family with two young children has spread a kilim on the warm stones of the wharf and is brewing tea in a samovar. I ache for them, and for the women crocheting lace inside the medieval walls.

Only sixty kilometres south of my parents' summer house and thirteen kilometres east of Ephesus is an exquisite mountain village named Şirince. Anatolian Greek writer Dido Sotiriou says in her book *Matomena Homata* (*Bloodstained Lands*) that Şirince was called Kırkıca or Çirkince until the second decade of the twentieth century. "If paradise can exist in this world, our village of Kırkıca was it," she writes. According to Sotiriou, it was a prosperous *Rum* (Anatolian Greek) village of 6,000 people with streets of marble and with two churches whose bells tolled on Sundays and feast days.

At Şirince Jean and I drink heady, rough, local wine on a terrace.

"How is it that there's still a winemaking tradition in this village?" I ask the owner.

"The people in this village are all immigrants from Greece," he tells me. "Some came from around Thessaloniki, and some from Crete. When our parents arrived here around 1924, they found the wineries that the departing Anatolian Greeks left behind."

"Are any of those émigrés still alive?"

He nods. "Günnihal *Hanım*," he says, and points to a little white house across the street.

A stooped old woman, Günnihal *Hanım* crouches on her balcony to talk to me. "I was four years old when we came here from Crete. My parents wanted to return to Crete, but the government forced them to stay and make the best of it. People longed for their own homes, but there was nothing they could do."

She grew up in Şirince, married the son of another émigré family, and stayed in the village. Her daughter and grandchildren still live there, working in fig orchards and olive groves. Her grandson works as a cook at the restaurant where Jean and I drank wine. She boasts that she still speaks Greek, but no one here remembers Crete or Thessaloniki anymore. "When I die, there'll be no one who remembers how our parents longed to return to those lands.

Dido Sotiriou says that before World War I the Greeks of Kırkıca and the Turks of nearby villages lived as brothers and sisters. The Turks would flock to Kırkıca on Christian holidays to feast with their neighbours. During the Islamic sacrificial holiday, the Greek Orthodox villagers would visit their Turkish neighbours to share the meat.

After the postwar upheavals, the people of Kırkıca who were sent to Greece eventually settled in a village built for them near Thessaloniki on the foothills of Mount Olympus and named it Neu Ephesos, New Ephesus. But they never stopped longing for the vineyards, olive groves, and fig orchards they left behind at Kırkıca.

In Şirince today, the light, the haze, the scent of mountain herbs — thyme, sage, lavender — intimate the blissful ordinariness of days before sorrow and bloodshed. Village women sell local olive oil, wine, and embroidered cloth in the streets. Magnolias and hortensias bloom in the empty courtyard of the small whitewashed church whose bell has been silent for seventy-five years — an empty shell of interest only to tourists.

I peer through the windows, straining to glimpse the remains of the frescoes near the altar, when a woman carrying a key chain appears in the yard. "I can open the door for you," she says in accented Turkish. Her name is Zehra.

Inside, she identifies the saints for me. "That's Hagia Yorgi. That's Hagia Yohannos. Of course, she's the holy Virgin Mary."

"How do you know all this?" I ask.

"I was born in Crete," she says. "My parents were ethnic Turks. They came here during the *mübadele* [ethnic exchange]. My parents spoke Greek at home, so that's my first language. An old Greek man came here a couple of months ago. His parents were from this village. Like me, he was a child during the exchange. He stood in this courtyard and wept."

How long do the spirits of people who have lived and loved on a piece of land linger over the olive groves and fig orchards they once harvested? How long do their sorrows and joys fill the stone yard of a church that now sits empty, its columns cracked, its frescoes of saviour and saints faded?

The noise and the debris of the technological age dull our memories. Even the land forgets, but I want to remember.

☾

At a magical garden called Cevizaltı (Under the Walnut Tree), Jean and I sit at tables beneath the branches of a giant walnut tree, cooking our own lamb chops on a small barbecue. The late-afternoon sun lights up the vineyards across the road, hens stroll beside our feet, and we talk about the contradictions in the texture of life in Anatolia. We notice once again the quality of light — hazy amber — as if we are seeing it for the first time.

"It must have been this type of light that engendered all those civilizations," I remark. "It's so joyful."

"Yet the Turkish temperament has a sombre side," Jean says. "Remember how people wept at the tavern. Maybe that was a remnant of the hardship of life in Central Asia."

"They also danced at the tavern," I remind him.

"Ordinary people are so extremely kind," Jean says. "You read about greed and corruption in newspapers all the time, about funds being transferred to Swiss banks, about bribes and kickbacks. We've never met anyone who might do those kinds of things. We don't rub shoulders with the rich and the mighty."

"We've certainly met people in dire need," I say. "Beyond the sensual colours and rhythms in this country there is a harsh undercurrent, a constant threat of economic crisis."

"I'm unemployed," I recall our village guide, Muharrem Kara, whispering to me in İncesu when Jean and I went there to see the carving of Cybele on the cliffs. "I used to be a construction worker, but construction has stopped. Please help me find a job."

The carving of Cybele is stunning, but Cybele's reign ended 2,000 years ago. Muharrem and his family are alive now.

As darkness descends on the vineyards and crickets begin their evening serenade, I am preoccupied with the soiling and spoiling of Anatolia, the impending plunder of its natural resources. Pine forests, vineyards, and olive groves on the Aegean and Mediterranean coasts will be razed for summer houses and hotels. Transnational corporations clamour to dig mines and build power stations and nuclear reactors in orchards and forests. Coca-Cola tins bob on the Aegean Sea. Plastic bags line the banks of the sacred Sangarios (Sakarya) River. Giant dams on the Tigris and Euphrates rivers engender terrible cultural and environmental costs.

I have heard with my own ears Turkey's minister of energy and natural resources saying that environmental concerns were an obstacle to economic development. "We'll mine the gold," the minister said. "It's essential that we rid this country of superstitions against cyanide." *Superstitions!*

"But environmental degradation is an issue in Canada, as well," Jean says to me now in Cevizaltı. "Perhaps it's less visible there because there's so much space ..."

"Yes, it's thirteen times the size of this country and has one-third of the population!" I say. "In Turkey there is no wilderness. No lake or river can be contaminated without depriving people of drinking water."

But there is something else. Canada is affluent. Affluent countries can afford to impose environmental standards on industries. When they do, the polluters set up shop in Asia, Africa, or Latin America where there are no such standards and no bargaining power. In Indonesia and Ghana, ancient forest reserves are sacrificed for mining. Turkey wants foreign investment. Foreign investors are giant corporations. They will rape the land and leave.

At a parliamentary hearing on a proposed new law on mining, which will open up all of Anatolia to transnational miners, I made a presentation on how the new law would violate European Union legislation. The executive director of the Normandy/Newmont gold mine accosted me in the hallway.

"You're hostile to the mining industry," he said.

Hostile. The word kept turning around in my head after I left him. I held imaginary conversations with him, explaining to him the need for a kinder, gentler way of living.

Night has fallen at Cevizaltı.

"Look, there's a bat," Jean says. "I know it by its strange flight. Bats are blind, you know. They do zigzags in the air."

The waiter begins to fold the tablecloths to hint that it's closing time. We put on our helmets and jump onto the motorcycle. To the house by the sea, it's a twenty-minute ride through citrus orchards and hills that have become charcoal shadows.

The night wind smells of thyme.

At middle age I have come to understand that invisible threads connect each of us to pieces of land and to history as though fine lines were tying generations, cultures, habits, rhythms, and loves to one another. My father and his mother, who I never knew, connect me to Anatolia's Byzantine past. My mother and her mustachioed father and uncles, Ottoman lords in Macedonia, connect me to the Ottoman Empire. Anatolia, the land itself, connects me to the people of the Stone Age, the Bronze Age, the Hittites, and the Phrygians. My two sons are making their way in Vancouver and Toronto. Invisible lines connect them and even their unborn children to Anatolia.

Anatolia, from the Greek word *anatol*, meaning "eastern" or "where the sun rises," is a word that resonates with history and prehistory. Nurturing, cradling Anatolia! Its soft light, temperate climate, and the flowers and fruits that grow so abundantly in its soil all incite pleasure. Here four different seasons can exist simultaneously. In November, while summer lingers on the beaches along the Mediterranean, snow might cover the mountains in eastern Anatolia, autumn rains might fall in istanbul, and the air might have the fragrance of spring on the Aegean coast. It is no accident that the earliest agrarian peoples lived here, that the Ionian civilization flowered here, and that Constantinople became a glittering capital while Europe languished in the Dark Ages.

Agriculture started in Anatolia and Mesopotamia and continued here longer than in most places in the world. Globalization and its instruments, the International Monetary Fund and the World Bank, are severing the last connections between people and the land by removing credits to farmers, by limiting sugar beet and tobacco production in order to sell surplus American produce, and by dropping the price of cotton. Investors want prime agricultural

A village girl sells wildflowers by a roadside in the spring in central Anatolia.

land for polluting industries. Agriculture is now a global industry that gives ownership of seeds and crops to giant corporations. Millions of people are migrating to the cities and transforming the social fabric of Turkey.

Anatolia knows that empires fall. The Hittite Empire, the Roman Empire, the Ottoman Empire have all reigned here, and all of them have turned to dust. But the Empire of Market Forces that rules over the world in the twenty-first century, indifferent to life, environment, history, prehistory, and memory, possesses weapons capable of destroying the planet.

The Garden of Eden is being spoiled. I am back in Anatolia as the world hurtles forward in a new millennium. Protests erupt all over the globe against the ravages of the New World Order.

Earth has entered a perilous phase. "We live in what the philosopher John McMurtry has called 'a war against the life-means,' wrote my former university instructor, the late Dr. Carl Ridd, in the United Church newsletter *The Eyeopener* just before his death in Winnipeg. He was referring to governments' and businesses' major project and policy decisions "that compromise the delicate global balance of the life-means."

The United States asserts its global dominance with increasing violence. Palestine, Iraq, and Afghanistan, regions of crucial economic and strategic interest to America, are embroiled in wars caused by ancient hatreds and the meddling of outsiders. Before the eyes of the whole world Iraq's thousands of years of human heritage were looted, burned, and shattered when the United States "liberated" Baghdad with bombs and troops. Perhaps no one will be looking when Anatolia's human heritage is dug up, submerged, or built over without fanfare. The mountainous land will forget the past. Memory is for people.

I sit in the living room of our apartment in Ankara, eyes closed, imagining the universe. Earth is a tiny sphere revolving around the sun among countless stars in blue-black infinite space that is an eternity of light, heat, motion, explosions, and other cosmic events far beyond my brain's capacity to conceive.

I visualize the tall aspens that shed their leaves around northern lakes every fall. I conjure up pitch-black nights that echo with the eerie laugh of loons. And I almost smell the fresh snow that renews the world on a cold night. Will I ever stop missing Canada?

In Ankara the heat of high summer is a memory now, the sun is gentler, and the air that moves the branches of the horse chestnuts in the park outside my window is sweet with the remembrance of fleeting things. I stare at the sparrows between large leaves like open hands and imagine their universe. Sheltering shade of leaves seen through sparrow eyes, huge, with large patches of mottled sunlight, and the sky, seen through sparrow eyes, creamy blue with tufts of opaque white.

Life continues — ordinary and magical. *Simit* sellers and fruit vendors shout their wares each morning. I have seen a flock of pigeons fly in orderly circles around the minarets of the Blue Mosque in İstanbul each evening, rising in a spiral against the glow of the setting sun, then descending as the light falls. Scarred with steel and concrete, stained with sulphur and cyanide, the dust-coloured land still bears olives and pomegranates, and I spread breadcrumbs for the doves on my balcony and listen to the whispers of an ancient land.

☾

Author's Note: While the manuscript for Porcelain Moon and Pomegranates *was being prepared for publication, my father, Samim Bilgen, passed away at the age of ninety-five.*

Selected Bibliography

Aeschylus. *Aechylus I: Oresteia (Agamemnon, The Libation Bearers, The Eumenides)*. Chicago: University of Chicago Press, 1969.

Akurgal, Ekrem. *Ancient Civilizations and Ruins of Turkey*. London: Kegan Paul, 2002.

Araji, Sharon K. "Crimes of Honour and Shame: Violence Against Women in Western and Non-Western Societies," *The Red Feather Journal of Postmodern Criminology*. Retrieved from *www.critcrim.org/redfeather/journal-pomocrim/vol-8-shaming/araji.html* on July 19, 2006.

Arnobius. Retrieved from *www.searchgodsword.org/his/ad/ecf/ant/arnobius/view.cgi?file=anf06-138.htm* in February 2002.

Ash, John. *A Byzantine Journey*. New York: Random House, 1995.

Aydın, Erdoğan. *Fatih ve Fetih Mitler ve Gerçekler*. Ankara: Doruk, 1997.

_____. *Nasıl Müslüman Olduk*. İstanbul: Cumhuriyet Kitapları, 1994.

Balter, Michael. *The Goddess and the Bull: An Archaeological Journey to the Dawn of Civilization*. New York: Simon & Schuster, 2005.

Barnett, R.D. *The Cambridge Ancient History (Fascicle):56: Phrygia and the Peoples of Anatolia in the Iron Age*. London: Cambridge University Press, 1996.

Başdemir, Kürşat. *Eski Anadolu Tarihsel ve Kültürel Süreklilik*. İstanbul, Kaynak Yayınları, 1999.

Bennett, F. *Religious Cults Associated with the Amazons*. New York: reprint of 1912 edition, 1967. Retrieved from *www.sacred-texts.com/wmn/rca/index.htm* in June 2005.

Berktay, Fatmagül. *Tek Tanrılı Dinler Karşısında Kadın*. İstanbul: Metis Yayınları, 1996.

Birdoğan, Nejat. *Alevi Kaynakları*. Vols. 1 and 2. İstanbul: Kaynak Yayınları, 2000.

Carroll, Donald. *Mary's House: The Extraordinary Story Behind the Discovery of the House Where the Virgin Mary Lived and Died*. London: Veritas Books, 2000.

Catullus, *Poem 63*. Retrieved from *www.vroma.org/~hwalker/VRomaCatullus/063.html* in March 2002.

Chapman, George. *Chapman's Homer: The Iliad and the Odyssey.* Princeton, NJ: Princeton University Press, 1998.

Childe, Vere Gordon. *Man Makes Himself.* New York: New American Library, 1952.

_____. *What Happened in History.* Harmondsworth, Eng.: Penguin, 1942.

De Bernières, Louis. *Birds Without Wings.* New York: Vintage, 2005.

Dinçmen, Kriton. *Şehir Düştü!* Trans. Yeorgios Francis. İstanbul: İletişim, 1992.

Eisler, Riane. *The Chalice and the Blade: Our History, Our Future.* San Francisco: Harper & Row, 1987.

_____. *Sacred Pleasure: Sex, Myth, and the Politics of the Body — New Paths to Power and Love.* San Francisco: Harper & Row, 1996.

Eliade, Mircea. *A History of Religious Ideas.* Vols. 1–3. Chicago: University of Chicago Press, 1985.

_____. *Shamanism.* Princeton, NJ: Princeton University Press, 1972.

Ergener, Reşit. *Anatolia, Land of the Mother Goddess.* Ankara: Hitit Publications, 1988.

Frazer, Sir James George. *The Golden Bough: A Study in Magic and Religion.* Abridged ed. New York: Macmillan, 1922.

Gimbutas, Marija. *The Civilization of the Goddess.* San Francisco: Harper & Row, 1992.

_____. *The Goddesses and Gods of Old Europe: Myths and Cult Images.* Berkeley, CA: University of California Press, 1982.

_____. *The Language of the Goddess.* San Francisco: Harper & Row, 1989.

Harris, David R., ed. *The Archaeology of V. Gordon Childe: Contemporary Perspectives.* London: University College Press, 1994.

Herodotus. *Histories.* Retrieved from *http://members.tripod.com/~ancient_history/works/hdt.html* and from *www.msu.edu/~tyrrell/Amazons2.htm* in May 2002.

Hoffner, Jr., Harry A. *Hittite Myths.* Atlanta, GA: Scholars Press, 1998.

Hürlimann, Martin. *Istanbul.* London: Thames & Hudson, 1958.

Imber, Colin. *Constantinople: City of the World's Desire.* New York: St. Martin's Press, 1995.

James, E.O. *Le Culte de la déesse-mère dans l'histoire des religions.* Paris: Éditions le Mail, 1989.

Kinross, Patrick. *Atatürk: The Rebirth of a Nation.* London: Phoenix Press, 2001.

_____. *The Ottoman Centuries: The Rise and Fall of the Turkish Empire.* New York: Morrow, 1977.

Kramer, Samuel Noah. *History Begins at Sumer.* New York: Anchor, 1959.

Krupp, E.C. *Sacred Sex in the Hittite Temple of Yazilikaya.* Retrieved from *www.sacred-texts.com/wmn/rca/index.htm* in May, 2003.

Lerner, Gerda. *The Creation of Patriarchy.* New York: Oxford University Press, 1986.

Mathews, Thomas F. *Byzantium from Antiquity to the Renaissance.* New York: Abrams Perspectives, 1998.

McCall, Henrietta. *Mesopotamian Myths.* London: British Museum Publications, 1990.

Medieval Sourcebook. "Travels of Ibn-I Batuta." Retrieved from *www.fordham.edu/halsall/source/batuta.html* in June 2002.

Mellaart, James. *Çatal Hüyük: A Neolithic Town in Anatolia.* New York: McGraw-Hill, 1967.

Mellaart, James, Udo Hirsh, and Belkis Balpinar. *The Goddess from Anatolia.* Milan: Eskenazi, 1989.

Ocak, Ahmet Yaşar. *Türk Sufiliğine Bakışlar.* İstanbul: İletişim Yayınları, 1996.

Patterson, Orlando. *Slavery and Social Death.* Cambridge, MA: Harvard University Press, 2005.

Pausanias. *Description of Greece, Book I: Attica.* Retrieved from *www.fordham.edu/halsall/ancient/pausanias-bk1.html* in February 2002. Also *www.theoi.com/Phrygios/Attis.html.*

Peristiany, John, and Julian Pitt-Rivers. *Honour and Shame: The Values of Mediterranean Society.* Chicago: University of Chicago Press, 1966.

Roller, Lynn. *In Search of God the Mother: The Cult of Anatolian Cybele.* Berkeley, CA: University of California Press, 1999.

Rumi, Mevlana Celaleddin'I. *The Life of Rumi.* Retrieved from *www.rumi.org.uk/life.html* on July, 18, 2006.

_____. *The Mathnavi.* Trans. Shahriari. Retrieved from *www.dar-al-masnavi.org/reedsong.html* on July 18, 2006.

_____. *The Rubaiyat.* Trans. A.J. Arberry. Retrieved from *www.khamush.com/therubaiyat.htm* on July 18, 2006.

Runciman, Steven. *The Fall of Constantinople.* London: Cambridge University Press, 1965.

Şener, Cemal. *Şamanizm.* İstanbul: Etik Yayınları, 2000.

Sharabi, H. *Neopatriarchy: A Theory of Distorted Change in Arab Society.* Oxford, Eng.: Oxford University Pres, 1988.

Shaw, Ezel Kural, and Stanford J. Shaw. *History of the Ottoman Empire and Modern Turkey 1280–1808/1808–1975 Cilt 1, 2*. Cambridge, Eng.: Cambridge University Press, 1997.

Shaw, Stanford J. *From Empire to Republic: The Turkish War of National Liberation 1918–1923, a Documentary Study*. Vols. 1–5. Ankara: TTK Yayınları, 2000.

Sobol, Donald. *Amazons of Greek Mythology*. London: A.S. Barnes, 1972.

Stone, Merlin. *When God Was a Woman*. New York: Harvest Books, 1976.

Thomson, George. *Studies in Ancient Greek Society: The Prehistoric Aegean*. London: Lawrence & Wishart, 1972.

Ünal, Ahmet. *The Hittites and Anatolian Civilizations*. İstanbul: Etibank, 1999.

Virgil. *Georgics*. Retrieved from *http://classics.mit.edu/Virgil/georgics.4.iv.html* in April 2003.

Walker, Barbara. *The Women's Encyclopedia of Myths and Secrets*. San Francisco: Harper & Row, 1991.